WHERE THE WATERS RECEDE

ROTIMI OLANIYAN

apex

A catalogue record for this book is available on request from the British Library

ISBN 978-1-9160263-1-5

Apex Publishing UK.

We have not finished telling
the stories from our past.

For our grandchildren,
And for theirs as well.

PROLOGUE

Lagos, Nigeria, Last Month.

The KLM flight from Birmingham had been routed through Amsterdam and finally arrived Lagos at 3.00pm. James Stephen Thomas felt tired and sore from the tiny seat he had been strapped into for the past six hours. He decided he would feel much better taking his jacket off. It was a hot and sunny day outside. He was surprised to find that the airport air conditioning wasn't working, and the heat that rushed to meet him as he stepped out of the plane and walked into the terminal building was such that he had never experienced in his life. He couldn't breathe and his entire body was already covered in sweat.

"Certainly, isn't England now." He muttered to himself as he joined a short queue for non-nationals that snaked across the open space, towards the immigration desk. He rolled a small cabin bag after him and had his passport and other essential documents in the inner pockets of the suit jacket, which he now realised was not a smart idea to have put on. When he eventually arrived at the immigration desk, he was attended to by a plump woman dressed in a brown uniform. She beamed a generous smile at him and asked for his passport.

"Welcome to Nigeria," She smiled." Have you visited here before?"

"No, this is my first time." He responded, patting about his trouser pockets for his glasses.

"Oh!" She exclaimed. "You must make sure you enjoy our food sir. Business or pleasure?" She added in a sudden official tone.

"A brief visit to Ife for a meeting." He replied.

He noticed her hesitation, unsure what to scribble onto the brown immigration card she had pulled out from in between his British passport.

"Business." He added, hoping she wouldn't see how nervous he was.

She smiled at him again and stamped his passport, almost knocking the stack of paper clips on her desk out of the way.

"Enjoy your stay, sir." She added, handing over his passport.

"Thank you." He said as he followed the hand gestures of another uniformed official, towards the baggage carousel.

As he waited for his luggage to arrive, he looked about the facilities at the airport. It was certainly not Birmingham International or Heathrow, but it provided the basics. This was a trip that had been over two years in the making. Now as he walked out of the terminal building to where a welcome party of two was waiting for him, he recalled how several members of his family and friends had tried to dissuade him from making this trip.

'Not safe, full of dodgy fraudsters, Boko Haram, Malaria!' The list had been endless. But he had been adamant and now he was finally here.

"Mr. Thomas?" A staffer sent by the cultural attaché at the British High Commission asked.

"Yes." He replied.

James nodded as he shook his hands. "How do you do?"

"How do you do? David Cassidy, I am with the Deputy High Commission here in Lagos." The man introduced himself.

"I hope the flight was pleasant."

"They offered a bit more than a sandwich." Thomas scoffed.

"Ah, shall we?"

"Most certainly." He said and watched as the man's driver attempted to collect both his bags.

"I shall hold on to this one." Thomas said, clutching on to the cabin baggage.

"No problem, *sah*." The Nigerian driver smiled.

Soon they were settled into the back of a dark grey Land Rover, heading out of the airport with Thomas grateful for the car's air-conditioning.

They drove in silence for a few minutes, cutting through heavy traffic and hordes of athletic street traders chasing after cars, displaying all sorts of merchandise to the windows of the passing vehicles.

"Is this allowed?" Thomas asked appalled.

"Well, no, and then yes." Cassidy chuckled.

"It's all a bit up in the air in this neck of the woods, though there is a method to the madness here. At least for the initiated."

"I see." Thomas replied, staring as a young boy who ran alongside the vehicle flashed him a recent copy of the Economist.

"Just to let you know that it will take us about three hours to get to Ife. Hopefully we shouldn't encounter too much traffic. Once outside Lagos and towards Ibadan, things will move a lot quicker." Cassidy said, changing the subject.

"Right."

"We have arranged an audience with his Royal Highness, the Ooni of Ife later this evening at his palace, where I am told a small reception has been arranged in your honour, with members of the Yoruba Studies Society and some academics from the Obafemi Awolowo University History and Cultural Antiquities Department."

"Thank you." Thomas replied.

"Most welcome sir. I must confess that it is a most intriguing affair."

"Well, you could say that." Thomas nodded in agreement. "But it is the right thing to do, wouldn't you say?"

He looked on at the civil servant who sat beside him. He understood that he was paid to serve the interest of the government of the day. The young man looked away and cast a polite gaze towards the road ahead. They returned to a moment of brief silence as the vehicle moved on. Finally, the diplomat said. "I do admire your sense of moral rectitude on the matter, sir. It has been an issue that has bred quite a lot of debate over the years. Very topical even during my post-graduate days while at St. Andrews."

"But do you think it is the right thing to do?" Thomas asked again.

"It depends, doesn't it?" Cassidy ducked, yet again, refusing to be caught in the vice of a definite position.

"Well, I certainly do." Thomas finally declared. "I think that we, as indeed all people with an ounce of decency, have the solemn duty to return the artefacts of a people taken away by our colonial governments, or our forebears, back to the people it belongs to."

Cassidy nodded, a smirk forming at the side of his face as he stared at Thomas. "Even when they are not able to have them kept in the best of conditions?"

"To be kept as they very bloody well please if you ask me!"

"Well, we all have a shared responsibility to preserve the antiquities of all civilisations. I would imagine that we all hold humanity's greatest relics in trust for the collective story of mankind."

"I would imagine that we do. So, help them build museums that can hold these artefacts."

"I can assure you that the government has been very generous in that regard." Cassidy replied with a show of official pride on his face.

Thomas laughed and carried on. "We could argue that we have no choice given our scandalous history of empire building."

Cassidy smiled, and after another length of silence, he asked in a hushed and contrite tone. "I wouldn't be able to take a peek now, would I?"

Thomas looked at him, then smiled as well. He placed the bag on his lap and very carefully removed a small leather pouch. He thereafter unwrapped the pouch and removed a carved figure of a half woman and half fish.

"It is an effigy of Yemoja, the Yoruba water goddess revered by her worshippers." He announced shortly after, in what he hoped was his solemn tone of voice. "It was given to my great-great grandfather as a gift by a Yoruba priestess in 1847 when he served as a missionary somewhere in these parts. He brought it back with him to England and it has become a sort of family heirloom ever since."

"Fascinating." Cassidy purred as he regarded the dark hard wooden carving.

Thomas nodded. "Yes, it is. The story goes that he placed a very deep value on it, but his only son died during the First World War and was not able to explain the symbolism to his three children who were still young at the time. So, my great grandfather, and later his son, my father, inherited this and a few other heirlooms without really knowing anything about it. The symbolism remained lost to the family for over a hundred years, until my sister and I, after some digging stumbled upon his private letters at the Church Mission Society Archives at the University of Birmingham four years ago."

Thomas watched as David Cassidy admired the primitive art then handed it back. He placed it in its pouch and returned it into his bag.

"Apparently, it had been his wish when he was dying that the figurine be returned to her or her descendants here in Africa someday. Sadly, we can never really know who she was or what became of her descendants."

"Very intriguing, so why the Ooni of Ife then?"

"Well, I did some research you see, and found out that the Yoruba see him as their spiritual leader, a sort of Pope. So, I reached out to his palace and they were quite helpful about it all. I would imagine it is right that the artefact is returned to him and his kingdom."

Cassidy nodded. "A very noble gesture Mr. Thomas."

Thomas looked out of the car window as they sped past the sprawling city of Lagos. He caught the contradiction of newly built modern housing estates that lay next to old urban slums and rickety rickshaws that queued up next to expensive SUVs at petrol filling stations. And there were giant billboards everywhere determined to sell everyone something.

"Yes, it is, isn't it? But it would seem that the old bugger grew deeply affectionate towards her." Thomas replied,

"Now, that must have been one remarkable story." Cassidy laughed as they crossed the bridge over the Ogun River. "How on earth did that happen?"

Thomas smiled at him and retreated in to his own thoughts. He had always wondered about the very same thing.

PART ONE (1821 -1826)

OMITIRIN

CHAPTER 1

AKINDELE VILLAGE, THE HARMATTAN SEASON, 1821.

I could feel the dry wind as it squeezed moisture from my skin. It meant that the *Asa* were fast approaching. Ma'mi had always told me that the birds were sent by their keeper, Oya, the goddess of the tumultuous dry winds, and the harbinger of the dry season. She sent them to warn us of the coming illnesses that descended with the departure of the rains. So, we could prepare ourselves. Yet, in my father's household, we all prayed for the coming of the season because it beckoned the start of the burning of old things.

Ba'mi, always said that a good farmer had to nourish the land back with the burnt offering of the last season's foliage. That way Olodumare, our creator and the king of all the heavens and the earth would be pleased and instruct Orisha Oko, the god of the diligent farmer to allow the rains to fall in the new season. When the rains came, the tender crops would be suckled to maturity and a season of dryness would give way to a season of plenty. It was the way the world was created, and the order that the pantheon of our Orishas gave to the way we lived.

Ba'mi was very wise, and I, proud to be his only daughter. He was not like the other fathers in our village who took to drinking too much palm wine out of idleness during the dry season while waiting for the next rains. He was gentle and kind. He loved to sit on his raffia mat under the old Kola nut tree, watching his children play while driving away the flies from his calabash of water with the fan my mother made for him. He was tall and had very strong hands. And though I was not supposed to know as a child of nearly fourteen harmattan seasons, it was obvious that a few of the women in our own quarters liked him. They kept a straight face about them whenever they came visiting my mother, but would behave like shy girls whenever he was around. Some of them treated me as though I were the Bale's daughter and not a mere commoner. It made me happy that they gave me things whenever they saw me playing with their children or running an errand for my mother.

"Omitirin," They would call out to me. "Are you hungry? Has your mother fed you yet? Ah! See her collar bone showing. We must put some meat about you o!"

Our village, Oko Akindele was known for our bountiful barns. Their richness could be surmised as being beyond our human endeavours. We were a small settlement of rustic villages and hazy hamlets bravely nestled amongst the forest trees and sprouting farmland along the banks of the mighty Ogun River. Our community had been established by my great-great-grand father, who the legend says floated down the river from Ibirapa not far from Ile-Ife, where the revered Ooni lived in spiritual dominion over the sixteen kingdoms of the house of Oduduwa. The legend goes that he had journeyed for many weeks down the mighty river in search of better fishing spots and had settled for the land where our village now stood because of the large amount of fishes he had seen as he arrived. Several years later when the catch had become sparse. The villagers decided to consult Ifa, our ancestral oracle. Ifa advised them to become farmers instead. Ifa promised that they would always be fruitful for as long as they made the required sacrifices as remedy for previous sins committed. Ifa fulfilled its promise. Overtime, our markets became prominent and traders from distant villages and even towns far beyond the great Olumo rock in Oko Adagba came to buy our crops.

I would sit with my mother, by our stall, and watch as they all went about their business, haggling more for the pleasure of brinksmanship, than to save a cowrie, because everybody knew that Akindele's tubers were always generous. Sometimes there would be a large entourage of the Awori people from Isheri near Eko where the mighty ocean had its shores, or from Ketu or Popo. They were worldly traders who brought all kinds of magical things from across Olokun's great ocean. Several people would gather around the strange objects, marvelling at the *juju* behind it. Ba'mi would warn us never to touch the items. It was all evil witch craft he would say, certain to take away one's good fortune and everyone knew that a person with a compromised Ori was finished in this world.

My Ori was good. My mother always told me that I had caused her no trouble, unlike my two brothers before me. 'Omitirin is the one who will redeem me.' She would always say, even though I never really understood what she meant by that. Ma'mi was not like my father. She was a trouble maker.

She was not the type to be given the task of sharing the kolanut, her friends would always tease, because it would never be shared equally. 'I came to this world to fight the unjust, ma'mi' would retort. 'I did not come to give more to those who had already.' Her friends would laugh, but no one ever dared stir her anger, not even my father.

She helped him with the harvest and ensured most of the items in our barn were sold off by the end of the planting season. It would leave us with just enough to replant the fields and feed on as we waited for the harvest to return. However, ma'mi's true passion was dyeing clothes in the communal dye pits at the back of our compound. There, she could be found with her craft group, spending long hours tracing out intricate patterns with bee wax on the cloth before subjecting it to the dye. The cloth always came out beautiful, each one unique in its' own story. She would sell the clothes on our market days, but always kept the best of the lot back, which she sometim*es* wore whenever there was a festival.

The sun had begun to set. I could already hear the crickets chirping in the distance, as they congratulated each other for surviving yet another day from the beaks of the unforgiving kites. Further on, by the banks of the great river, the toads joined in with their noisy croaks. If for no other reason than to remind us that they too lived amongst us. There were fewer mosquitoes at this time of the year. They didn't thrive in the harsh evening cold. So, it left us with the opportunity to lie on our raffia mats under the old Iroko tree by the side of the compound. There, once settled and comfortable under the canopy of hazy stars, we would send the more mischievous amongst us to coax one of the elderly patriarchs to come tell us stories.

Arologun Oloto was the best story teller in our village and he lived next to our quarters. He was so old that most of his teeth had fallen out, but he still had the childish glint of wonder in his eye. He was wicked with his tale too, knowing when to scare us and when to make us laugh. And even though his voice would sometimes croak like those of the frogs from the river when he sang, his songs were always amusing. Several times he would nudge at us to tease out a moral he wanted to teach us. It sent us into debates way into the night, arguing amongst ourselves as only children could. It was the way we learnt what they were meant to teach us.

It was my duty to bathe the younger children in our compound. I would have fetched the water in the big calabash, earlier in the day and prepared the black soap made from cam wood and soda ash as I bathed them. I would scrub hard with the brittle fibres of a fresh day-old *Kan-kan* sponge and snigger as they cried out with pain as it scraped the grime off the tender skin on their buttocks. I walked towards the spot by my father's younger sister's hut, calling out to the children to report quickly. Today I wanted my chores done on time because it would be one of those evenings when Arologun Oloto entertained us with a tale.

With my chores done, I walk over to my best friend's mother's hut, calling out to her as I approach. Ayanke and I were age mates, though she liked to remind me that she was a few months older. Her parents had counted almost fifteen rainy seasons for her. We spent most of our time together, roaming around our homestead, playing, singing, doing chores and staring at the great Olumo rock in the far distance. We took turns wondering aloud who amongst the younger men in our community would fancy us enough to one day ask our fathers for our hands in marriage. We had known each other all our lives and even though our mothers were not particularly good friends we almost felt like we were sisters.

Ayanke comes out to meet me and together we make our way to the old Iroko tree carrying our mats under our armpits. As we settled on to the mats, other children in the community join us, some carrying small boulders which would serve as seats. The ones who come late do so with oily soup dripping down their chins, wiping their dirty palm oil stained fingers on their bald heads.

Arologun Oloto came a while later. He had a wrapper around his waist which exposed his frail torso to the harmattan wind. Today he chose to come along with his walking stick. This we usually considered with a great deal of apprehension. By now we knew all too well it would have a part to play in the telling of today's tale, while also serving as an instrument with which to lash out at the recalcitrant amongst us. One of his several grandsons came along with him carrying a small apoti. Ayanke and I giggled since this meant the old patriarch wanted a comfortable sitting rather than a quick perch. It meant that we would be entertained for long this night.

We all rose to greet baba. The girls knelt before him in greeting while the boys prostrated flat on their bellies. Baba greeted us back and sat himself down with an exaggerated sway. We all giggled, knowing that the story telling had begun. He looked around taking in our faces, as though gauging his audience and deciding which one to pull out of his quiver of delightful stories. He cleared his throat, looked around, then announced in his knowing husky voice.

"Our story tonight begins in the heavens. Orun up there beyond the stars, where our creator, Olodumare the owner of all the heavens resides in all his glory."

Baba paused and peered at us to see if we were all paying attention. Satisfied that we were, he coughed a little, then continued.

"You see, one day Olodumare decided that it was time for him to create the earth and our people. So, he prepared a chain made of iron and cast it from the heavens down to the void below. The chain was long and it would have taken a mortal man several lifetimes for him to have descended it, but it would take the Orisha only a moment. The chain's end landed at a point which today we know as Oke Itase in Ile Ife. Olodumare then commanded his two sons Obatala and Oduduwa to descend and set about creating earth. While coming down, Obatala went wayward, but Oduduwa brought with him a cockerel with five feet, earth dust which he kept in the shell of a snail and a single palm kernel nut. There was at the time only primordial waters all over the earth. As he came down, Oduduwa took great care to ensure that he poured the earth dust onto a point on the waters, then, he instructed the cockerel to spread the earth dust all over the waters so that land might be formed. Olodumare was pleased with this so, Oduduwa took the precious palm kernel and buried it into the earth that was formed and it began to grow into a mighty tree that bore sixteen branches. It is those sixteen branches that represent the first sixteen kingdoms of our people to be found across this world."

Baba stopped and asked us if we understood. Most of us nodded only out of fear of his walking stick. Knowing better he carried on all the same.

"You see, Oduduwa is our father because he obeyed Olodumare, owner of the heavens, unlike his elder brother who chose instead to go in search of drink. It was he, Oduduwa, who had the courage to plant something that bore good fruits, and it is for this reason that he and his descendants' rule over our people till this day."

Baba continued into the night. He regaled us with stories of our forebears and the Orishas who we worshiped as spirit gods. Each in charge of an awesome force of nature, and all with clear instructions from Olodumare as to their purpose in our lives. It was Orunmila he ordained his chief prophet and messenger to mankind. He gave him the important work of speaking to man through Ifa. Baba explained to us that contained within Ifa were the secrets of Olodumare, and Orunmila had revealed them to the great priests amongst our ancestors so as to help us to be at peace with this world.

Baba laughed as he watched us soak in his every word. "Ah!" He sighed, enjoying himself.

"That there is peace in this world should start from our homes and even the homes of gods, should it not?" He asked no one in particular. Then he sniggered and carried on.

"Let me tell you another story about the great Sango, the god of the sky and thunder. During his lifetime on earth, Sango had three wives. But before he married the third, there was his first wife Oba, who was the goddess of the mighty river of the *Tapas*, and his second and favourite wife Osun, who was the goddess of the river in Osogbo. Sango loved Osun very much because of her mastery in cooking. She was also very good in some other things but you are too young to understand these things as you are all children." Baba admonished, but the older girls amongst us laughed knowingly.

"Any way children, one day Sango sees this new woman in the market place. Her name is Oya, and she is the most beautiful thing that he has ever seen. It is said that her beauty was not of this world and Sango being a magician himself at once knows that she is no ordinary woman but a spirit woman with special gifts. He then decided to secretly follow her and find out what the secret of her powers were. He followed her all the way and watched as she entered the forest and transformed by wearing a wild animal cloak before returning deeper to her home in the forest."

We all gasped with fright at the thought, which allowed baba to catch his breadth. He continued. "The next day Sango trails her again, but this time he goes ahead of her and takes away her animal cloak from where she hid it. Oya later arrived at the spot and started looking for her cloak without knowing she was being watched. When it started getting late, Oya who was known to be tempestuous started raining evil incantations on whoever stole her cloak. Alarmed by her temper, Sango jumped out of hiding and calmed her down. He is enchanted by her, so he professes his love for her. He however refuses to return the cloak because he insists that she is prettier without it." Ayanke and I smiled. I wondered just how beautiful she must have been. I sometimes wondered if I was beautiful.

"Sango's words calm her down." Baba continued. "And the tempestuous Oya finally warms to her suitor. Sango asks her to marry him, but Oya initially refuses because she is aware that Sango himself is equally tempestuous. She has heard stories. She knows that the thunderbolt that emanates from his mouth when he gets angry is also Sango's most deadly weapon in his arsenal. Oya fears that the union will not work and his anger will destroy them both. But Sango is adamant. Eventually Oya agrees to become his third wife, but they both swear a secret pact not to ever reveal each other's magical powers." Baba took a sip of water, then continued.

"After they had been married several years, Oya did something that the two other wives never did. She persuaded Sango to entrust the thunderbolt magic with her for safe keeping, as a way of protecting them all. Sango reluctantly agreed, but warned that she must never keep the power close to her womanhood because it would weaken the power of the thunderbolt and could even render the magic impotent forever. Oya promised to handle the powers with appropriate care. In time, Oya would not keep her promise. One day she keeps the thunderbolt next to herself. Sometime later, Sango's authority is challenged by one of his subjects in his court and in an effort to deal with the subject he summons Oya to bring his thunderbolt to him. As he strikes the subject, Sango realises that the thunderbolts' power has severely diminished. This enrages him and in that moment of madness he summons every ounce of power left within the thunderbolt and within himself and destroys his entire palace, killing every one present, including his own children. The great Sango is distraught and flees his kingdom in grief and shame. He disappears mysteriously from that day on, never to be seen nor heard from again."

Arologun Oloto shook his head and sighed. He watched us as we clucked our tongues in horror. "There is a lesson there for all of us in the way we live our lives, and the choices we make." He said quietly to our horrified faces. Then he prayed for all of us. "May Olodumare teach us to be wise." He said.

I slept deeply that night, covered against the cold with a mud cloth. I slept as I usually did, in my mother's room, by the foot of her own sleeping place facing the alcove where she placed the personal Orisha figurine that she worshiped. Ma'mi's favourite Orisha was Iya-mapo, the patron deity for creativity and women's art and craft, such as pottery and the dyeing of cloth. The alcove was her shrine to Iya Mapo and in it she kept an effigy, an assortment of cowry beads and bales of her best mud cloth. She was very devoted to Iya Mapo and would start her day every morning with a song as she offered a sacrifice of fresh fruits, a cowry, and cloth work. She sang in exultation:

> Iya Mapo, I reverence you.
> May the dye produce well today
> you our protector
> is this not the activity
> that has earned for you
> the gift of plenty?
> Iya Mapo, you have never allowed
> your daughters to go hungry
> Iya Mapo, I reverence you.

I dreamt. I saw myself singing to Sango. Softly imploring him not to worry about his thunderbolt. I was dressed in my mother's best dyed cloth, feeling beautiful like the goddess Oya. And when it seemed like he stirred, I saw myself preparing a meal of white Lafun, from the innards of well ground flour, with darkly green Ewedu leaves, and blended Gbegiri bean soup. And in it was the richness of well-seasoned antelope meat that was fit for the god that Sango was. I served it in a decorated earthen ware. The type the Dahomey women brought from their country to sell at our market day. Intricately patterned with beautiful murals that told the story of their fierce love. I offered Sango fresh water from a drinking gourd carved out of an animal's tusk. I dreamt that Sango had peace and was happy as he looked at me.

~

11

The gentle grating of dried coco-yam leaves against our water pots woke me. It was the moments just before dawn and I had beaten the cockerel to it's morning crow. It was much colder at this time of morning and I sought to draw the covering closer to me. As I tried, I felt a wetness about me, and though it was dark, I managed to muster the light from the flicker of the oil lamp by the feet of the door to orientate myself and look about me. I felt the wetness much more this time and noticed that it came from between my laps. I pulled the covering away from me and crawled off my mat to grab the oil lamp so I could take a closer look. I touched myself where the wetness was and inspected my fingers, helped by the light from the flickering flame. I saw blood. I wanted to scream, but I stopped myself and thought the better of it. It was very early and the entire compound was asleep. It would be at least till the crow of the cock before the women and children arose. What was wrong with me? I wondered. Why was I bleeding down there? I looked over to where ma'mi still slept. Even though she hadn't woken up, my movements had made her stir. She coughed wildly and readjusted herself. I crawled towards my mother and gently tapped her awake.

"Ma'mi...ma'mi! ma'mi!"

She opened one eye and squinted at me through it.

"What is it?" she asked.

"Blood," I said. "I am bleeding."

She opened the other eye and was focussing her attention on me much better now.

"Blood?" she asked a bit taken aback. "Where?"

"From under me, ma'mi." I pointed timidly.

She dragged herself out of bed with a single motion I hadn't ever seen her perform before. She grabbed the oil lamp from me and positioned it so she could get a better look. She did not look for more than an instant and then I saw her nod her head and look at me again. I am not sure what emotion I read from her face. It was an emotion I had never seen before, but she touched me gently and whispered beaming with pride.

"Ah! Omitirin, let Olodumare be praised! You have found favour with Yemoja. You have become a woman. Come now." She said as she took my hand and led me to the backyard. "Let me take care of you."

CHAPTER 2

AKINDELE VILLAGE, TWO MONTHS LATER.

I could not have ever imagined that so much could change about and around me at the mere sight of feminine blood. There had been hushed whispers about me, from the lips of all the women in our village. It seemed that the men now looked at me differently. My best friend Ayanke too seemed to have become distant, even if it was in a respectful way. I felt it was all strange that Ayanke should react to me like that. She was older than I was after all, and had experienced what I was now going through several months earlier than I had. I had needed her to share this experience with me. To celebrate my becoming a woman as Ma'mi was quick to tell me. I missed Ayanke's banter and constant teasing. She didn't spend as much time with me as she used to anymore and every time I called to her, she would claim that she was on one errand or the other for her mother.

My mother had resulted to restricting me to our compound most of the day. I was made to sit on a new raffia mat, playing with pebbles and drinking fermented pap infused with herbs. When evening came, I would look on with envy as the other children ran towards the old Iroko tree, preparing to be scintillated by another tale from old Akogun's wise lips.

I had my elder brothers to help me. They had become more protective towards me in recent days. Ogundare, who was my mother's eldest child, who had never seemed to care what I was up to, these days sought to share his piece of meat with me whenever we ate. He would make small banter as he passed on the sinewy piece of antelope, and watch as I bit off a piece and handed him back whatever remained. If anyone were to suggest that he could so easily part with some of his roasted bush meat, that person would surely have had his forehead checked for signs of fever. Ibidokun, who was my father's favourite amongst his two sons from my mother was the one who first smiled at me and let me into the conversations that seemed to have commenced about me. One afternoon after running an errand for our father, he sat with me on the mat and called me 'Iyawo' which meant wife. He said it teasingly; as though he had found out I had a secret admirer. It might have been a slip on his part, because he quickly scuttled away after he had called me so. Was I to be married off at the first sight of blood? I wondered, appalled at the thought of leaving my father's household at such a tender age. What did I know yet about men? What did I even know about women yet, for that matter!

It seemed that news about me had travelled far indeed. Two weeks after my mother had made me wash myself with cold water scented with herbs and given me fresh cloth with which to pad myself, a strange woman visited our home. She came very early in the morning of the day before our market day. That morning my mother had prepared the pap from the finest bushel of grains we had in our barn and the bean cakes she fried were flavoured with expensive crayfish from her special secret pantry where she kept her cherished spices. The palm oil was fresh, and shone bright red. It gave the cakes the look of rich kernels. All this to serve as a befitting breakfast in honour of this strange woman who came calling. Even ba'mi had not been so well served in recent times, but it did seem like he agreed with the preparations as I could see that he had arranged a few of his best yams into a decent heap by the side of the entrance into his own quarters. They were to be offered as gifts. When the woman came, she walked into my father's quarters with deliberate steps that were only seen from those with authority. Had she been a man she definitely would have been a high chief or perhaps she was a member of a privileged order. She was dressed in an impeccable white buba and wrapper; she threw an intricately woven shawl decorated with cowrie beads across her left shoulder. She was adorned with beautiful indigo beads, and carried a long beautifully carved staff on her right hand.

Her greetings with ba'mi were short and seemed perfunctory. She gave him the obeisance of half a curtsy, and ba'mi was far more eloquent with his greetings than he usually was with other women her age. She was elderly, but she was not old. She carried herself with so much dignity that I watched her, enthralled by her social graces. It was to my mother's quarters that she came directly she was done with the niceties. Ma'mi had ensured I was appropriately bathed and dressed in one of her brightly designed indigo mud cloth. She had shooed me away from her room, but instructed me to wait by the vegetable patch by the side of her quarters so I could come quickly the moment she summoned me.

I did not have to wait long for the call. As I walked in, the elderly woman stared at me, her steely eyes burrowing into me as though she wanted to inspect my very spirit. Ma'mi beckoned me to come close and greet. I did, with the full yet meek aplomb we reserve for the very venerable and very powerful, and even sometimes our deities. The woman looked at my frame as I knelt before her and then she greeted me by my *oriki*; my praise name; Abeni (we begged Olodumare to have her). Ba'mi had told me that our oriki were given at the time of our birth as eulogy to our progeny and a poetic source of inspiration to one's destiny. Mine was Abeni:

> *Precious daughter of Akindele,*
> *the one whose mother swaddled*
> *her with colourful dye clothe*
> *When she came in tears*
> *Progeny of Akinfa of Ibirapa*
> *The ones who listened to Ifa*
> *Orunmila said they should swim*
> *down a long river*
> *They obeyed*
> *and left the river for its bank*
> *Dutiful progeny of Akinfa*
> *who replaced a life of hunger*
> *for mighty barns of grain.*

My oriki was given because my mother had wished for a daughter after she had borne two sons. It is said that she had asked Orunmila for a special intercession, and he had granted her special favours in the manner of my birth.

"Come closer my daughter." The woman beckoned. I crawled closer towards her on my knees and she hugged me lightly. Her grip was gentle but firm. I felt the weathered toughness of her palms upon my wrist, she smelt of cam wood.

"You are very blessed amongst women." She said to me.

"Thank you, ma." I replied, watchful, as she inspected my face.

"You are very beautiful too." She added before turning back to my mother with approval. "You have brought her up well."

"Thank you Iya." My mother accepted the compliment with grace.

"Tell me Omitirin, do you know who I am?"

"No Iya." I replied

She said nothing as she continued to study my face intently.

"She has her resemblance as well." She said finally, in what sounded like an important verdict. I felt my mother re-adjust her posture, using her palms to wipe off imaginary specs of dust from her laps in approval.

"I am your mother's very old friend and elder sister." The woman said to me. She clicked her finger to accentuate the length of time they had known each other.

"We grew up together and have been friends from just about when we were your age, not far from this village. Your mother and I made an oath to each other many years ago before you were born and we thank Iya Yemoja that we have both lived to see the day when our oaths will be redeemed."

I looked at my mother, who sat there expressionless.

"Omitirin, I am going to be like your mother now. Your second mother. Would you like that?"

I turned to look at my mother yet again, searching her face for a clue to all this, but I found none.

"Don't be afraid my child." the woman said smiling as she sensed my unease. "I might have no child of mine, but I have many daughters like you. Your mother told me that you saw your first flow two weeks ago. Is this true my child?"

"Yes, Iya." I nodded, again startled at how this piece of news had spread.

"Then you are truly blessed Abeni, my daughter. It means that it is time for you to come live with me and the other women who will be your sisters."

I looked up at her, confused by all what I was hearing, and willing my mother to speak.

Iya finally rose to her feet and asked my mother.

"Do you have the cloth?"

"Yes." My mother handed her the cloth with which I had cleaned myself on that first night, neatly folded into a parcel and tied together by twine. I watched as she took the piece of cloth and put it into a pouch she carried. She left her pap and bean cakes untouched. She left as she had come, with such a deliberate stride for a woman her age, escorted by carriers bearing the best tubers of yam from my father's barn.

That had been two months ago. Now I sat quietly outside my mother's living quarters, on a wooden stool carved out of timber. My feet rested on the brightly coloured raffia mat that had been my place of solitude all these weeks. My hair was being shaved by my mother with a supporting party made up of female relatives and friends. They were singing. It wasn't the loud and raucous type of singing we engaged in during the harvest festivals, but rather mellow and thoughtful and deep. There was a rhythm about it that was comforting. It was a praise song. They sang to 'Iya O' as Yemoja was affectionately called by the women of our community. They sang her praises and told of her exploit, and begged her for her favour. I listened to the words of the song and watched as my hair fell to the ground. I was lost in a near trance of mixed emotion. Sad to see my hair go, bewildered by the honour ma'mi said was about to be done me and our family and afraid of what the next few months might hold.

~

Not long after the Iya left, ma'mi had called me into her room and sat me down again. She took me in her embrace and rocked me gently, the way she had always done when I was much younger and she had to nurse me back from the fever.

"Omitirin, my redeemer." She whispered and then, she began to sob. I could not remember if I had ever seen her cry in recent years.

"What is it ma'mi? Why are you crying?" I asked bewildered. "Did somebody die?"

"N-no." She sniffed, wiping her nose with the edge of her wrapper. "Must somebody die for a mother to cry? There is nothing wrong my daughter. These are tears of joy. I know that you do not understand Omitirin. I know that all this might seem strange and confusing to you, but these are good days for our household."

Ma'mi left my side for a moment to draw herself a drink of water from our earthen pot by the corner of her room. She returned with a small calabash in her hands.

"Omitirin, it is time for me to explain all this to you." She said as she took a sip. She sat next to me then cracked her knuckles loudly.

"Many years ago when I was not even the age you are now, I was promised by my mother to the convent of priestesses of Yemoja. My own mother had suffered as a child because she would not stay in this world. She was an *Abiku* child. She would reach the age of seven then leave this world, only to return a few years later through her same mother. She caused her mother so much pain that one day after the death of yet another daughter, my grandmother, who is your great grandmother finally decided to consult Ifa about her predicament. The Ifa priest told her that the only thing that Ifa said could stop all this recurring death of her daughter, was if she submitted the daughter to the Orishas by dedicating the daughter to the service of one of the female deities. When my grandmother then asked which female deity specifically, Ifa replied that the choice had to be hers from amongst three."

Ma'mi lifted her hand and counted on three of her fingers. "There was Oya, the goddess of the great Tapa River and deity of the tempestuous harmattan wind, Sango's warrior queen, who wielded his thunderbolt in her palm and went into battle wielding her cutlass before him. There was Osun, the coy goddess of the cool waters of the Osun River, the consort queen and giver of sweet and beautiful things, lover of children and protector of her worshippers from epidemics and finally there was Yemoja, the deity of our own river here; the Ogun River. The greatly endowed mother of all gods, who blessed women with fertility and the land with abundance."

Ma'mi brought her hand down and touched me lovingly on the shoulders before she continued with her story.

"The priest mentioned that your great grandmother would be given three months to make up her mind, after which she would return to make her sacrifice to her chosen deity. Your great grandmother left and spent the next three months meditating on which of the three Orishas to choose."

Ma'mi paused to search my face. I was listening with rapt attention.

"Was it a test ma'mi?" I asked.

My mother looked at me curiously. "Yes," She replied. "In a way, it was a test. But only the type your great grandmother could find an answer to by herself. There was never going to be a right or wrong answer. There was only going to be her choice on the matter. Because as you may not know, though all three Orishas were river goddesses and great wives to Oduduwa's sons, they were also very different in their qualities, their *ase* or spirits, and the powers they each possessed. Ifa was asking her to go and reflect on how she would choose to worship her creator and it was a choice she had to make for herself as much as it was one she would have to make for her daughter, my mother as well."

"Your grandmother chose Yemoja didn't she?"

Ma'mi nodded gently and sighed. There was a lurking sadness within her that I did not understand. She fell silent for a while rocking her body gently like one who felt the weight of a burden that had been carried for too long.

"Yes, Omitirin." she continued, as she cupped my face in her cold hands. "Our great matriarch chose that her daughter would serve Yemoja as priestess in her order. Yemoja the great mother of all who birthed the sixteen realms of Ile Ife, where Oduduwa himself descended from heaven to create the earth as we know it today. When she returned to the Ifa priest to report her decision, it was said that Ifa received it well and her sacrifice was accepted. But it was there that Ifa then told her that the covenant must be passed down from one generation of daughters to the next. That on the first sighting of her menstrual cycle, every first daughter of the successive generation was to be bound to the service of

22

Yemoja as a priestess in her order. Only in agreeing to this would her daughter live and not die prematurely.

My grandmother agreed to this and as Ifa promised she had my mother two years later. My mother came into this world when her own mother saw her thirty-eighth harmattan, but this time she stayed as it had been promised. Twelve harmattan seasons later, her mother kept the covenant with Ifa and ensured that she entered the convent to train as a priestess as was promised to Ifa. It is said that my mother served Yemoja diligently for eighteen harmattan seasons until she died when she was birthing me."

I sat there in silence, watching as my mother told me the story, amazed at how so little I had known about our family and our history. I understood now for the first time in my life why certain occurrences in the past, which had seemed so innocuous at the time, had elicited heated argument among the grownups in our household. I was however still left confused about another issue. I did not know my mother to have ever been a priestess of Yemoja. It was as though ma'mi, had read my thoughts. She gave me a wry smile and lifted the edge of her wrapper once more towards her face. She wiped her forehead and readjusted herself where she sat facing me on her mat placed on top of an elevated mound of earth. At this moment, as I watched her tell me these things, ma'mi seemed older and fatigued. The wrinkles now looked deeply etched into her forehead and worry lines stood pronounced around her mouth. Her usual stern demeanour had faded, brought about by the relief of sharing a burden that had been bottled away for too long.

"I had no mother to carry me, Omitirin." She eventually blurted out remorsefully. "I had no mother to speak the truth of life to me and guide me in this world. I was an only child so I grew up with my grandmother who was not pleased with me. It was she who watched over me but she was overcome by the grief of the passing of her beloved daughter, for whom she had suffered for so long. She would sometimes blame me for my mother's death. She would accuse me of being sent to spite her, but how could that be. How could my *ashe* be that evil as to plan the death of my own mother?"

My mother was weeping by now. The tears flowed freely down her cheeks and stained her wrapper with her pain.

"Esu plays wicked tricks on us in this life, but I know my ori is good." Ma'mi said wiping the tears from her cheeks. "When I saw my first flow, I went to my grandmother to tell her the good news expecting that I would also be given to the service of Yemoja, but mama rejected me and rejected Ifa. She said that Ifa took her daughter away despite her sacrifice and covenant, that I was not a replacement in her eyes. Till the day that she died, she denied me the privilege of entering the convent of Yemoja, because she said I killed her daughter. She laid me bare on the anthill of misfortune to be devoured by all who cared. For over five harmattan seasons, I would go to the entrance of the shrine begging to be let in but only to be denied by the sisters for fear of enraging mama. It was on one of those occasions that I met Iya Metu, the Olorisa who came to see you. She was much younger then. She had already been given to the sisters many years earlier and had started receiving her instructions in the mysteries of Iya wa. She knew my story and took pity. At great risk to her place in the order she befriended me and became like an elder sister to me. It was at that time that I asked her to swear to me that should I have a daughter, and she came of age, she would take her into the order and guide her in the mysteries of Yemoja, our great mother who my own mother served as priestess until she died having me."

24

I was crying as well by now. I found my heart heavy also and caught up in the pain, shame and self-guilt that I never realised had haunted my mother all her life.

Ma'mi hugged me. "Omitirin. Ah! Omitirin. My redeemer. That is why I gave you this name, you know? *Ibi ti omi tirin si.* Where the waters recede and are at their lowest ebb. Because you came at a time of personal sorrow. But wipe your tears." Ma'mi said. "I have cried enough tears for both of us all these years ago. Now is the season of redemption for us and our mothers before us."

I nodded my head in a heavy acceptance and took the edge of the wrapper off her. I helped wipe the tears from my mother's cheeks.

~

Ba'mi had come to see how the preparations were going. Never a man for many words, ba'mi glanced my way and nodded his head as if to approve of my sudden baldness. The singing had reached new levels of fervour and more people had begun to arrive at our compound. The drummers who would add to the cadence of the ceremony were to be seen drinking in the distance. I knew one of the drummers. He was my brother's friend and had once mentioned to me that the fermented drink they took helped to loosen the hand when it began to beat the talking drum. I was told that the Olorisa Iya metu had arrived with her entourage of sixteen women from the order. My mother had explained to me that she was now the third most ranking priestess in the service of Yemoja all over the various realms of the Yoruba. She was sought after by several other orders because of her deep understanding of the mysteries of our great mother. Ma'mi told me with great pride that Iya metu had summoned the sixteen women from various orders around our community to represent the sixteen cowries of Ifa's divination beads. The sisters she had summoned were here to support me when I began the ceremony and be my escorts as I began the solemn procession towards the Yemoja's shrine of seclusion and convent. The convent was tucked away in a remote part of the forest by the bank of the great Ogun River. It was here, far away from the prying eyes of men, non-initiates and my family that I was to spend the next three months being cleansed and initiated into the spiritual mysteries of our great mother, Yemoja.

I was beckoned onto my feet by one of the women present. By now, my head was completely bald and I felt sores in a few spots where the sharp knife had unkindly cut into my scalp. A wet cloth was used to clean my scalp and a light blend of palm oil and rock salt was rubbed on it as a balm of sorts. I watched as a younger woman who had all along been grinding some whitish cam wood into a wooden mortar with a small pestle, now brought the prepared paste towards me. I was covered in a simple white cloth, tied securely around my armpits and dropping just below my knees. My breasts were yet to fully ripen so the cloth clung to me snuggly making me look more like a playful child. The women took turns dabbing my exposed body with spots of cam wood. The patterns they made were ticklish, but dried quickly and soon my skin looked like the patterns on the skin of a spotted white hyena.

Iya Metu finally arrived and inspected me. She asked that a few things about me be adjusted and soon held my hand and began to lead me towards the communal square. The drummers had joined in by now and the festivities were well underway. My mother and her entourage all followed behind, singing in a choral harmony. Some swayed to the pulsating rhythm of the shrill Bata drums while others clapped in concert with the wooden clave dutifully tapped upon by one of them. There were several parties of onlookers about, mostly our kinfolk. They called out to me as I walked past them. The women prayed for me and poured water at my feet, while the men and the children simply stared.

We finally reached the edge of the communal square, where a larger crowd was gathered. I spotted my brothers perched on tree tops amongst the crowd, intently watching the proceedings. I wondered where my father was. Then I saw Ayanke. She was standing next to her mother looking at me curiously. Our eyes met for an instance and then I saw her look away. Startled by her reaction, I had not noticed that Iya metu had placed her two hands on my shoulders to stop me. When I looked up, she brought out a native clave and began tapping a new rhythm. The women who were to be my escorts filed towards us making a semi-circle, and began to exalt their deity:

Ashe o Iya mi Yemoja!
Mother whose children are fish
Who inhabits the great river
Mother whose salt runs in our veins
you give life when ours have drained
you are the mother
who lives in our tears
revealing your benevolence
in both our darkest
and happiest moments.
You are the great begetter
and mother to other gods.
You curve the river like the wind
and sculpt their travels in stone.
Even the mountains
cannot stop you on your journey
and there is no obstacle

you cannot circumvent.
There is nothing
that can block your way.
Even the hardest and strongest
will give way.
Ashe o Iya mi Yemoja!

Iya metu looked over to me and whispered loudly. "It is time for you to start your journey our precious bride. Hug your mother and bid her farewell."

She placed a large calabash on top of my head. It was filled with two mirrors, parcels of cloth, a yam tuber, small bags containing yam flour and salt, a vat of palm oil and a small bag of cowries. They were items I would need to take care of myself while at the convent. I balanced the calabash on my head and turned to face ma'mi. She was beaming with joy and pride, yet tears ran down her cheeks. She took hold of me and said,

"I have something for you Abeni." she had addressed me by my oriki which underscored the importance of the moment. She pulled out something from within the pouch in her inner clothing where women kept precious and sensitive things, and placed it in my open hands. I opened them to reveal an intricately carved figurine. It had been carved in dark hard forest wood, and covered in mud cloth. It had the head and body of a woman. Her face was etched with the distinct tribal marks of the Ile-Ife people from where we all descended. Her torso showed an ample bosom. Her neck was adorned with cowrie beads. Her lower body was carved to show a pair of generous buttocks, but rather than legs she had the tail of a fish. She held two children in her arms; a boy and a girl, and it looked as though they were both being breast fed.

"It is the symbol of Iya Yemoja, our great mother and giver. It belonged to my mother and her own mother before her, when it was given to her at the time of her promise to Ifa. Keep it safe and honour her well Abeni so that we both may be redeemed and our mothers before us."

I did not know then, that it would be the last time I would set eyes on my mother.

CHAPTER 3

I t had been agreed with my mother that my stay at the convent of our great mother would last three months. Iya Metu would explain to me later, that after those three months, I would be allowed to return to my family for a little while. I was to return to the Popo to continue my obligations in the service of the Orisha. My Awofakan, which was the ceremony where I graduated from the first level of understanding would be at the start of the rainy season, and coincide with the planting season. It would offer an opportunity for me to witness Yemoja's benevolence of fertility in the renewal of crops for her devotees as we watered plants with waters drawn from the great Ogun River.

Her shrine was constructed of fine swish-mud, and enclosed within an enclave of tall bamboo trees, that made soft wailing noises when the thick harmattan wind coursed through them in the evenings. In front of the shrine were carved wooden columns and totem poles with staccato etchings and motifs burnished with dye. The walls of the shrine also had motifs depicting fishes, snails, tortoises as well as ferns and large water lilies. No man was allowed anywhere near the Popo, nor were children, except on special occasions and ceremonies.

My new life at the convent of the shrine was filled with cleaning and clearing of the light brushes that surrounded the enclave. I joined the other younger women in the harvesting of coco yams and the preparation of meals which were served to the elderly priestesses or those devotees who came on special pilgrimage to perform special prayers and sacrifices to Iya wa. In the evenings when it was much cooler, I would gather with the younger women at a spot by the river to sing hymns and songs of praise or to listen to Iya Metu or her Ojugbona, explain Yemoja's ashe or spiritual essence to us. We were shown the several special herbs which were to be used for treating various ailments, including specific treatments for women's infirmities such as excessive bleeding, fibroids or even barrenness. We learnt how to prepare them for adults, as well as how to make the bitter concoctions sweeter so children would not spit them out.

The Iyalodes, as the elderly women among us were called, spoke about the mysteries of Ifa. We would listen as they recounted various verses of the Ifa; the Odus which were the allegories of the creator of the universe itself, as revealed to humans through the teachings of his trusted prophet Orunmila. They had been passed down orally through generations, to guide us today, just as they had guided our ancestors. We were women, Iya metu would remind us ever so delicately, and as women, our own powers existed in our ordained place within the mysteries of the Orishas we served.

Our order she explained was in obedience to Yeye Yemoja, the mother goddess and divinity of the great Ogun River, the ancient daughter of Obatala and wife of Agayu, who herself gave birth to several gods.

We were women and would be wives, the Iyalodes would say, so we had to be careful and seek *ashe pele*, and *ire rere*, which symbolised the spirit of peace and goodwill.

"Yemoja hates death so we must stay away from quarrels, fights and violent atmospheres. We are creators of life and solutions for our communities therefore we must avoid death." the women admonished.

"Avoid those who wield daggers, knives and swords because they destroy Yemoja's ashe and corrupt our harmony with her." Iya Metu had warned us.

We were instructed not to loiter on the corners of paths, or crossroads as other idle minds might do in search of gossip, so that Esu the trickster Orisha would not deny us our fraternity with our mother deity. But above all, she admonished that henceforth I must make it a duty to regularly visit the great Ogun River to offer thanks and prayers to Yemoja by giving her bean cakes, which was her favourite food.

It reminded me of my mother who I had always been convinced made the best bean cakes in the whole of Akindele. I now understood why she had spent so much time making sure she taught me how they were made. I could not wait to return to her to regale her with tales of my experience at the convent.

There were evenings such as today when we were left alone to do what we pleased. I found it strange that the convent though not so far away from our village, could offer such an enriching life experience so different from what I had back home in my father's compound. I recalled that it had taken less than half a day of trekking for the procession to get here. The walk had been slow and certain portions of the path were far from well beaten tracks which meant we had to circumvent great boulders or snake infested craters. We came across wild boar and antelopes several times, but no one stopped as men would usually do to see if they could track the game for meat. On this evening, I walked to the river bank and sat there in silence, allowing the harmattan breeze to hit my scalp that had barely begun to grow back hair. I had the figurine my mother had given me. I carried it with me everywhere now. It was wrapped in the same cloth that it had come with. I spent most of the free time examining the carvings and admiring the beautiful workmanship that had gone into its creation.

The figurine was the length of half the distance from my elbow to the tip of my longest finger, and it required my two cupped palms to just about cover its width. I noticed that it had chipped slightly at a portion of the tail, perhaps from the altar that it must have been kept. It was the most prized possession my mother had ever entrusted me with and that fact sometimes frightened me. I had never seen it with my mother until the day she handed it to me, nor had I ever heard any stories about it from anyone in my family. I wondered what my great grandmother would have felt when she was handed the precious symbol by the Ifa priest who read her odu for her. It must have cost her a fortune to have it made. I wondered if the two children who suckled on the nipples were twins. There was a song the new brides in our community always sang when they became eager for children to consummate their marriages:

It is children that own the world
It is children that own the world,
Orunmila please give me children
Though there may be difficulties in this world
I am not afraid o ye
I am not afraid to birth twins

I cradled the figurine and sang the song softly to myself, just above the rustle of the river reeds which seemed to approve with their own harmony. I knew then in my heart that since Yemoja loves me I would always talk with her during my chores and in my playtime to remind her about my mother's pain and beg her to give her peace and redeem her *Ori* by giving me my own children that she could be grandmother to. They would be twins, sired by a strong, handsome and hardworking man. Maybe he would be a prosperous farmer, with barns filled with good harvest or a craftsman. Perhaps even a leader in a great royal court, maybe he would be like Sango and lord to a kingdom of his own. Yet whoever he would be, I would bear him twins, many strong sons and then a daughter who would follow in my footsteps...

"What are you doing day dreaming my daughter?"

I turned to see Iya Metu walking towards me clutching some leaves in her hands and a chewing twig that darted about in her mouth.

"You are like your mother, truly." She laughed as she sat on a fallen trunk just away from me. "But you are more perceptive and gentler of spirit."

I knelt to greet her and then rose, quickly wrapping the figurine away. She waved me to sit.

"Yes, she really was more a woman of trade, but you, I see by the way you grind the herbs and the way you stare at the water's edge that your ashe is more towards the water than your mother's. Perhaps that is how Ifa wanted it all along. Did your mother ever share with you what Ifa divined at your *Ese te aye* ceremony on the seventh day after your birth?"

"No Iya mi," I replied. "I was never told."

"Hm! It is between you and your parents and Ifa anyway. May you fulfil your destiny."

"Ase." I replied.

She looked at the figurine then pointed at it, smiling. "That, you must keep well. I first saw it with your grandmother when we served our great mother together. She treasured it deeply and served it as best she could. There was an altar made for it in her husband's house at the time, your late grandfather's. She would adorn it appropriately and serve her with water and shells and bean cakes, very well spiced Efo vegetable. She would sprinkle drops of palm oil once every two weeks in supplication." She paused for a short while then gently shook her head. "It is strange sometimes the way of the Orishas, to call home quickly those for whom they have a particularly fondness. I sometimes do wonder if that wasn't your grandmother's case. May she continue to rest well with her ancestors."

"Ase." I replied.

Iya metu rose and waved me to join her as she began to trek back to the enclave.

"Tomorrow will be your eighty-ninth day here and the day after will be your ninetieth when you are to be released from seclusion and returned to your parents to visit. So, in preparation you must go and bathe yourself in the water, to cleanse yourself of your old ways and take on the new anointing of Iya Yemoja. Tomorrow is to be a special day my dear daughter." Iya repeated as she feigned a symbolic bata dance step. I giggled as I watched her dance and discovered a new fondness for her and her devotion to the mysteries of Iya wa within me.

"Come quickly." She continued. "You must sleep early so you can dip just before the first light, when the water will be cool

35

and *ire rere* will be abundant, so you and the sisters can prepare to return to your people later in the day."

CHAPTER 4

Iya Metu had told me the night before, that my mother had brought me to a spot by the river and offered me to Yemoja herself. She had come alone one morning just like this one, when it had been quiet and the water cool and unperturbed. She had prayed to the deity for mercy and life, and had promised me to her service when the time came. Iya metu had said that such prayer would always be answered because it was offered at the best time of the day. It was early in the morning that one should seek the face of Yemoja, when prayers and exhortations could be whispered quietly into her ears rather than shouted across the din.

I had come alone, as Iya metu and the sisters had instructed me. I brought the figurine along with me, as well a decorated calabash filled with perfumed soap and ash. I had draped a white wrapper around myself and taken from the twig she always chewed to clean both my teeth and tongue.

The first light of day had barely broken through, and the forest was silent and at peace. I took off my wrapper and cast it onto a nearby shrub. I scanned the area looking for a safe and comfortable spot within the river to dip. I found a spot not too far off where it seemed like a tree trunk had fallen in. It was hedged on the side by a few round boulders. I thought perhaps it had been used as a cloth washing spot by a few before, but that was highly unlikely given how remote the spot was. The river ran gently at the spot, its current broken by the log as well as the boulders. They had smooth round contours polished over time by the current. The river wasn't deep which suited me. I was barely a good swimmer, but I could waddle in the water. I carried the figurine and calabash in separate hands and made my way to the boulders. The water was just below my breasts and the coldness of the current hardened my nipples. I placed the figurine carefully in a crevice between two of the boulders. It offered to secure it against the flow of the current, while I placed the calabash on top. My nakedness shone beneath the waters as the beautiful first light now cast a silver streak upon my reflection. I opened out my palms to scoop water and poured it over my head. I lathered myself with the soap, using simple circular motions to knead the sweet-smelling potion deeper into my pores. I began to chant the *odu* I had been given by the priestesses. I asked Iya to look upon me kindly and to find me worthy in my devotion to her. I traced her antecedent as a cherished ancestor and canonised goddess among our people. I recognised her as first amongst all women and hailed her fertility through the years. As I poured water on myself, I made sure to pour an equal amount onto her effigy as well. I prayed and sang and washed, grateful that I would be reunited with my mother and father by this time the day after tomorrow.

It was at that moment that someone grabbed me and flung me away from my perch, further into the river bed. Startled by what had just happened, I screamed. I raised my head above the waters and saw a full-bodied man in nothing but bloodied loin cloth swimming towards me, clutching at a dagger. His torso was massive and he had death in his eyes. His teeth though pure white was stained dirty brown at the tip and his face when I saw the light shine on it was decorated with tribal patterns that I had never seen before. They were not like the tribal marks our people bore. These were painted lines and patterns. He made to grab me while speaking a strange language that I had never heard before. When he finally reached me, he swung the butt of his dagger with such force. I remember screaming as loud as my voice could muster as I made out two other men grabbing at me just before the blow landed on my head, and a darkness come over me.

My head throbbed when I awoke. I felt sharp pains at my wrists and ankles and through the haze and agony I looked to find that I had been shackled with iron chains. I moaned deeply, again shocked to find that I was suspended from a thin wooden pole carried by two men on either side, the way hunters carried home their game after a successful hunt. My neck was raw with pain and my face was barely an arm's length away from the dirt path that we seemed to trek along. I could make out a few people ahead of me. They were also chained at their wrists and ankles, but they were walking, barely staggering of their own volition. They were all bound together in a chain gang. They were sobbing and cursing in our language. I raised my head yet again to see what was behind me. I saw another line of shackled captives and further back were four men dressed in flowing robes and dark turbans that covered their heads and faces. They were carrying whips and long swords which they used frequently to strike the captives ahead of them as they admonished them to walk faster.

The sun had fairly risen, but it remained hidden away from full view by the broad crest of tree branches and forest fauna scattered all about us. There were so many fleas and mosquitoes preying on us, and the distant call of monkeys, and other wild animals echoed. I cried out in pain and fright, asking where I was, and what it was that these people wanted of me. I screamed out for my mother and Iya Metu, and thrashed about intermittently in my suspended state, as I tried to release myself from my shackles. I was stark naked. The two men who carried me were equally shackled. They said nothing to me as they each balanced the end of the thin pole that bore me on their shoulders. They seemed disoriented and despondent. Sweat poured from their naked torsos and I saw as they grimaced with pain every time I moved my bulk.

I did not know who all these people were, but I slowly came to realise that I had been captured by slavers. It was a rarely mentioned occurrence in our homeland. I had heard the stories of how people from different towns raided errant villages and hamlets that they were at war with.

It was said that those hamlets that had no protection from the Orishas, nor our rulers, had their people captured and sold away to the slave traders who then resold them to the white people from across the mighty ocean. These were stories I could never really understand. Mere myths I had believed, brandished by our parents to scare us, and that we carried in our heads as children to keep us on the straight path. Things we believed only happened to other people, and never a course of event that would be one's own destiny. This was all a mistake. In fact, I was sure I was having a night mare that I would soon wake up from. The priestesses would all be looking for me by now, and I would make my way back soon. A deeper wave of dread and anguish fell over me, as I contemplated the thought of being separated from my family. I thrashed about like a bound hyena screaming for my mother and Yemoja to save me and fainted.

The taste of cool water tickled my palate and soothed my patched throat. I swallowed it hungrily, willing my bound hands free so that I may cup them and draw more of the water into me. I opened my eyes to see one of the captives aiding me with a drink of water. I had been dropped on to the ground, though still shackled and bound to the pole. My two carriers sat like sacks of heavy millet on the ground beside me, all life ebbed out of them. They watched as the woman who stood over me fed me water and splashed some over my forehead. She had marks on her cheeks that suggested that she was Yoruba from Oyo land. They were thick and prominent. She said nothing to me at first as I struggled to swallow and open my eyes to take in my new surrounding and situation. The sun had gone down and the party had been settled into a tight group in a clearing next to a stream. Our captors surrounded us in a full circle, brandishing swords as well as bows and arrow. Two of them carried Dane-guns, which they slung on their shoulders. There must have been eight of them. They shouted their conversation across to each other while using their eyes to guard us. Very often, one of them would get up from the floor where they stooped, and whip one of the captives without warning. The others would snigger at how the person cowered from the sting of the whip. They shared kola nuts amongst themselves shouting their strange language.

I uttered a weak thank you to the woman. She nodded and returned to where she sat with a boy half my age. I noticed that he had been whimpering. His nose was running with mucus, while his eyes were rheumy and weary. It made me think of my mother, so I started crying as well. I did not feel the first sting of the whip when they landed on my body. It was the evil look in the man's eyes revealed from within the

41

turban he wore that frightened me even more, causing me to wretch even deeper. I threw up on myself. Not much came out because I hadn't eaten anything all day. Rather, I produced a pale mixture of bile, water and self-pity. I raised my arms to protect myself from the whip as he struck at me again and again, shouting his strange language at me. One of the men barked something at him and he stopped for a moment. Instead he grabbed my chin and forced me to reveal my teeth, which he then inspected carefully. He seemed to be pleased with what he saw and dropped my chin.

It was impossible to sleep that night. Every evil that lurked in the jungle came out in search of prey I thought. The men killed snakes and scorpions about them, and even a congress of baboons came to share the warmth from the fire that was built to keep our captors warm. I heard a few of the captives speak amongst themselves. I understood most if not all of what they said even though the dialects were slightly different. They were mostly Egbado, and Oyo dialects. One of the captives told the others that he had been sold by his own father in lieu of a payment of debt his father had owed to a courtier, an Ilari at Ede. The courtier hadn't had need for him, so had sold him to one of the slavers instead. He said he bore his father no grudge, as he was confident that he would pay his way out of debt and return to his village. The woman who had given me water, kept watching us curiously as she listened to the captives speak. She would sigh ever so often. A big heave which brought her bosom out before it returned to where it had come from. Her son now slept by her side, breathing loudly and waking often in startling fits which caused him to cry out, only to be pat on the head back to sleep by his mother. Eventually she spoke in a deep guttural Oyo accent. 'Fula' she hissed out loud. She told the others that our captors were Fula slavers from far north of Oyo-Ile where the Alaafin of Oyo ruled most of Odua land from. They had raided her hamlet of Lagelu two months ago, and killed her husband in the process. She and her son had been with the slave party for over three weeks now on the trek to the port town of Eko where we were going to be sold to the white people who came from across that mighty ocean. These slavers did not worship our gods she told us but rather faced the East to pray five times every day calling on a god they called Allah. They had powerful amulets they wore on their fore arms which gave them powers to see ahead of mere mortals. She had witnessed how when a marauding party had tried to snatch away some of the captives from them, they had followed and caught the rustlers and ruthlessly killed each one of them with their daggers. These were terrible people and were to be truly feared she said.

"What will become of us?" One of us asked aloud. "Surely the Orishas will save us?"

I saw one of the men who had carried me shift his massive frame where he sat staring into the night. His face had a deep gash that ran from his temple down to his cheeks and stopped by his chin. The Oyo woman had whispered that he was a convicted murderer who had been sold to the Fula slavers by the Ogboni cult in a small town outside Remo, as punishment for his crime. He sneered with despondence, showing a gap in his gums where teeth had once been. His tongue darted about and then he spat.

"Ours is finished." He said as he looked over his shoulders to where the captors watched over us. "Are we not the ones the Orishas have forsaken?"

43

We trekked alongside the river bank for two painful days, on our journey towards the coastal town of Eko, until we finally reached the river crossing at Isheri, the village of the Awori. Isheri was a large village with more thatched huts than I had ever seen. They all nestled close together in the harmattan as though sharing warmth from each other on both sides of the river. My mother had told me that they were once prosperous fishermen and traders. Then the white people had come from across the great ocean and now offered them their wares in exchange for slaves. They bought the *eru-* slaves from all over the hinterland and as far as the desert planes in the far north. They carried them across the river in great canoes to various slave markets along the shore of the great ocean. There, they handed them over to the white men for cowries and cloth. I had always stared in disbelief as ma'mi told my brothers and I these stories. Shocked at how strange such a trade must be, not for once ever imagining that I would be a victim of such in my life time. Ironically, it had been my brothers who she had always been more worried about. The two of them were ever so adventurous, wandering off into the thicket and on occasion even deeper into the dense forest that surrounded our homestead to set traps and snares for porcupines, bush rats and even the occasional antelope. On such days when good fortune shone on them with a worthy kill, they would come back into the village like conquering heroes. They would skin and gut the animal and lay its meat onto ma'mi's table at the night market in front of the Bale's house. She would beam with pride as she helped them sell the meat, and yet fuss over them at the risk she felt they took at times. "There are dangerous tribes out there." She would quip sternly. "They don't like the Egba for who we are. We must all be careful." She explained that the Awori had originated from Ife but they changed ever since they had been ruled by the

44

Ado people from far away Ado land. Ma'mi had warned us that the Ado were cannibals and practiced vicious witchcraft which sacrificed small children to heathen gods. They were to be feared she had said, and like the Ijebu, never to be trusted.

I saw canoes of different sizes resting on the water's edge, and people engaged in lively banter. The sort you heard in a market place, where the trade was brisk and the margins were good enough to be haggled for. Our captors bound us together tighter and inspected every inch of the iron shackles that restricted us. I was now able to walk on my own, though I limped slightly as I had suffered a cut to the side of my left heel. We approached what looked like the gates into a market. The floor was black with murk and the place stank of shit. I saw children playing with goats and poultry as their mothers tended food stalls. Men sat on wooden logs and make shift benches hurriedly scooping morsels of corn starch which they dipped into watery soups before swallowing hungrily. I heard dialects and languages of all sorts as we were marched passed groups of slave traders towards holding pens crudely constructed in the middle of the market square.

A thick plume of smoke rose like a massive column of black clouds in the distance and I could hear the distinct sounds of people wailing in anguish. I began to cry again, afraid that I was about to die. There were women and children in the pens just as men. Like us, they were all stripped of any covering and left shackled together. We were herded into a small pen and instructed to all sit on the floor. I fell in exhaustion and used my hands to knead the side of my thighs and feet, hoping to thaw away the pain I felt. I was hungry and thirsty and as I looked around me in fear, I wondered what was about to befall me. A small crowd gathered around our kernel observing our every demeanour and posture, the way we would observe goats and poultry at the weekly market back at my village. There was a crowd made up of young men in dusty work robes, and middle-aged women who tied their head cloth around their fallen breasts. I watched as they approached the Fula slavers and enquire about us. They made animated hand gestures to compensate for not being able to speak each other's language, then dispersed as quickly as they had come.

It seemed like they kept us there for all eternity, as new crowds also gathered and then dispersed. Some with rowdy laughter and others with sneers of disgust at what they perhaps considered an exorbitant price placed on our heads. We were fed as dusk began to settle. They gave a few morsels of corn starch meal with a dash of palm oil wrapped in banana leaves and a small gourd of water. I stooped to a huddle with my back to a post and wolfed my tiny portion down ravenously. The Fula who had been tasked with the responsibility of feeding us, watched me as I ate. He was much younger than the others, perhaps not many years older than my eldest brother. He had his turban off which exposed his curious eyes, his face was painted in bright colours. I noticed his eyes wander down towards my breasts and then gaze even further down. I stared back at him chewing on my food and licking the palm oil off my fingers. I felt the sudden crack of the whip as it tore through my back, knocking the breath out of me and tossing me unto the floor. It was the evil one amongst them, who once again came at me intent on inflicting pain. He shouted words at me that I did not understand, and pushed the young Fula away from where he stood watching me. I raised my arms just in time to protect my face from the second lash of the whip. Whatever remained of my food had been tossed into a nearby puddle. I screamed in pain as the third lash landed on my belly and tore the flesh open. The young Fula hurried back to join the others and I broke down weeping. Another group of three women came towards the kernel, attracted by the spectacle of my being whipped so viciously. Two of them had large calabashes balanced on their heads, while the third carried a log of fire-wood. They gesticulated at my tormentor and then watched as he turned towards the others. He waited only a moment before he then took hold of one end of the chains that bound us all together, and gave it a strong pull, dragging us all towards the edge of the kernel so we could be better inspected. He brandished his whip even more menacingly and motioned two of the men in our party to come closers towards him.

The women took turns examining one of the two men. They checked his teeth and asked him to stick out his tongue. I watched through my tears as he obeyed meekly. One of the women clasped his jaw and spent an inordinate amount of time inspecting his tongue. The leader amongst them then checked his hands and finally grabbed his genitals and squeezed hard, causing him to double over and wince slightly for a second. I noticed as she checked the tip for any signs of disease. The two younger women who had observed the proceedings burst into a giggle and a sharp exchange of banter amongst themselves. Perhaps not satisfied, the elderly woman called out to the evil one amongst the slavers and haggled some more. They must have eventually come to an agreement of some kind, because the man was released from amongst us and handed over to the women in separate chains. The women forced him to drink a potion, and then waited patiently for it to take effect before they led him away from us in a state of delirium.

We passed the night in the slave market kernel at Isheri village by the bank of the Ogun River. I barely slept. I tossed and turned in my sleep, tormented by visions of death and anguish that came to me. I saw Ayanke casting a spell on me, and the contorted apparition of an old woman who must have been the grandmother I had never met, calling me into the abyss where a whole congregation of troubled souls wailed in anguish. I sought out my mother in my nightmare pleading for her to save me, but she did not come to me. It was the scream of the Oyo woman that woke me from whatever respite I found in sleep. I opened my eyes, where I lay on the murky floor to see her screaming and tearing out her hair in a fit of maniacal hysteria. "He is dead! He is dead!" She kept screaming as she fell on to the ground where the body of her son lay by her side. She shook his lifeless body vigorously, as she called his name. His eyes had entered into its sockets and his tongue now fell out of his mouth and dangled like that of a strangled dog. His body limp, cold and silent as she shook him like a tattered piece of rag in the harmattan wind.

"Olodumare, what have I done to deserve this?" She screamed into the quiet of the night. Her eyes were fiery red like madness, mucus ran down her nostrils and she sounded like a wounded hyena. I saw in it the hopelessness of a mother from whom everything had been taken, so I went to her side and held her and cried with her.

On the second night of our stay at Isheri, I was awoken yet again, but this time by the Fulas themselves. It was the evil one amongst them who came into the kernel and separated my shackles from among the others. He yanked me off from the floor and lifted me by the armpit and led me out of the kernel towards a group of three young men who stood beneath a kola nut tree discussing in hushed voices. They spoke in a dialect of Yoruba that was a little foreign to my ears but easily discernible and it seemed as if there was an argument going on among them as to where they should head to before first light.

"*Ma bo ba yi*" one of them kept saying to me; "Come with me this way."

He carried an oil lantern which gave a meek source of light, and barely lit the pathway we took towards the river embarkment. There we saw several canoes tethered together and bobbing up and down to the river's gentle waves. The call of bullfrogs echoed clearly in the night, and joined with the sound of water lapping the sides of the dugout canoes, to create a moment that would otherwise have seemed peaceful to me. But I was petrified. Unsure of what was about to befall me and disoriented by suddenly being yanked from what had been my only sense of routine and order since I was kidnapped. It helped that I could understand them. So, I asked. "Where are you taking me?"

The one with the oil wick simply looked at me but remained silent. He beckoned me into a large canoe, where another shackled young man in tattered loin cloth already sat waiting, tied to an anchor within the canoe. He seemed distant, lost to the situation around him, or perhaps resigned to his fate. He offered me no acknowledgement. He sat there staring into the distance.

"Please, where are you taking me?" I asked yet again, suddenly overcome with a new wave of chilling fright. It caused my legs to buckle and I choked on my words as I fought back a wail that was brewing from within my belly.

"You must be quiet." The man with the lamp finally retorted, as he shackled me firmly to another anchor within the canoe.

The men entered the river and pulled the canoe away from the embarkment before jumping on board once they had advanced towards deeper water. They grabbed hold of wooden paddles which lay on the canoe floor and then began to row methodically, pushing the canoe further along into the river.

"I-I am cold." I complained, as I hugged myself wanting them to pay me some attention.

They ignored me, so I fell silent and watched them row. Ours was the only canoe journeying at this hour. We glided effortlessly downstream through the brackish waters of the river, leaving the slave trading kernels at Isheri behind. I thought only about the Oyo woman and the terrible death of her son that I had witnessed. I prayed to Olodumare to help her, and I asked him to save me also from the bad dream that was manifesting before my own eyes. I stretched out my hands to the water and let the current flow through my open fingers, then cupped some to throw on my face. This was Iya Yemoja's River and I could not understand why she would forsake a girl like me when I had opened my heart to her worship. I surmised that I must have done something wrong either in this life or perhaps in my previous one. I must have killed someone, or possibly even a child. I let the waters run through my fingers and began to cry. It was painful and I was despondent, tired and afraid. The tears streamed down my cheeks and face, and stung me as they passed over the lacerations on my stomach where I had earlier caught the whip. The four men in the canoe, three free and the other enslaved, watched me. They all seemed unperturbed by whatever it was that I was doing, but I didn't care anymore. I jumped into the water, content on Iya taking my life. It was a futile effort, as I soon realised that the chain which shackled me to the canoe's weighty anchor would not allow the whole length of my body to be submerged in the water. I had only half my body in the water and the other outstretched hand caught in an uncomfortable pull by the side of the canoe. I trashed about with my feet and free arm making a splash. Movement rumbled the canoe. I screamed at the top of my lungs, begging for someone to come and save me from my captors despite knowing that we were in the middle of a large river. I felt the fight leaving me as I was dragged back into the canoe and dumped onto its' floor in one heap. One of the men slapped me on the head and shouted at me to behave myself otherwise they would gut me open and feed me to the fishes. Was that not what I wanted in the first place I wondered to myself? Yet, I no longer had the heart to tell them to their faces? I recoiled even further into myself. Heaving painfully and calling my mother's name so I could find some peace.

When I awoke from the slumber I had cried myself into, I saw that we were approaching a landing with a long protruding jetty made of bamboo sticks. The sun had begun to climb, casting early shadows about the canoe. There were few people standing by the jetty. I counted three canoes tied to stakes that were pushed deep into the sandy embarkment to hold them from floating away. The men manoeuvred our canoe towards the jetty so it could rest on its' side, making it easier for us to disembark. They brought me out first and secured me to a tree while they attended to the other slave. The few people standing by the jetty did not look our way, more interested in their banter, than our affairs. We left the jetty and marched along a narrow footpath past tall reeds and tiny ponds filled with dirty water that spawned several tadpoles. They darted amongst the water lilies in bloom. Their glorious big green leaves opened towards the sunshine for playful dragonflies to admire.

As we moved further inland, we encountered more people going about their daily business. No one really paid our party any attention, except the ones my age, particularly the females, who stared at me with a curiosity I did not fully understand. Eventually we ended up at a large homestead with several huts. By the largest hut before us, where a massive tree provided shade, was a veranda filled with fishes left out to dry. An old man sat on a mat beside the display of fish, eating a meal of water yams and smoked fish. He looked up as we approached him and accepted the obeisance of our two captors, who both called him father.

I listened as they both took turns in briefing him about their expedition to buy good merchandise at Isheri. They complained that the Popo's had not arrived with a good stock of slaves by the time they left, so they were forced to select from a kernel full of poorer stock from a few Ijebu dealers as well as a small party brought in by the Fula. They then pointed at the male slave who had barely said a word throughout our journey. They explained to their father that they had bought him off the Ijebu for a good price. Then they pointed at me and explained where I had been sourced from. The old man listened and nodded as he chewed on his fish. He cast long glances at both of us before returning his gaze to the food before him.

"Take them inside to the back and hold them with the others," he said. "Maybe tomorrow we will take them to the white men by the sea."

The two men stood up quickly and moved towards us.

"The girl, what happened to her?"

The two looked at each other nervously. "What do you mean father?"

"The girl," he said again. "She obviously looks poorly kept. Look at all her scaring."

One of them muttered something about my being a stubborn goat."

The old man raised his hand to signal that he didn't wish to hear of it.

"Which child ever comes willingly?" He smirked. "Keep her with the others for a few weeks. Make sure to clean and fatten her up well. The white men like the young girls, the ones with good teeth, growing breasts and firm buttocks. She is the type that will fetch a good price."

CHAPTER 5

The endless crashing of angry waves against the stretch of white sand, overwhelmed me with fear and astonishment, while the curious taste of salt enticed my lips. I had never seen so much water in my life. I stared at the great ocean that lay before me. It reached out into the horizon for as far as my eyes could see and met the morning sky in a close embrace at a place I was sure only *Olokun* the Orisha of the deep waters could ever touch.

I dropped to my knees and scooped the sand beneath my feet. The fine sand slipped through my fingers and returned themselves to the abundance of the shoreline. I knelt there transfixed, marvelling at the tiny mischievous crabs with funny legs that darted across the froth, stealing small fragments of food from each other. I had heard stories and descriptions of the greatness of the ocean told by the itinerant traders who visited Oko Akindele on our market days to buy farm produce and regaled us with worldly tales from their many travels. They had however, not prepared me for the amazement that I felt at this moment as I stared at the abundance of water and the majesty of the mighty ships in the distance, that danced on top her. How I wished that Ayanke were here with me to experience this. We would have run around the sand screaming playfully with delight and throwing sand at each other. We would have teased our toes with the splashing waves and marvelled at the massive shells that lay about the beach and provided play things for the sand crabs that crawled about aimlessly. Sadly, it was not the way I would have wished it. Instead I knelt at the spot alone and terrified. Shackled at my feet and neck, about to be sold off to the white men who lingered in the distance and unsure of where I would be taken next.

I had ended up spending over three months as a domestic slave in the quarters of the old slave trader and his sons at Ikorodu. My life with them had revolved around gutting, cleaning and drying the fish brought back from fishing expeditions by his fishing canoes very early every morning. The family traded the fish for slaves and other produce from slavers from the hinterland. The work was tedious and laborious but it kept me fed and clothed, and placed a roof over my head. He must have owned over one hundred slaves, all of whom he camped in his slave quarters scattered around the fishing settlement of Ebute Ikorodu. Every week, a dozen slaves would be taken out to be sold to the white men, and immediately replaced with a new consignment bought in from the slave markets at Ikosi, Isheri and sometimes as afar as Oudiah near Dahomey where, I later learnt he had a second wife.

There was some respite in the fact that life at Ikorodu had been less brutal than that while under the Fulas. We were fed generous portions and sometimes allowed to approach and talk to the other women and children encamped within his family quarters. I had made a new type of friend with one of his daughters. Her name was Bisagbo, and she was much older than I was. Her father owned me, yet her friendship had helped lessen my sorrow at being separated from my family. She would steal extra portions of Amala and Ewedu soup for me at the end of the day and she also helped to groom my hair as it grew back. She told me stories of her father and his generosity towards his slaves. My story would end well she would always console me. I asked her where it was that the slaves were eventually taken, but she claimed she didn't know much. The little she did know was from when she had once overheard her father telling a story of one of his encounters with a slave of the white man who himself had once been sold as a slave but now returned as a worker of one of the white men. He had Yoruba tribal marks and could speak the language of the white men fluently as well. The man had told her father that there was a great land across the sea at a place called Bahia, where our people worked as slaves for white men who had mighty farms of sugar cane and tobacco. The sugar cane they would turn into strong drink and sell to various ships that came to their land from distant places. He had said that the white men were very wealthy and had houses and palaces built with wood and stone. Their women wore trinkets and strange but beautiful clothes and their children played with all sorts of things. I asked her if they worshipped our Orishas but she said the man had said he did not know.

I stared at the great ships. They were the size of small hills with their masts tethered securely. Surely, I thought to myself, Olodumare would prevail in their land as well. Surely Olokun the Orisha who dwelled in the deep of the ocean, would be well instructed to ensure that all those who crossed on those ships would do so safely? I could see as smaller canoes bearing crews and cargo were rowed from the shore towards the vessels.

There were people about the shore and the distant exchange of banter came from the direction of wooden barracoons erected on the sand docks, where our party headed. Five vicious looking white men with rotten teeth stood guard at the gate with muskets which they immediately pointed at us the moment we were within a shouting distance. I looked at them with amazement, how odd they looked? Pale white like *afin* albinos, with ugly raw red patches like those seen on the baboon's bottom. Whatever happened to their skin, I wondered? How could a human be so light skinned, and their hair were not black and curly as I would expect of humans, but brown and the texture of the *Bere* raffia? Our handlers raised their right arms to the sky and with the other pulled out a piece of white cloth which they duly waved at the direction of the guards. The eight of us; six slaves and two handlers, were made to kneel on the sand while we watched as a sentry approach us. One of the handlers called out to him in their language and then pointed at us. The sentry studied each one of us carefully and called back to his colleagues.

Two other white men appeared from within the barracoon a few moments later and walked towards us. Each one had a long whip in his hands, the like of which I had never seen before. Our two handlers stood up as they approached and walked towards them waving the piece of white cloth. They exchanged what seemed like perfunctory greetings and began a conversation that seemed to take the better part of the morning. I could barely hear them over the splash of waves, nor could I understand what they were saying, but I hung on to the movement of their lips and a growing sense of foreboding overcame me. These strange white men did not seem like farmers to me. I began to whimper with fear and finally I saw that they were pointing in my direction. I felt a weakness envelope my entire body and I urinated on myself. The warm water ran down my inner thighs soaking the loin cloth with which I had covered myself and dropped on to the sand in a trickle. I looked down feeling ashamed of myself and began to cry.

The white men came over and lifted me by my armpits. One of them studied me, starting with my hair which he checked for lice and then my face. He pulled back each eyelid and peered into my eyeballs. Satisfied, he moved towards my nose and followed the contours of my thick nostrils with his thumb and index finger and plucked away at the tip with a snap. He then opened my mouth and stuck a finger in which caused me to gag. He grabbed hold of my neck and gave it a stern squeeze and worked downwards towards my torso and cupped both my breasts in his rough hands. The other laughed and I wanted to spit on him, but I held my mouth. He groped my entire stomach, and ran his fingers over the receding scars that had been formed from the bite of the Fula whip. I felt the white man thrust his finger into my private part. He was rough and wanton and I feared that I would bleed. He threw me down onto the sands and I watched as he brought his finger up to his nose to smell me. I would have wished to be taken and cast into the sea and left to the fishes and other creatures that dwelled in the deep with Olokun. I curled into a ball and covered myself with nothing but my two arms and shame. They were clearly not sufficient to neither drape my humiliation nor hide my pain so I took solace in the cool wetness of the beach sands and the playful crabs that danced about me. My tormentors continued to talk amongst themselves. I suspected that they were haggling on what would be a fair price for me. In my young mind I wondered how much I would fetch the old Ikorodu slave dealer. Surely my father would have been able to offer an equal amount in fine farm produce. I wondered if I should tell them that. It seemed strange how the memory of my father's produce brought comfort to me as I lay there waiting for my destiny to be decided by strange white men. The moment finally came when I was handed over to them along with three other slaves. Our erstwhile handler left with two unsold slaves, a sack of cowries and a wooden crate of sundry merchandise, while the four of us were marched into the barracoon.

There was a young boy about my age in the cage we were thrown into. He sat in the corner of the room singing softly to himself, but stopped to look at us the moment we were marched in. He watched us in silence as we gathered ourselves into a familiar huddle on the floor in the far corner of the room.

Finally, he spoke to us in Yoruba. "You are welcome. Don't be afraid." His dialect was different from mine but I could understand him. We nodded, but still chose to keep to ourselves, wary of any movement from him.

"Where have you come from?" He asked.

"From far." One of us answered.

He nodded politely. I watched him closely. He couldn't have been more than fifteen or sixteen harmattans, but he looked older.

"Where have you come from yourself?" Someone else in our party asked.

"From Osogun, near Iseyin in Oyo." He replied. "It is far from here."

"What is your name?" I asked him.

He looked at me and smiled gently. "My name is Ajayi Omo Alapere. What is yours?"

"Omitirin." I answered. "You are a son of a weaver?"

"Yes." He nodded. "My father was a weaver in our village. Where are you from?"

"Oko Akindele, near Ake."

"How did you get here?"

"I was captured by Fula slavers while I was bathing at Yemoja's River."

"Fulas." He sighed. "It was they who raided our village, along with the Muslims from Ilorin. They took us all away." There was so much sadness in his voice.

"They brought you here?" I asked.

"No, I have been taken from my father's compound for many months now. They sold me from one slave trader to another. My last owner was an Eko slave trader who bought me from another from Ikosi where I crossed a big river. I was with him for over three months in a slave house, but he sold me to the white man only a few days ago to be taken away."

"Just like us." I whispered." We lived with an old slave dealer in Ikorodu for three months but we were brought here today."

"I heard some people talking in the other cages that the white men are in a hurry to leave Eko. They say that a big ship filled with white warriors is coming to free any slaves taken by them."

"I do not understand," I quizzed. "Which people are these? Do the white men have people among them who oppose this?"

Ajayi drew closer towards me. He whispered in a conspiratorial voice. "It would seem so. I do not fully understand this myself, but it was said by a few of those here who know their ways. We must prepare and pray that the Orishas will protect us from them."

I watched his lips as he whispered. He had striking facial features that you would not forget quickly and his eyes were broody. His nose was very thick set.

"You talk of the Orisha with much affection." I prodded curiously.

He looked at me and smiled. "Do you not worship any one of them?"

"I serve Yemoja." I replied. "I serve her though I wonder why such misfortune should have befallen me. How can I have been snatched from the river on the day I went to perform my absolution? I find it troubling that Iya did not protect me, or am I not found worthy?"

He was silent for a while. Perhaps so he could contemplate his answer to what was otherwise a difficult question for people our age.

"My parents told me that when I was born, Ifa gave them a prophesy that I would be a great servant of Olodumare. When my mother prodded the priest to tell her which particular Orisha I would serve, he could not reveal any. This troubled my mother for many years. Then one day when I was eight or nine harmattans, my father's hut was engulfed by a terrible fire and he couldn't put it out. I was but a child then, but I ran into the burning hut and was able to save all my father's idols which I handed to him and my mother. It was from that day that my mother said she then understood what the prophecy implied. That I was destined to go beyond the service of all the Orishas and thus serve Olodumare himself."

I stared at him in amazement. He sounded so wise for a boy his age.

"But like you I find myself here." He continued. "My father has been killed by the slavers, and I have been separated from my mother, sisters and brother. I am reduced to an animal about to be taken to a land that I do not know. How can this be from Olodumare? How can ones' Ori be laden with so much misfortune?"

I noticed that tears had welled in his eyes. So I raised my hands to touch his face.

"I have asked myself the same questions, brother. I wonder whether this is my destiny."

"Yes...yes." He said sniffing and wiping his eyes quickly, as though he was embarrassed that a young girl had seen him cry. "The answer must be in what my mother always told me when we tended our poultry. It is the guinea fowl's destiny to lay eggs and no amount of sacrifice will change that fact. So, does it not serve the fowl better to accept her fate and become renown as a fowl that lays fine eggs?"

CHAPTER 6

EKO COAST, THE RAINY SEASON, 1822.

S o, it was that during the reign of Oba Osinlokun of Eko, the son of Ologun Kuture and father of Oba Kosoko, I met Ajayi Osobogun, slave boy, weaver's son and predestined by Ifa itself to become a servant of Olodumare. The white men who watched over us behaved strangely all day. They were mostly drunk on rum. It made their gaze shifty and they sweated a lot. They seemed afraid of something that lurked in the horizon and conducted themselves like thieves would, worried that they were about to be caught. They came into our bamboo cage and separated the women from the men. They took us into another hut, and left us chained by our feet rather than our necks like they had the men. They fed us Abala, a meal made from ground corn and palm oil and a gourd of water. Then, they left us alone.

I knew from the moment that we spoke to each other that Ajayi's *Ori* was good and he was destined for greatness. He was handsome and fiery eyed yet gentle with his words, quick witted, yet filled with so much inner sadness. I had never met any young man like him in my village, nor did I believe I ever would as I lay on my back day dreaming about him. I had hoped that perhaps we would be boarded on the same ship and sail to the white man's world together. He would protect me from the evil and wickedness of this world and I would cook for him and perhaps if Olodumare sanctioned it, perhaps become his wife. I was certain that my father would have approved of him. My mind drifted between places as I lay on the cool sandy floor listening to the crackling voices of white men shouting instructions at themselves and slaves calling for their maker. I was no longer as afraid, even though I still felt sadness in my heart every time I drifted to the thought of my mother, I noticed that it didn't hurt me as much. I resolved that I would keep myself strong through the voyage to the land where the women wore fancy dresses.

When morning came, I noticed that the white men had quickened their paces and were screaming at each other at the top of their lungs. The other females and I kept in the bamboo cage drew ourselves nearer towards the walls and peeped out through the crevices to get a sense of what was amiss. I saw that they had several slaves and native porters who were hurriedly transferring their possessions unto several canoes moored at the nearby jetties. Several chained slaves had been lined up and were being pushed along into the waiting canoes. Many of them resisted as they came in contact with the ocean. They drew back terrified, cursing and screaming at the *Oyinbo* as the white man was called. A few white guards threatened them with whips, while others pulled them by the chains attached to their neck. It caused several of them to choke and whimper. Eventually, they followed as they succumbed to the punishment meted out at them. It was remarkable how quickly the entire barracoon was being emptied out. I watched as one cage after another was opened and the inmates marched to the waiting canoes to be transported to the two ships that waited further out on the great ocean. Then, the guards reached the cage I had been in earlier. I saw as the line of slaves staggered out into the early morning sunshine, bound by chains. I saw Ajayi Osobogun squint his eyes and then rub the crest of his head with both his palms. I called out to him and he turned to stare, adjusting his eyes to compensate for the sudden burst of light. He must have made me out from behind the bars of bamboo because he smiled and waved his hand at me. He called my name.

"Omitirin." He said. "Are you all right?"

"Yes." I replied. "What is happening?"

"I do not know."

"They are loading people on to ships." I warned him.

He looked towards the ships, nodded then turned to the boy behind him, to explain what was happening. He turned to me hurriedly and shouted. "If Olodumare spares you this ordeal please help me find my mother and my sisters in Iseyin. Tell them that I live." And with that he was marched away to the canoes.

I fell to the floor of the cage and tried to make sense of what Ajayi had said to me. It neither made any sense, nor did I feel pleased by it. It was my hope that we would journey together to where ever it was that the white men were taking us. I expected that we would join the party soon. So, I moved hurriedly towards the locked gate of the cage. In my hurried action I jarred the chain that bound the next slave to me at the ankle which caused her to rain curses at me and even threaten to kill me. I apologised by kneeling. She was much older and bigger than I was, and besides I had meant no harm.

"The ships are leaving." I announced. "Are they not coming for us?"

No one answered me, as they themselves contemplated their fate. So, I asked again. "Are they not coming for us?" There was desperation in my voice.

One of the women looked at me and sniggered quietly. "Are you in a hurry to leave my daughter? Where is it that you know you are going?"

I looked down at the floor downcast. I wondered why my legs suddenly felt weak, so I sat on the floor by the side of the entrance and waited for the white men to come and get us.

They did not come that morning, nor that day. I watched as several other cages were emptied out leaving ours and a few others. The canoes stopped coming towards the early part of the afternoon and the barracoon became but a shadow of itself. Most of the white men had left, crating all their cargo of slaves and woven cloth from Ijebu, black soap from Badagry, peppers from the surrounding pepper farms in Awani and several sacks of palm kernel and vats filled with palm kernel oil. Those of us left behind were watched over by our own kind, native watchmen who would be paid with liquor and trinkets to keep us in order till the next ship arrived.

Night fell, and it rendered an eerie silence about the barracoon, punctuated intermittently by the thunderous sound of crashing waves in the distance. It had become difficult to feed us as the canteens established at the back had been packed and most of the workers disengaged. The native guards about, resulted to handing each one of us a cob of corn boiled in a large vat of sea water. I chewed on the cob and intermittently spat out a mouthful of sand and an occasional worm that had burrowed into the cob. I heard several women regurgitate and curse. The pen where we were held now carried the stench of urine and excrement. I chose to remain by the side of the bolted entrance. It pulled taunt on the chain which caused the shackle to cut deeply into my ankle, but I chose to bear the pain and willed myself to hope that our ship would arrive in good time.

There were fourteen of us in the room and I must have been the youngest. I succumbed to sleep, drifting into short spells of unconsciousness only to be startled awake by the angry chorus of vicious mosquitoes inflicting painful bites all over me. I slapped at parts of my body intent on ridding myself of the anguish but to no avail.

Suddenly, two of the white men who had apparently been left behind stumbled into the room. They reeked of liquor. The one holding the whip fell over as he attempted to unlock the shackle of one of the women. The commotion woke her. Startled, she asked what he was doing. He grunted in an inaudible accent, swaying from side to side as he struggled with the lock. The other man, welding a short cutlass, was better comported and grinned as he watched and urged him on. The sound woke the other women in the cage.

"What is it you want?" The women asked in a chorus.

The men if at all they understood, did not reply but kept at their mission to release the woman's shackle. They eventually succeeded and dragged her by the arms out of the room. She trashed about screaming "*E ma gba mi!*", save me!

Another half an hour passed before the doors to the cage room opened again. The two men staggered into the room again. This time, each lunged at the woman nearest to him.

One grabbed my neck and lifted me off the floor. He released my ankle shackle with a dagger in his free hand and dragged me out of the room. He was enveloped with the smell of liquor. I wanted to scream but his hands were locked on my throat. Eventually he cast me to the ground in a space which served as a piazza of sorts. I saw other women on the ground, their legs flung wide open and men on top of them grunting like wild animals. In my mind's eye I saw my mother face aghast with shame and horror that I would be defiled in such a manner, to lose the virginity that we had been taught to keep for our future husband ever since we were barely girls. In our village there was a special ceremony on the night that a new bride was taken into her husband's house. It was a solemn and private one where the women in the man's house were allowed to inspect the new bride to see if she had truly come unblemished. It was unheard of for a maiden girl from my village to have ever been found wanting. The shame that she would bring to the family of her mother would last many generations and her story would become the communal lore for promiscuity and dishonour. It was better to die than bring such shame to one's family and here I was about to have my destiny destroyed. I screamed and tightened my legs together as he clawed at me like a beast. He slapped me several times, still I held my legs together like a priestess possessed then I started to curse him from the inner depth of my consciousness. I cursed his mother and his entire lineage. I cursed his children, both born and unborn. I spat invectives laced with terrible Odu as he tore my legs apart and made to thrust into me. I was crying but I did not stop cursing him, not even when I felt him suddenly go limp like a sack of corn. I felt warm liquid pouring all over my chest. It took a while, but I finally realised that it was blood, and that a dagger had been plunged into the temple of his face. I screamed in horror as someone tapped and resolutely called out to me. Scared out of my mind, I fought to get away from the touch. This caused the man's body to roll off me.

"My child…. my child." It was a woman's voice." You must leave this place now. You must run away from this place."

I looked closer to see the middle-aged woman I had earlier asked about the ships, looking over me with a bloodied dagger in her left hand.

"We must leave this place now." She said to me with such urgency that I immediately rose to my feet. I stared at the body of the dead man as he laid there, face down on the sand. There was blood everywhere. It poured from his temple onto the sand. There was blood all over my neck and chest too.

"Come with us." The woman whispered. She grabbed my arm and dragged me from the piazza, where men still grunted with pleasure and a few other women screamed with pain, unknown to them that a man lay dead in the darkness just a few feet away.

Five of us fled through a crevice and an open gateway where a guard would otherwise have stood watch. Before us, we saw the mighty ocean, with waves breaking violently on to the shore. It was too dark to see beyond, to where the ships had been only a day earlier. Three women left on their own. I followed the woman who had rescued me, and we soon disappeared into the darkness. She dragged me towards the shoreline and asked me to wash myself quickly. I did as she had instructed, afraid to approach the water yet desperate to rid my body of the blood. It was still warm and sticky and in my terrified state I screamed in anguish. The woman hurriedly cupped my mouth and shook her head. "We do not have much time my daughter. We must leave this place at once, before they come looking for us."

I nodded. Scooping the cold waters of the Atlantic with my cupped palms, I promptly began to scrub, using sand as I would a sponge, to ensure that I was clean. The woman stooped beside me, dropped the knife onto the sand then began to wash her hands with a careful and deliberate motion.

"Thank you for what you have done for me." I said staring at the knife."

She simply nodded then rose to her feet. "We must leave now. I have someplace I know we can go."

"Did you kill that man, Iya? Is he dead?"

She turned to look at me strangely, and then I noticed that she was laughing. "No child, it was not me who killed him. It was you."

I n the year that I killed a man, the kingdom of Awani or eko which the white man called Lagos, did not know peace because there was war amongst brothers. Ologun Kutere the late Oba had borne two sons; Osinlokun and Adele. Osinlokun was the elder of the brothers and according to tradition the rightful heir to his father's throne, but for some reason Adele had succeeded their father and ruled over the kingdom for ten years. Some say that Osinlokun who was already a wealthy man at the time of their father's death had given his brother the privilege of the throne because he did not want the distraction of ruling the kingdom at the expense of his trade. However, he changed his mind and sought to depose his younger brother and win the crown for himself. Osinlokun's quest to forcefully take away the crown was then made easier by the follies of his younger brother who had fallen out of favour with the chiefs of the kingdom. They accused Adele of becoming arrogant, stingy and imposing strange customs on the people. The Ifa devotees also accused him of having opened the gates of the entire kingdom to the religion of the Muslims who now claimed an ardent following of worshippers which hitherto was unheard of in the whole kingdom. The people deserted Adele and invited Osinlokun to return to Eko as ruler and inheritor of his father's stool. In the fighting that ensued between both camps, Adele was roundly defeated and banished to Badagry where he remained in exile. Yet no sooner had Adele established himself in exile and made himself regent of Badagry, did he commence the waging of regular and intermittent attacks against his brother and his own people of Eko. Even though Adele did not succeed in taking back the crown, he had created a network of spies who fed him with reports on the state of affairs in the kingdom of Eko. Several of these spies had been trusted palace slaves of his while he had been at court. They were known as *Ibiga*. Though slaves, a trusted few had become exceedingly wealthy in the course of doing their masters bidding. They tended the king's farms, or conducted his trade which also included the trading of slaves. While several of his *Ibiga* had fled to Badagry with him, a few remained behind and lived seemingly innocuous rehabilitated lives as artisans and fishermen among the people. At night however, they would make the journey into the creeks of the lagoon where under the cover of darkness they passed on information to runners who then relayed the messages back to Adele in Badagry.

It was to the home of one of such men and apparently a kinsman of the Badagry woman who had helped me that we fled that night. We trekked through the night heading for the settlement of Addo which the woman claimed was at the tip of the adjacent mainland. The woman moved confidently through the bush paths past deserted market stalls and family huts and more imposing edifices, the like of which I had never seen. We finally got to the bank of the lagoon that separated both land masses. We searched for a canoe which had a pair of oars as canoe owners usually took the oars home with them. As we searched through the canoes I asked her how she had known the way. She told me she had visited the kinsman many times in the past when she had come to trade. Then had come the unfortunate incident in her life when she had been accused of witchcraft by a rival trader at Apome near Ijebu. The trader had owed her cowries, but refused to pay back and accused her of evil as a way of reneging on her obligation. She had been forced to swear an oath and drink the bitter liquid truth potion given to her by the herbalist called to interrogate her on the matter. The potion would identify if she truly were a witch by killing her instantly or turning her mad, and leaving her unscathed if she were innocent. She had neither died nor gone mad but she had fallen very ill. No one believed her even when she fully recovered. Her enemy claimed that she had survived because she had invoked witch craft. Not too long after that incident, the adjudicators had sold her off to a slaver as part of a consignment of debtor slaves brought to the coast to be sold off to the white man.

We eventually found a pair of oars. So, we stole away in one of the smaller canoes and paddled through the night till we eventually landed on the muddy banks at the other side of the lagoon.

"It is not far from here." She told me confidently as we weaved through a cluster of mud huts and raffia sheds towards the adjoining settlement of oyingbo. When we finally found the compound, she could not be certain of which hut exactly her kinsman lived in so she knocked on the most likely one anyway and waited for her prayer to be answered.

A man's voice growled. "Who is it that at this ungodly time of night?"

She apologised and mentioned that she was looking for Fadipe the fisherman.

"How much does he owe you that you should choose to lay siege on him this early in the morning?"

"I have urgent word for him is all." She explained.

"Then, you must be evil!" The man retorted. "Words brought in the dead of night cannot bode well for anyone."

"Even if his relative has just had twins?"

There was silence for a while. Then the man appeared from behind the wooden door. He peered at us cautiously. "And who are you both?"

"Family members." The woman said as she knelt down before the man in greeting. "Please forgive us. We mean you no discomfort, but we have been sent to find him. If you can please point out his compound we shall immediately be on our way and trouble you no longer"

"Just beyond that cursed *Egungun* masquerade house." The man said.

"You will see his compound. His house is the one with mud fish traps stacked in front of it."

We thanked the man and fled in the direction of the compound. Fadipe was home asleep with his family when we knocked. Initially reluctant to open the door till he was seemed convinced that it was indeed her voice he was hearing.

"Iyabo!" he muttered in shock when he saw her.

She threw herself on the ground and started rolling back and forth, pouring sand on her head and wailing softly.

"A thousand sackful of evil have been visited upon me my brother" she wailed.

The man looked about the compound nervously and immediately ushered us into his hut and shut his door.

CHAPTER 7

Back home at Akindele, I would lay on my mat, by the side of my mother's watering pots on clammy nights. The breeze that came through a back-door post served as a welcome relief to the itch that came with sweat. It would gently caress my thighs, giving me a sensation that I enjoyed about my body. On nights that I was cursed with restlessness and could not find sleep, it hid me away from the view of my mother and my father when he came to visit her on days that were her turn.

Ma'mi was always apprehensive of such visits from my father. It no longer seemed to be as regular, but on the occasions when he was to call, I noticed that she would take great care to prepare herself. She stayed longer by the stream when she went to bathe and she would seek more luxurious potions of cam wood and other blended oils which she applied carefully about her body. It made her skin to shimmer in a hue of dark bronze that glittered in the evening sun. She always seemed to spend more time around her breasts. She would sigh as she assessed them and then pack them away into her inner vest as though they had become fragile and were no longer part of what was to be offered.

I always watched, curious as to her ritual and the effect it had on my father. I would lay there and feel as the breeze tickled the inside of my thighs. I wondered what it felt like to submit one's self to a man. I imagined it must be like the cool breeze made one feel. The young wives never spoke of pleasures, nor did the elderly women in the compound ever offer any help. But they all glorified the carrying of a pregnancy to full term. They whispered about their labour in a conspiracy of sister-hood and saluted their bravery on the birth of their big-headed children. I had never thought to question the basis of how a woman submitted herself to a man because it had never seemed possible that I would somehow not be able to have one found for me. In the same way, it had never seemed possible that unusual circumstances could ever befall me.

I became sick in the days after we were harboured by Fadipe, the *Ibiga*; Iyabo's kinsman. We were fugitives of the white man and had become *'asaforige'*; homeless dependents now beholden to him and at the mercy of his generosity. They kept me in an inner room where he stored the better part of his merchandise. There, Iyabo and his wife fed me *ogi*, the sour pap made from fermented corn, in which they had infused bitter herbs that would help the fever to break quickly. I floated above my body in a state of delirium. In the nightmares that ensued, I felt my joints ache and saw myself drowning and being raped by drunken men whose laughter rang out and echoed as though I were trapped in a hollow chamber. I called out Ajayi's name hoping that he would save me. Yes, I dreamt about him and the coolness of the evening breeze. Yet he never seemed to be able to reach me from across the big river where he stood with his hands outstretched over the body of a dead guard with blood pouring from the deep open wound on his temple. Iyabo would tell me later, that I had been given up for dead by the fifth day of the sickness, but the fever finally broke on the morning of the sixth and my sleep became less laborious. Fadipe's wife offered me a kan-kan sponge and suggested that I bathe with the Eworoworo shrub to cleanse my skin of its warts. I was very weak and had lost so much weight that even I was shocked at my reflection in the calabash of water that was placed before me. I recalled what the old Oyo woman who had lost her son to death at the Isheri slave market had said to me as she sought comfort in my arms at her time of grief.

'Olodumare cannot be this wicked but for a reason.' She had said at the death of her son. 'Good must come out of this or how am I to continue to worship him? It is not enough to fear god, but are we not to love him also?'

I sat on the floor with my back to a sack of smoked mud fish, managing what I could swallow from the bowl of pap before me, and suddenly grateful for where I now found myself. I was healing and I was about to be free. Was this not the good that Olodumare had offered me?

In the days that followed, Iyabo and I became eager to leave Addo and return to our individual homes. Fadipe asked me about my village and I rightly explained that Oko Akindele was to be found in the Egba forest. While no one seemed to have heard about Oko Akindele, everyone knew where Ake was, and I tried to relate the journey that I made to get to Eko. I was left confused however When Iyabo and Fadipe's wife explained to me that I could not be on my way home yet until a solution to a problem at hand had been found. Returning home would not be as easy as I had thought. Fadipe mentioned that even though we had escaped the barracoon we were bonded and still property of the white men, unless we could somehow be ransomed or freed by them or the Oba's authority. The trading of slaves was the most lucrative endeavour in Eko and had made the Oba exceedingly wealthy even before he had become king. The Oba and all noble men in his council made up of the titled Barons, The Idejo, the Akarigbe and the war generals of Eko, the Abagbon, all protected the trade. There were strict rules of conduct on the matter of how the trade was administered, and the matter of runaway slaves and other fugitives was taken seriously.

Fadipe lamented that the matter had become complicated because we had now brought him into the fray. He was willing to help for Iyabo's sake he said, but he had to be careful. While it could be possible for him to turn a blind eye and let us flee, he told us plainly that it would be foolhardy on all our parts. We would be caught in no time by the several spies that the Oba had all over the travel routes. He also said that given his position and the on-going dispute between the current Oba Osinlokun and his master, the former Oba Adele, who was the rightful Oba of Eko, he could not afford to have allegations of his abetting the escape of slaves levelled against him. The truth was that Oba Osinlokun received a generous poll tax on all slaves bought by the Portuguese and Spanish slave dealers and to encourage the escape of slaves would be detrimental to his commercial interest. Fadipe also worried that while he was seen by the few who truly knew him as a servant and loyalist of the former Oba Adele, the current courtiers at the *Iga Idungaran* palace and Oba Osinlokun himself, still thought of him as a law-abiding subject of the kingdom who lived his simple life of fishing after Adele's exile to Badagry.

A solution would have to be found, and one which would protect every one. He asked us to be patient as he made his consultations on the matter. With no other choice but to wait, we devoted the next few weeks to being as helpful as we could be while not attracting undue attention to ourselves. The time was spent cooking and cleaning and helping the family prepare merchandise for the markets at Ido and Ebute Metta, where three lagoons connected each other, and where the Awori's favoured themselves over others who lived amongst them. On those long evenings I would sometimes wonder about Ajayi, and what his current fortune was. The humidity and the abundance of water made it easy for one to day dream, but I made great efforts to snap out of it and focus on the tasks at hand. I only missed my mother more on the tedious days and now I had begun to think about the idol of Yemoja that I had been forced to leave behind by the boulders in the river. I dreaded to think that it had been found perhaps by an itinerant fisherman or farmer who would not know of its importance to me or my family. On some days I would recite an Odu from amongst the few that we were taught. It shamed me slightly that it was becoming difficult to remember some of them but I consoled myself in the hope that I would return to the convent soon to complete my instructions in the mysteries of Iya.

I once asked Fadipe's wife which deity she served, and I was astonished to hear her reply nonchalantly that she was not a devout follower of any. They had neither shrine, nor a figurine in their house but they offered casual verbal supplications to an Orisha once a while. What was even more curious was that occasionally she would speak glowingly about a Muslim *Alfa* or preacher who they sometimes went to listen to at Isale Eko, where a big Muslim prayer ground had been established. She told us that on every seventh day a special prayer was observed. It was almost like a festival. A large congregation of the *Imoles*, as those who touched their foreheads to the ground were referred to, met there to pray just after mid day. "They come wearing flowing robes and dab themselves with sweet smelling scents and share fruits and dates." She had said. There was also a festival where they would fast for thirty long days and nights until a new moon was sighted and they would end with a big feast. I marvelled at descriptions she offered but wondered at how this could be allowed. Would Olodumare not be angered, so I asked which God they worshiped and then she said the god was called *Allah* from a language of the Tapa and the Fula at which point I froze.

"Nothing good can come from them." I whispered fiercely and perhaps having sensed my apprehension, she left the telling of the story for another day.

One day Fadipe returned home from the lagoon later than usual. He was evidently troubled when he came into the compound. He did not greet his wife, nor did he ask about the welfare of the children. He would not look at Iyabo's eyes directly and as for me, I had long resigned myself to the fact that he saw me only as an inconvenience. He sat himself down under the canopy of an old tree. We all sat at a safe distance watching him and waiting for him to make the first move. He eventually did towards the very late hour of the night when those who fished for crayfish would usually set out.

He called Iyabo, and his wife, who by now was drifting into sleep, to join him. I was not invited so I sat waiting and watching them nervously. They spoke in hushed tones for an hour. It reminded me of the several times that tragedy was about to befall me when I had been a captive of slavers. When they eventually dispersed, I stood up at once waiting for the news which I knew would be bad, as it always was.

"What is it, my big sister?" I asked Iyabo as she walked towards me. Iyabo walked passed me and merely sighed.

"Go and sleep." She said as she brushed pass me. "We will finish the talk in the morning."

I did not sleep. I contemplated several things in my mind and imagined several more outcomes, none of which turned out good. I considered sneaking out of the compound and running away in the cover of darkness. For I thought, could it not be possible that the plot was on to return me to the barracoon and the murderous rapists who would be glad to get their hands on the girl who killed one of them?

Many long hours later, an impatient cock crowed in the distance. Soon, the muttering of early risers could be heard coming from nearby compounds. It was Fadipe himself who shook me awake. It was not a rough and angry shake. He rarely called me by my name, choosing instead to call me slave girl. I had taken offence the first time he had called me that but Iyabo had told me not to take any offence by it. He meant it in an affectionate way she had said, as an ode to my story. This time, it was different.

"Omitirin." He called. "Wake up. You and Iyabo must come with me."

"Where are we going?" I asked him fearfully. When evil lurks, it does so in the morning I thought.

"There is an elder we must all go and see." He said.

"An elder?" I asked as I searched his face for hidden clues and traces of deception. "What elder is this?"

He tapped me one last time and stepped away, "You ask too many questions for a child." He snapped. "Did they train you to question your *agba*?"

I apologised at once. "Forgive me, my father. I am afraid Is all."

He nodded in understanding. "You have nothing to be afraid of *aburo*. But you must pray that God continues to favour you."

At that moment I realised that Fadipe Ibiga, himself once a court slave to a powerful king but who had somehow through the strength of his own character and loyalty to his master fought his way to some standing within the scheme of things, was indeed a good-hearted man. I thanked him and payed him the full obeisance of staying down on my two knees.

"Not to worry slave girl." He said." I want both of you to follow me so you can be presented."

They said that no Oba in Eko ever ruled in isolation. They sought to carry their chief council of noble men along as a way to assure loyalty and the stability of their reign. The Idejo who were the early settlers were recognised as the highest-ranking noble men in council in Eko, and had been so ever since the Oba of Ado had sent this son to establish his dominion over the Awori's in Isheri and later Ebute.

We arrived at the house of one of the Abagbons or Eko warrior generals. He was a man with thin incision marks on the sides of his temple. He sat on a stool on a small elevated platform in the centre of his living quarters. He was surrounded by sacks and spears, oars and rods, large gourds of protective fetishes on the wall, two massive elephant tusks and several other appurtenances of his calling for inflicting pain, death and destruction on his enemies. I was stricken with fear as we were ushered into his presence by his chief slave.

Fadipe went ahead of us and lay flat on the floor in obeisance to the aged general. He greeted him to his hearing, calling him by his praise name.

The Abagbon motioned him to stand, but Fadipe chose to rather crouch on his toes, his head bowed.

"My father," he began. "Our elders say that when a man carries a load, the excessive weight of which bends his neck, he will do well to seek those can help him dismount it."

"Or help him carry it if fortuitous." The general remarked at once.

"That is true." My lord, Fadipe retreated. "That is true. Indeed, it is how one presents his load that determines how others help him carry it."

He looked back at us. He coughed and carried on, "It is a delicate matter my lord, concerning my two younger sisters who had some misfortune visited upon them."

"Yes?" the general muttered a bit impatiently as he cast Fadipe's head a steely gaze.

"The two were caught at different times and sold to the Portuguese slave buyers some week back, but by some circumstance beyond their own understanding they were able to retrieve themselves and found their way to my humble homestead. They have been gravely ill, otherwise they would have been presented much earlier."

Fadipe stole the general a cursory glance to see how he was doing. He could barely tell, so he added. I brought them as soon as they could get up from their sick mats my lord, for this is a matter beyond my station."

Two other men entered the room and proceeded to pull out idle stools which they promptly sat upon then turned their attention to the proceeding. The general watched them settle themselves in, apparently pleased by their presence.

"So, what is it you seek from me Ibiga Adele?"

I saw Fadipe stiffen slightly at the way he was addressed. For Adele's name to be so quickly mentioned was not a good omen.

"They have come to throw themselves at your mercy my lord. In a matter of this nature they require the powerful yet benevolent and merciful. A man like you who has the Oba's two ears."

That was the cue we had been earlier given to then approach and throw ourselves on the floor before the general in a plea for mercy. Fadipe's wife joined us with a basketful of prime mud fish, cleaned and seasoned and already skewered on long bamboo strips, so as to save the general's household the trouble of preparing them.

The general watched the display patiently, then turned to his two associates to gauge their reactions to what they had seen. They shifted on their stools and coughed as though sharing a secret between one another.

"Eh Fadipe, Ibiga Adele," the general began, in a firm yet generous tone. "Your steps seem well appointed. You are welcome. I know you as one who served his master Adele loyally. Your master was a friend of mine and I loved him like a brother. But yes, brothers must sometimes disagree with each other."

The two adjuncts grunted in agreement.

"Adele was a good king when he began, but then a man sometimes becomes his own worst enemy. May Ogun who we both deified forgive us all our follies." He shook his head and looked to the basket of fish. There was a resounding chorus of "Ase."

"I have heard what you have said about these two." The general stopped and grunted for effect. "Runaway slaves, ah! That is a very serious matter."

"Very serious indeed!" One of the men seated echoed for good effect.

"Kabiyesi Osinlokun is a man unlike his brother. He is a man who takes his cowries seriously and this matter affects him greatly."

One of the two men spoke out to every one's hearing. "There is talk that has been on for weeks about a girl who they say killed one of the white men at the barracoon. It would seem we have finally found her."

Fadipe froze where he crouched and turned to face both Iyabo and I. He had an incredulous look on his face. While Iyabo looked away in distress, I stared back at him fiercely. He turned back to face the general.

"We hear a lot about things at the market my lord, but who knows what is true. Who does not know the inordinate amount of liquor that these people drink?"

One of the observers laughed. "A man can forget his own mothers name after consuming that potion." He cracked, but the general didn't find it amusing.

"This matter has reached the *Iga Idungaran* palace, and I know for a fact that Kabiyesi has not taken lightly to the report of slaves running away and killing their captors. What will happen if every slave or indentured servant in the whole of Awori land does as he or she pleases?"

"Ah, that one is a recipe for disaster!" The other adjunct spat rising to his feet.

I laid there on the ground wishing the earth would open up and swallow me whole.

"The palace cannot but adjudicate this matter, Omo Adele. You did well to bring the two fugitives here and for that you will be rewarded."

A stunned Fadipe watched as the two adjuncts swiftly seized both Iyabo and I and pressed daggers into the nape of our throats. Fadipe's wife, Omolara began wailing and rolling on the ground.

"My lord." Fadipe said, at last finding his voice. "You cannot be questioned in such a matter. Your wisdom supersedes mine ten-fold, and even then, I cannot be said to have started to comprehend issues as you do. I am a slave who found mercy in a king's household and today I freely roam the creeks and lagoons of this kingdom. Some say that it was my destiny. Should that not be how such a delicate matter is decided in the long run? Should this not be a matter for Ifa's guidance?"

The general looked up at Fadipe and smiled. "Spoken as Adele would have spoken himself. Ibiga, you have truly spent time with courtiers. That is what I will advise Kabiyesi himself to do. He will be wise to have someone look into the calabash for him on this matter. But that I will leave to him. I will advise that you leave these two with me for now. You may excuse yourself."

Fadipe nodded and picked his wife off the floor. He glanced over at Iyabo and held both his hands to his chest in a gesture of goodwill. Then he left, leaving the basket of fish where it had been placed before the general's feet, without paying me as much as a glance.

That night, we were marched to one of the several slave warehouses adjourning the *Iga Idungaran* palace of Oba Osinlokun. As I entered the big hall-like building which was made from mud, fortified with rocks and thick logs of wood. I cursed my Ori and cursed the day of my birth. I did not cry nor did I fear. I was resolved now to take my life at the earliest moment that the opportunity presented itself. This world was no longer that which I had envisaged it to be. The laughter of playmates in open farm fields and mothers who fed me morsels of sweet food had blurred into the distance and now I existed in a place where the wickedness of people was all too common and had become revealed to me in such a personal way. There were several of us chained to each other and left to sit on the dirty floor. I spared them all barely a moment's glance. As one of them cursed, I remembered what one of my fellow captives had once said, *'are we not the ones that that the Orishas had forsaken?'*. I retreated into the place within myself that I had now become accustomed to. There, I swept away the cobwebs that had grown since my last stay and prepared myself a place where I could rest my dejected spirit. There I could let my mind wander in the quiet darkness of a certain despair that yet comforted me because I knew now, that I shared it with my wretched destiny.

CHAPTER 8

'A dín dí Òdí, a dìn dì Òdí .
Let us understand the case of Eji Odi
Who hides the message in heaven,
And Ifa who reveals it on earth.
He says, no matter what you say about me,
The place of the Esuru yam
Is not in the mortar.
He says, no matter what you say about me,
The place of the Eminẹ seed
Is not on the grinding stone.
He says, no matter what you say about me,
It is a taboo of the Olodumare.
The palm oil used to fry the palm kernels
Will never come through their shells.
He says, no matter what you may say or do,
you cannot harm me.

I knelt before his Royal Majesty, Oba Osinlokun, the wealthy. Oba of Eko, the son of Oba Ologun Kuture and father of Kosoko. As the Ifa priest cast the divination cowries and chanted the *Odu meji* upon which my divination from within the mysteries of Ifa had fallen, I saw the king's eye widen, startled, and then fall.

"Kabiyesi." The Ifa priest coughed as he picked up his *Okpele*. "This one is unusual. Particularly for a child."

The priest wondering whether he still had Kabiyesi's attention paused to look at the king, perhaps to be guided by his demeanour. The Oba remained, silent playing with his royal horse tail, deep in thought.

"My lord, Ifa warns the girl that she is in the midst of enemies, but assures her that she will see victory. Ifa tells her that her destiny is assured so long she makes her sacrifice and holds on to Ifa. But the Odu has a deeper message my lord."

"For whom?" Kabiyesi asked curiously.

"For the girl, Kabiyesi."

"I thought the divination was for my benefit." The Oba snapped.

The priest snapped back. "Ifa speaks to us all Kabiyesi. Kings as well as slaves."

"Ifa has marked her as one who should live under special conditions. For that is where her *Kadara* is revealed as strongest."

"Special conditions?"

"Yes, Kabiyesi. I marvel myself, but this one seems destined."

The king rose from his throne and walked towards me. He had a stiff gait and wore a bored expression.

"What is her name?" The question was directed at the party of Abagbon Gbolahan who had led Fadipe Ibiga and his adjuncts to present us to the king.

Fadipe answered. "She calls herself Omitirin, Kabiyesi."

"And do you know where she is from?"

"She is Egba my lord. Though I am not clear about her village."

The king looked at me and grinned. "How is it that this one can strike a blow that kills a grown man? Oshodi Tapa should we not be ashamed for these white men?"

No one said a word. They looked on instead at the king's trusted slave master and emissary to the white men.

"It is ironic, is it not? " The Oba continued.

"You are merciful my lord." Abagbon Gbolahan was quick to add.

"It is Olodumare that is merciful, Abagbon. We simply must find out his true wishes and obey."

Everyone in the room grunted a respectful approval and hailed the king.

"Kabiyesi! May your crown rest for a long time on your head and may your royal sandals adorn your feet for several years to come."

"A murderess." The King mused as he took my jaw in the grip of his hand and twisted hard so I could feel pain. I cried out softly.

"What is it that you advise on the matter?" He asked the priest.

"My lord, if it is left to Ifa, this one is trouble for the throne. Ifa says that this one should be left alone to make her peace with her Ori."

One of the king's white cap chiefs rose from his stool and coughed.

"You harm yourself if you lay this matter down so easily, my lord." He was an Idejo chief from the higher ranks of council. He was dressed in impeccable white robes and head attire made of the same white cloth. He had a giant coral bead laced around his neck, and carried a long staff.

"Oloye Ibikunle, I recognise you." Kabiyesi said with good nature. "What is your concern?"

"Trade, my lord." Oloye Ibikunle declared. "How are you to explain this to the White men? That those who they offer you as protectors of their merchandise can so wantonly be killed by children who are then so easily set free? Kabiyesi, you and I know that the white man's King has ordered that this trade be stopped. We do not have the level of trade we once used to have, even before you became king. I urge you to carefully consider the implication of your actions."

The hall fell silent again. Chiefs who sat on lofty stools re-adjusted themselves or took sips from the gourds of drink placed before them. Watching with cunning eyes for who would pick up the thread of the argument at such a tricky moment. There was a burly man who stood by the far corner of the room. He had watched the proceedings with interest and amusement and as the silence now seemed to have reached palpable levels, he punched at it with humour.

"The arse of the *yindi-yindi* fire ant is very tiny indeed, but it still births hundreds of ants my lords." He joked.

Several of the men in the room sniggered, while those closer in rank to the king laughed.

"And your point exactly, our visitor, Balogun Ijeru?" kabiyesi asked.

"That which seems inconsequential and innocent can still wreak havoc, my lord."

"You refer to the girl?"

"Yes, my lord. I have seen many battles as you well know and I can tell you that in those wars I have witnessed much havoc wreaked on strong forts by what we would have considered weaklings. This girl knifed a man my lord. These are not the virtues of a child."

The Oba looked at me anew. It was obvious that he was taken by what had just been said, so he turned to face the burly man who had just spoken. The man's accent was very different from the others. His was a thick Oyo accent similar in many ways to the accent of the old Oyo woman who had lost her son. He had tribal marks that defined his face and he was dressed in the *danshiki* and *sokoto* of the northern Oyo. The front of his dress was adorned with several leather pouches which were how charms were worn by the warriors of the various Oyo tribes. He stood tall and dangerous. A man who had killed several and one who should be feared.

"Balogun Ijeru, you are a respected guest and a trusted customer to this palace. I am curious to hear how you would handle such matters in Oyo land."

The man laughed and smacked his chest with both his hands.

"My lord, let there be no mistake. I am here to sell you slaves and buy the white man's gun powder for the Alaafin troops. I am a warrior in the service of the owner of death himself, *Iku Baba yeye*, your brother king, the Alaafin of Oyo. I am leader of the vanguard that protect the northern side of his great kingdom and I have drunk dead men's blood from the same gourd as the Are Ona Kankanfo. Warrior of a thousand battles and the general of generals. You ask the wrong man if you are seeking advice of how to show mercy."

The king stared at him and nodded. He sighed and then he said, "The ship that came for the consignment had to flee. A report reaching them mentioned that the white King had sent his cursed ships to capture the Portuguese ship and stop the trade."

"*Espiransa, my lord*" one of the palace scribes interrupted, "the white man's ship was called *Espiransa*."

The King stopped abruptly and beamed proudly. He pointed at the young scribe. "He is learning the white man's language and now writes my letters to my friend and customer, the Oba of Bahia across the great water."

The room filled with grunts of admiration.

"The white men told us that the ship was eventually caught by the white king's warriors and the slaves on it loaded on to another ship that headed to the Saro country to free them. The trade has entered very difficult times and profits are dropping. These are troubling times indeed that require fewer troublesome people. Balogun Ijeru you make a good point. I concede. I can no longer afford this kind of behaviour."

I had not heard what the king had said as my heart had leapt for joy at the knowledge of Ajayi's possible freedom. It was as though I had suddenly been awoken from a deep trance that had weighed all over my fatigued soul. A wave of relief, joy and hope that now washed over me and offered me a momentary lease of life. I praised Olodumare silently.

Then I heard him utter his damning verdict.

"Return her to the Portuguese." I suddenly heard the Oba say. "That is her destiny."

He began to walk away from the chamber as I wailed in anguish, rolling on the ground in my chains. Fadipe quickly ran to hold me down and muttered sternly to me to behave myself and not to get him killed.

"My lord you err gravely!" It was the Ifa Priest in a loud voice. He rose from the earth floor where he had sat casting his cowries. His old legs swayed ever so slightly as he grabbed his walking stick to steady himself and approach where the Oba was exiting.

He began to chant an Odu loudly to the hearing of all present, while he tapped the stick on the floor for emphasis:

> There is only one home
> to the life of a river mussel
> There is only one home
> to the life of a tortoise,
> There is only one truth to the soul of man
> If a child cannot call on an elder for mercy
> Who else will save the child.
> This is what Ifa says
> The cycle of mercy must not be broken
> For that is destiny too
> the king of gods asks Orunmila
> Who else will save the child?"

The room fell silent yet again and every one now looked at the King. He had stopped walking and had his back to everyone as he had reached the door way to his chambers. He stood there for what seemed an eternity, brooding, and then turned to face his courtiers. His eyes were misty and his forehead furrowed with worry. Then he cleared his throat and spoke with the authority that God had given to kings over men.

"Ifa speaks, yet Ifa teases me, baba. I am merciful, but my brother Adele was not. I listen to Ifa, but my brother Adele did not. I have heard this Odu before and it brought me good fortune in a loyal slave. But I have no need for another." He looked around his court evidently troubled. Finally, he looked at the warrior from Oyo.

"Balogun Ijeru, I offer you this girl as a gift of mercy. Take her with you when you return to Oyo and do with her as you please. I have been merciful." The Oba of Eko said, then he stormed out of the chambers, leaving his courtiers to turn their gaze towards me as I screamed with fear.

CHAPTER 9

AGODI IBADAN, THE OYO EMPIRE, 1826.

M a'mi had once told me that mad men do not sleep at night. It was a thought that had always frightened me. We did not have any mad man in our village, so I never really could observe to see if this was true. But now as I was laid on the floor, with my entire body wracked with pain and confusion, I realised that there was some truth to what my mother had suggested to me. Mad men do not sleep. They lay awake instead, gazing at their genitals, marvelling at their own madness and laughing at themselves.

Balogun Ijeru lay on top of me, his torso heaving as he panted each time he thrust himself into me. I thought that if I screamed, it might perhaps make the pain go away. But his calloused palm covered my mouth, making it impossible to do so. I was hoarse from whimpering and sore with pain. So,

I cried in fits, as wave after wave of the pain ravished my body. I wondered if I could will death to come and take me at that moment. If only to save me from the shame that this brutal man had forced upon me. I closed my eyes in defiance, determined not to give him the pleasure of seeing me weep. Yet the pain that I felt betrayed me and the tears came by themselves. His face was contorted in a mask of pleasure and madness; It accentuated his tribal marks which ran deeply etched across his temple and cheeks. His teeth were unevenly chipped at several points and darkened by the kola nut, while his tongue smelt of liquor and gun powder. He was bald from shaving and I could see the scars from where the medicine men had made incisions into his scalp and rubbed the charms that were meant to protect him from being killed by his enemies. He was probably older than my father, but unlike him, he was brutish and unkind and now he owned me.

I cursed him as he lay on top of me. I cursed his marks and cursed his household and I almost cursed Yemoja for reducing me to such a sorry state of misery. She, who I had sacrificed sweet things to in rivers. She who I had vowed to serve.

Our journey to Agodi from Eko had been uneventful and commenced the day after the Oba of Eko had handed me over to the Balogun. His convoy of porters and soldiers had hauled wooden cases of muskets and kegs of gun powder through the dense forest, as we made our way through the hidden pathways and across tiny back waters far removed from the usual trade routes. It was a ruthless party much accustomed to such stealthy travels. They were different from the slavers I had earlier travelled with. They ate less, talked less but rather communicated amongst each other through a series of coded noises and hand signs. When they made camp in the evening, I could tell that they were confident about the night, even relishing it by the way they deftly climbed on to the top of trees to survey the landscape and the night sky. When the baboons howled, they would howl back with laughter.

The Balogun travelled on horseback, a black mare with hoofs the size of my entire head. Her tail had been decorated with brightly coloured raffia ropes, while an amulet hung across her neck. He was attended to by four soldiers within the party. I was made to walk alongside him, often trailing back when exhaustion set in. It helped that I was not bound, nor shackled as I had become accustomed to in recent times. That made the four-day journey bearable. Farmers walked towards their farms early before the sun came out, and weeded in between the ridges, to reveal the rich and dark soil that nourished the crops that fed the people of Agodi. The sprawling fields of green and Kolanut trees told the story of a once peaceful people who loved the shade of the trees. A motley clan of story tellers and proverb swappers who had lived within high walls that kept thieves and the Fula's out. But Agodi had long changed and had now become a military outpost for the Alaafin of Oyo. It was here he kept his most ruthless generals and warriors at lavish expense. Always no more than a moment's notice away from the next rebellion that needed to be quelled within the empire, or village of errant subjects who needed to be sacked for having fallen behind on the payment of their tributes to his coffers. Agodi had become a settlement for warriors and murders. Valiant generals and the old trusted herbalists; *Babalawos* who concocted the potent potions that toughened their skin and won them victory and glory in vicious battles fought against kinsmen who spoke the same language.

I had been given to a mad man to do with me as he pleased, and it pleased the Balogun of Ijeru that I joined his household to serve as a domestic slave and a trophy addition to his harem. He refused to call me by the name my parents had given me even though he had asked me. He chose instead to call me *Yindi-Yindi* after the tiny ant he had alluded to at the Palace of the Oba of Eko. Sometimes he would mock me and call me '*Omo Oba*' or Princess, because I was handed over to him by a king. There wasn't much affection in the man's ways, nor did I ever for once truly believe that he was capable of demonstrating such qualities. I was, after all, but a mere possession of his, another filly to be mounted when he felt the urge to. I was exhibited to his guests and lieutenants as a murderer of white men and a gift from a great king and benefactor. My name spread across the garrison as I became the animated equivalent of one of the general's swords. A beauty to be admired, yet dangerous enough to kill.

The Balogun rolled off me sweating profusely. He wiped his brows and then cupped himself with both palms as he glanced at me.

"Yindi-Yindi." He sniggered, "What will I do with you this one? You will not kill me." He glanced down at himself and started laughing. He ignored the fact that I was weeping. I covered my nakedness with my arms and fell into a huddle by the corner of the room. I could hear the hunter dogs barking at the moon outside. They barely masked the muffled curses of drunken sentries who had lost their cowries at the gambling table. A lizard darted back across the embers, as though it had been waiting patiently for it to be over. Yet the Balogun lay there on his side touching himself and laughing. How else could I explain Balogun Ijeru's qualities, if not but to chalk it all up to madness?

I snatched the blood-stained loin cloth that I had laid on and draped it across my nakedness. I fled out of the room and into the surrounding darkness of the night.

"Return to me at once!" I heard him say. I defied the fear that coursed through me and ran instead across a field of Coco yams and Ewedu vegetables. My heart pounded as I ran. My feet stung from the stones that lined the walk way, cutting deeply into my feet. I stumbled and fell many times bruising my palms and elbows, but I was determined to escape the clutches of the mad man I had been given to. As I ran further into the night, I could swear that I saw the apparition of my mother in the distance. Ma'mi was willing me on, and holding on to the figurine of Yemoja that she had given me. I didn't understand it. I cried out to her but she was gone as suddenly as she had appeared to me. I called out terrified at the thought of being in this strange predicament by myself. With each stride I took, I became despondent and soon my pace was reduced to a slow trot. I was tired and the hope that I had carried inside me now seemed distant and strange, faded and tattered like the joy of childhood I once knew. So finally, I resolved in my mind that I had nothing else left to live for but to hand myself over to death instead.

PART TWO (1826 - 1841)

GRAHAM THOMAS

CHAPTER 10

ISLINGTON, LONDON, AUGUST 26, 1826.

The muffled sound of slow trotting horses as they pulled ornate coaches along cobbled streets mixed with the hushed excitement of children eager to escape the watchful clutches of their parents. The boys ran off into the surrounding meadows chasing butterflies and showing off their cart wheels, while the little girls in their dainty bonnie hats darted after the pretty ladies hawking sweeties. The lanes were filled with chatty people, out and about, eager to enjoy such a rare beautiful summer day. The village of Islington was famous for it's leisurely country walking lanes and fresh milk that came from the several dairy farms within the borough. It didn't seem out of place for families to head to the nearest tavern on a glorious afternoon like this, if only for a pot of roast and pint of ale. Such a wonderful promise brought on by the smells of peas and broth that wafted above the conspicuous hedges of lime green shrubby hare's ear, the chunky deep purple of lavender and the shimmering array of golden oats. While silly dogs pissed on the barks of stubborn oak trees just barely missing the spot where love sick teenagers had chiselled the names of their sweet hearts for all the world to see.

Graham Wilson Thomas sauntered into one of such taverns that dotted the lane between Angel and Highbury fields, looking to buy himself a modest meal. He was a young man of nineteen years, with an unruly mop of brown hair and a day-old bristle covering a rather determined chin. There was a quiet confidence about him that belied the truth about who he was. In truth he was a stranger, still new to the wiles that could only be found in London. Graham had been born and lived most of his life in his village of Abbeydale, which was further north in the Yorkshire dales and moors. There, his parents were livestock farmers and self-professed botanists who could trace their lineage to a clan of ancient Viking druids. He had only recently completed the course of elementary studies at the local parish school. On the prodding of his Vicar, he now sought to continue his instructions at the Parish school at the church of St Mary, the virgin, in Islington, under the guidance of his distant uncle, the Vicar, the Reverend Daniel Wilson.

He had his letters of introductions safely tucked in his pocket, a ruck sack stuffed with a few clothes, a bar of soap, two ounces of cheese carefully wrapped in a piece of brown paper, a family bible and a few hard-earned shillings his mother had given him to get by with until he could find himself a wage paying job.

As he dipped a chunk of bread into the bowl of bone broth placed in-front of him, he looked about the tavern and watched as others ate. Most other customers had meat on their plates, a luxury he knew he wouldn't be able to afford for a while. Not with the little he had to get by on. Growing up in Abbeydale had been hard enough. The family raised sheep which they sheared for wool. It was tough work which kept them outdoors most of the winter. At other times they joined the village as they all gathered and threshed the rape. A crop which they grew for its' seed pressed into oils, while the forage left behind was fed to the livestock to help fatten them.

While food hadn't always been abundant growing up, liquor certainly had been, and as a *'preemer'* boy to several wool croppers, he had claimed his own fair share of drunken brawls. That was until he had started paying more attention to the Vicar's Sunday sermons and become enthralled by the stories visiting missionaries and *expeditionists* told of their courageous adventures across India, Indo-china and the dark continent of Africa, where they spread the gospel of Jesus Christ to the heathens in those lands. They told stories of tigers, exotic plants and delicious berries that gushed out nectar so sweet that women cried. Those stories were rivalled by tales of never-ending rivers and fish the size of sheep, bright evening stars and warm winters and gold hidden in deep crevices that only the courageous ever dared explore. Graham was drawn to the possibilities of a life of adventure and greater purpose beyond the rolling hills and quiet meadows of Yorkshire where very little ever happened for a young man like him.

He finished his meal quietly and left the 'Boars Head' tavern for a short walk along upper Liverpool Street towards the Chapel of Ease that was attached to St Mary's church. He had been advised by his Vicar that to be adequately prepared for a missionary life, he would do well to seek his maternal uncle's help. The Church Mission Society to which his uncle belonged, had established a parochial school of learning within the parish for the instruction of intended evangelists and missionaries. They had also achieved great success in bringing young Indian and African natives to be trained for the work of accompanying English explorers through the dark continents as well as saving their fellow heathen souls.

Graham finally met with his uncle and benefactor just as evening tea was being served in the old vicarage. He was ushered in to the room, clutching his rucksack tightly, unsure of how he might present himself in such an appointed circumstance. His uncle peered at him through bifocals and smiled as he pointed him to a chair. He was chatting with a few elderly parishioners who by the look of what Graham could see, seemed rather enthralled by his manners. His uncle ignored him and the letter he presented, as he engaged in casual banter with his guests. The elderly ladies nibbled on scones, sipped exotic oolong tea and giggled politely at the anecdotes the Reverend told. He laced it with generous compliments and was gracious enough to personally refill their tea cups.

"You mustn't despair Edna." He admonished one of them. "The good lord works in mysterious ways, and I dare say that the Right Honourable and Earl of Liverpool has been a most accomplished Prime Minister and given the circumstances has served as a good influence on his majesty the king if I might add."

"Quite." Another of the ladies nodded curtly. "God help us all if he hadn't." She added.

"I do worry that the society may not be able to get the royal commissions required from the Palace to send another contingent of missionaries to India in good time." Edna sighed.

"I do worry that the gluttonous fool that George has proven to be, will always prefer a tart and a bottle to a sermon and good politics."

"I'm sure it will be fine ladies. We must not forget that the Tory party secured a resounding victory over the Whigs which undoubtedly will strengthen the government's hand in these matters. India after all is of vital importance to the crown." The Vicar assured. "More scones?"

"Delightful treats." Another of the ladies cooed.

"Freshly baked this morning by the good women in the parish bakery." The Reverend added proudly.

"Saints, all of them!"

They chatted on for some time with Graham seated with his head politely bowed. He was torn between getting a drink and perhaps some of the scones on display. He stole glances at his grand uncle; his mother's uncle on her paternal side, as he sat self-assured, cultured and courteous. It was almost impossible to believe that this man and his mother and her siblings had once been raised in the same homestead in a Yorkshire hamlet to share croppers and lead miners. A family so poor that they barely survived the great famine. He was only eleven years older than his mother who had stayed back and married the first man who offered her a future, whatever that future, might have been. The Reverend on the contrary had fled, first up north to Edinburgh and then later down towards London where he had clawed his way first through a Presbyterian education, then later found his place within the Church of England. He never returned to Yorkshire though, choosing rather to write letters and send money. Graham had ever only met him once. That had been several years ago when he was a little boy still bouncing off his mother's lap. A fairly well-off great aunt had died in Edinburgh and left a small inheritance for the family. The Reverend had still been in theology school then and had come for the service and the reading of the will.

"And this young man is a distant relative." Graham looked up to find that the Vicar was standing in front of him and had patted his shoulder. "Ladies, allow me to introduce Graham Wilson Thomas."

He jumped out of his seat, almost knocking the Reverend off balance.

"Sorry about that, sir" Graham blurted in his thick Yorkshire accent.

"Now then, we must be more aware of ourselves, mustn't we?" the Reverend quipped. The women were making their way to the door slightly bemused by his clumsiness. "How do you do young man?" They asked curtly and then they were out of the door and gone.

The Reverend took him by the shoulder and stared at him for a minute. "Yer have yer mother eye." He smiled as he broke into a Yorkshire accent that Graham was more familiar with. He looked up startled at the remarkable change in accent and met sympathetic yet humorous eyes staring back at him.

"Yer 'ere to addle some brass, I hear." The Reverend smiled. "Yer have lots to learn about the art of getting on so." The Reverend said. "We'll see if we can make a grand job of yer as a soldier for Christ. Now come along and put wood in t'ole!"

He led him out the door, past the imposing chapel of Ease which had been built in 1814, based on a design by the respected William Wickings, who was at the time famous for his design of churches and cathedrals. It was designed as a typical Georgian six bay brick box house with tiny windows and a solemn crypt.

They crossed the lane towards a newly built structure with open balconies and painted balustrades that over looked the chapel and its beautiful gardens.

"Our new school for the instruction of Christian soldiers." The Vicar announced proudly. "All of us are chuffed to bits."

"Here you will find room and board, hot meals to warm yer belly and the good news of Jesus Christ to lift yer soul. Yer Vicar tells me that you have become a bit of a brawler now have yer?"

"I... I... I." Graham stammered.

The Reverend laughed, "Not to worry son, isn't every young *sprog* in Yorkshire, but here if yer attend to yer duties and yer instructions, the mission will straighten yer out. Come now let me introduce yer to the house master."

They climbed up the stairwell and walked across the corridors to the house master's office. The Vicar didn't bother knocking as he walked in. They found a lanky gentleman standing arms akimbo poring over a set of large maps carefully displayed on the wall. They had 'The London Cartographical Society' boldly inscribed on them, but it was difficult to tell where exactly they showed. A couple sat on two adjoining seats sipping tea and nibbling on similar scones as had been served in the vicarage, while also staring at the maps.

"Good evening, Vicar." The lanky man greeted cheerfully.

The Reverend nodded curtly. "Damian."

"May I introduce our friends visiting the parish from the Sierra Leone, the Reverend Thomas Davey and his lovely wife Mrs Davey."

"Ah" the Vicar responded, turning on the charm and switching to a more southern English accent, "How do you do Reverend and Mrs Davey How nice to meet you?"

"How do you do, Reverend?" The visitor replied.

"I have heard of the remarkable successes you are achieving for the gospel in Africa."

"It is by His grace only Reverend." Davey replied

"Yes, indeed, Reverend. Yet, achieved against such inhuman odds."

"The Reverend Davey and his lovely wife have just been updating me." Damian explained. "The society hopes to start an industrial school soon at Freetown to provide an education for slaves freed from the clutches of the Portuguese slavers in the various territories of the Fante, Oudiah and the Bight of Benin. It seems great progress is being made in stopping the slave trade and converting the freed slaves to the Christian way."

"Great news." The Vicar purred.

"I must caution that we have barely put a dent in their evil intent, gentlemen. The Portuguese are such crafty buggers and their schooners are fast. Despite the diligence of his majesty's navy the slavers keep devising new ways to evade our efforts."

"It doesn't help that the heathen natives are quite up to their eyeballs in the dreadful trade themselves. I suppose it leaves us with little else to do than celebrate each cargo we are able to set free and pray for more."

There was a bit of silence in the room as they all seemed to reflect on the thought.

"Alas, that his name may be glorified." The Vicar added before carrying on.

"Damian, may I introduce my nephew, Graham Wilson Thomas."

"Graham comes to us recommended by his parish Vicar and an old friend of mine, as a man in search of a life of mission."

Damian said, "How do you do?" and extended him a hand.

Graham took it and shook it politely. He noticed that his hands were stronger than Damian's. He released it and fiddled his rucksack nervously.

"Graham also has the peculiar benefit of being from a long line of ancient viking druids. And his Vicar tells me he has fascinating skills the society can put to good use in places like India or greater China someday; a thing for plants."

"How fascinating. The study of plants." The Reverend Davey interjected. "I suspect that you might find his skill more suited to Africa, Reverend Wilson."

The Vicar glanced at Reverend Davey. "Well, I am not entirely sure I am conversant with the terrain, Reverend."

"An extraordinary array of plants and fauna exists, Reverend," Mrs Wilson chipped in. "Most yet to be appropriately catalogued and only a few botanists have attempted the journey to Africa given the dreadful toll on Christian lives of course."

"Intriguing thought, but perhaps still a little early, given that we still have a Christian conviction to hold of him."

Reverend Davey smiled. "That, Vicar we *all* spend our entire lives building up." He stroked his beard and then patted his wife's arm. "Mrs Davey and I have been blessed by the almighty to witness even the most unlikely of native souls come to Christ and build their faith day by day sometimes with the most admirable of human spirit that puts even educated men to shame. Even now on this trip we joined with two young Africans who hold such remarkable promise that they may benefit greatly from an exposure to the English Christian way of life."

"How delightful." The Vicar said thoughtfully.

"Yes indeed, Vicar." Damian acknowledged. "Two bright souls I just met. They have been sent down to the infirmary to be examined before we place them in the hall with the other Africans."

"The church has been most generous." The Reverend Davey added. "We look forward to these two spending a few months under the instruction of the school. Mrs Davey and I hope that they will be able to return to Freetown with us at the end of our passage."

"I don't see why not." Damian mused. "Now young Master Thomas, tell me about your own ambitions." He asked turning to Graham.

Graham glanced at his great Uncle and touched his eye brow nervously. "I-I am a hard worker sir." He muttered.

"I'm sure you are. Tell me how you feel about the lord?"

"I-I don't have anything against the lord sir and I keep myself out of trouble."

"So why do you seek a life of mission then Master Graham?"

Graham took a deep breath and dropped his ruck sack on the floor carefully. When he eventually brought his gaze up, he locked it on Damian's. "Because I want to see the world sir. I'd be one to climb mountains and track animals, and if there is any wounded to be carried I will not be one to spare a thought before I carry them to safety on me bare back sir."

"Interesting thought." Damian commented, looking away for a moment to cast a glance at the Vicar. "An explorer and a hero." Damian announced curtly.

"And a botanist." The Reverend Davey joined in lightly.

"So it would seem." The Vicar finally commented casually. "Perhaps you can get him settled in with the other lads now, Damian." It was said more as an instruction.

"Certainly, Vicar." Damian replied falling in to step." Now, Master Thomas, perhaps you will like to come along with me, let me show you to the halls." He added as he led the way out of the office.

The Church Mission Society was founded on the twelfth, of April 1799 as the then Society for Missions to Africa and the East. The inaugural meeting had included a group of activist evangelical Christians famously known in London circles as the Clapham sect. Many of the society's founders made up of such distinguished men as Thomas Scott, Henry Thorton, John Venn and William Wilberforce, had become renowned for their efforts at stopping the slave trade in Africa as well as promoting the education of Africans. William Wilberforce, who was perhaps the most famous of the early founders, had been a member of parliament, relinquishing his seat as MP for Bramer only two years earlier.

In the years after the formation of the society, he had become the leader of the abolitionist movement determined to have the House of Commons declare slave trade an illegal act. In addition to the ambition of fighting the scourge of slavery and spreading the gospel to all corners of the British Empire, the society also drove an activist agenda of social reformation within British society as inspired by the example of the famous Methodist, John Wesley. The work of the society had become significant in the years after it was formed, and they had become successful in attracting a large pool of patrons who donated generously to their various causes. Unfortunately, the same could not be said about their ability to attract and recruit English missionaries to join their adventures in Asia, and the Gold coast of West Africa. Several of the early volunteers to their expeditions had either returned with illnesses or perished in the tropical reaches of Africa, having succumbed to the fever. An illness so severe and unforgiving that it had now become known to several people as the white man's curse.

Reverend Davey had himself become afflicted with the fever a few years earlier, when he first visited West Africa as a member of a Lutheran exploratory mission to the Susu people of the Guinea. There had been seven Europeans at the start of the expedition which had lasted four months. He alone had survived the illness. Sadly, the others had perished and been buried one after the other by the banks of the Guinea River. He had prayed through his bouts of delirium occasioned by the high fever, while his head felt as though it might erupt and scatter into a thousand pieces from the headaches. Sometimes there were cold spells that threatened to throw him into convulsion. It had been the natives who had cared for him and had fed him on a strain of sour pap infused with ground leaves from specially picked plants they swore would help him. He had agreed to swallow the concoctions, unlike the others who had refused, calling it a witch doctor's brew.

When his fever eventually broke a few days later, he had lain on his back in a make shift bed made of tied bamboo sticks dressed with raffia fronds. Conscious that he had survived the near impossible, he became convinced that he had been spared by the almighty for a reason. He found the justification for his purpose in the need to ensure the gospel of Jesus Christ was spread to the negroes of the harsh continent. His faith and resolve renewed, he threw himself back into the work of the Church Mission Society in Bathurst and later Freetown in the Sierra Lone where alongside a few other European missionaries, they established industrial dormitories for freed slaves. In addition to teaching them how to read and write in English, the men were taught carpentry, while the women were taught dress making.

Graham sat next to Damien and the visiting Reverend Davey at one of the several long dining tables within the school refectory, listening to the Reverend Davey as he told his story of the missions work in Freetown. Dinner was cabbage soup, black pudding, farmers bread and fillet fish served with an array of vegetables. The hall had erupted into a din of chatter immediately after the blessing had been offered by one of the school masters. There must have been about a hundred and fifty young men in the hall, all about Graham's age or slightly older, seated in groups of twenty across the several tables and poking fun at one another as they dunked sour bread into their soups.

The Reverend Davey was explaining that the colony of Freetown was growing rather fast as each successive shipload of freed slaves arrived the port under the supervision of the British navy task force stationed there. He was concerned that if not properly looked into, the overcrowding could give rise to an outbreak of disease. There was already a need to divert more resources to the colony, and while it fell on the British government to provide a large part of what was required, the Church Mission Society and its band of donors needed to help cover the gaps. He wondered if there was a way the message could be passed to the appropriate quarters in time for necessary assurances to be given before he returned to the colony in the next few months.

"The man to see will certainly be Mr Henry Venn." The Reverend Daniel Wilson advised. "Now that Mr Wilberforce has sadly become a bit indisposed, Mr Venn's submissions are very respected by the other leaders of both the Sierra Leone and Church Mission Societies and he gets much done. I also have it on good authority that he is viewed as a future Secretary of the CMS."

"He is undoubtedly a remarkable man." Damian replied. "A true Christian gentleman like his father. A chip off the old block."

The three men munched away in silence. Graham who had been given the privilege of dinning with them wondered what it must be like to free slaves from slave ships.

"Beg your pardon sir, but it must be dreadful what these slaves go through." He addressed the question to the Reverend Davey.

The Reverend smiled at him.

"You will find Master Graham, that there are indeed very few indignities that may be considered worse than being sold into the forced servitude of others. Most of the slaves we see returned to their freedom in the good colony of Freetown, were benign native folk captured by African slavers themselves during raids or inter-tribal wars waged within the hinterlands and then marched to the coast to be sold off to the Portuguese and French who then shipped them off in deplorable conditions to the plantations in the Americas."

Graham stared at the Reverend his face aghast. Damian nodded and picked his teeth with his index finger before he joined the conversation. "It is my understanding that these tribal wars are more predominant in the kingdom of *Eyo*?"

"How right you are sir." Reverend Davey applauded. "We see several of the Yoruba stock as they are also called, captured within this evil trade, particularly their women. There is the legend that they being of very fertile constitution are quite a good investment for the plantation owners."

"Good God!" the Reverend Daniel Wilson bellowed. "Not even the pits of hell will be good enough for these serpents. To breed humans like animals?"

"The lord himself is indeed a patient God." Reverend Davey replied. "That he should not see fit to bring instant judgement on the vile ways of men."

Damian asked. "What tribe would the two freed slaves who are to be with us belong to?"

Reverend Davey stroked his beard casually and replied rather thoughtful, "One of them is Ashanti I believe, while the other younger fellow Samuel Crowther is Eyo or Yoruba depends on which linguistic interpretation you follow. Now he is a very gifted soul I must add. He has taken to his education and the word of God with such zeal."

"Samuel Crowther?" The Reverend Wilson seemed puzzled. "Isn't that...?".

"Yes." Reverend Davey interjected and smiled, as he read the Vicar's mind. "His baptismal name is taken after *the* Samuel Crowther. The respected Vicar of Christ Church Newgate."

"How thoughtful." Said the Vicar, genuinely intrigued.

"I agree. Chosen himself with guidance from Mr Raban who is one of our missionaries. I believe the young man's native name was Adjayi. *Ehem*, native names, unbelievably complex and unpronounceable."

The men laughed.

"An excellent choice, nonetheless." The Vicar re-affirmed. He raised his tin cup as he proposed a toast. "Gentlemen, to Samuel Adjayi Crowther. One more native soul for Christ."

Graham Thomas raised his tin cup along with the others in the toast. He drank and then placed his cup down on the table. The din from ongoing chatter had continued unabated throughout the course of the meal and everywhere he looked he found young men just like him, from all corners of the three kingdoms, eating heartily, laughing at one another's jokes and a few even back slapping in a spirit of camaraderie he had not witnessed back home in Abbeydale. It seemed that they all took joy in the knowledge that they belonged to something eternally greater than their individual lives. Plucked away from the obscurity and tedium of rural English life and being prepared to extend the frontiers of the Church across the empire's furthest reaches. Adventures deep into the hinterland of heathenism, where a world of thick jungles, rapid rivers, and natives who could force you to gulp witch doctor's brew waited for the valiant and the devout. Graham was not sure he understood what sort of love made other lads wish to sacrifice so much of themselves to seek such a precarious future, but within his heart he knew his.

For him, it lay in the opportunity to someday return to his local parish in Abbeydale with the stories of his own adventures. Stories which he could tell to the young lads and lasses in the county. Especially those that would win the admiration and love of the lovely Georgette Harrows, the baker's pretty second daughter, with curly brunette hair and pale blue eyes, and skin that smelt of lavender. She was the only girl in the whole of Abbeydale who made his young heart ache with pain at just the thought of holding her by the hand. Graham wished Georgette could see him now, seated on the same table with worldly men and talking about Africa. He looked across at his uncle as he ate his meal. He suddenly understood how lucky he was to be here and given a chance to be part of this. So, Graham raised his tin cup. This time of his own volition and spoke without much of a stammer.

"Sir," he began, as he held the cup just below his eyes. "Thank you for your kindness sir. I will find more *darkies* and drag them to church if I have to. I promise."

He did not quite understand why the two men both burst out laughing. But as each man gave him a hearty back slap, and a cheer of hear, hear! He sensed he must have said something right. He only wished that Georgette could have been there to see what a fine young man he had become.

CHAPTER 11

My dearest Georgette

I sincerely hope that this letter meets you with happy thoughts. Not a day goes by that I do not think of you, and while my time in Islington might have been filled with new adventures and thrills and much learning, I confess that I turn to my bed at the end of every night with the gentlest thoughts of you. I have become a better learner of the bible and a much better writer as I hope is evident by this very letter. You will also be pleased with my better praying tongue. Mr Damien says that I have the constitution of a priest within me. The days are long here and filled with so much instructions and duties, but I tell the lads in my hall that they are nowhere near what is required to breed sheep or tress wool back in Yorkshire. I do hope your father's affairs are dandy and his business profitable. I can only say to you that were he to have his bakery here in London, he certainly would be a wealthier man. I have never seen so many people gathered in one city in search of a living and a happy time, surely, they all must eat bread.

I am hopeful that I will return to Abbeydale for the Christmas this year. Mr Damien says we are all deserving of a jolly Christmas, which is much more than I can say for the two Africans and three Indians we have amongst us. You will be surprised to find that they do not celebrate Christmas in Africa. They have all sorts of heathen ceremonies instead.

One of the two darkies is called Samuel, though he still holds on to his African name of Adjayi. He is a very interesting lad indeed, a freed slave but very quick of learning and eager to adopt our English ways. He is very good with his hands too, and perhaps as good a carpenter as any might be within the school. He sings to the lads in his African language, songs he claims are about being good to others and being good to the earth. They are quite a spectacle the two Africans, but surely Samuel the more remarkable of the two. His English is fast improving and he reads the bible too.
Mr Damien and the other masters have taught us about the good in Britain abolishing the trading of slaves amongst Europeans and the Africans themselves. It is such a noble endeavour Mr Damien says, and fraught with the dangers of adventure and duty to God and our king.

My uncle assures me that time will come after my studies for me to join a mission to India to bring the heathens there to the way of God and trade with our sovereign. I cannot tell you how excited I am about such prospects. But for now, I must study hard and prove myself worthy of such responsibility.

I am afraid that I must stop here my dearest. I find that you have become my source of joy and if I may be so bold, I dream of the day that I may find the courage to walk you to church. For there cannot be for me a greater delight, than the thought of you happy in my arms.

Forever,
Graham

≈

Dear Graham,

I am happy that you have found something gallant to do with your life. I am sure that the life of a missionary will suit you well. My father is well thank you, and we are grateful for the little that we make at our shop. The parish continues to thrive and Sunday school certainly just the way you might last remember it. I do hope you enjoy your studies at Islington.

Sincerely,
Georgette Harrows

G raham folded the letter back and slipped it into his pockets. He sat there in silence for a while wondering what to make of Georgette's reply. Surely, she could have been a little more forthcoming, a little warmer in her response perhaps. He stared at the lads playing cricket in the surrounding open fields behind the school refectory. They were a hearty bunch, jumping about and catching balls, but terrible bowlers by the look of it as no wickets had yet fallen.

It was autumn and the mulberry trees had already started shedding their dark orange leaves. As he stared into the distance, a sullen look etched across his face, he remembered the rolling hillsides of Abbeydale. The fierce icy winter winds that came gushing down from the North with a vengeance, banging on the rafters of the otherwise cosy cottages with their crackling fireplaces. There, families huddled together with their hot toddies and burning whiskies that sent liquid fire coursing through the body and kept everyone indoors warm. He had always pictured Georgette against the backdrop of a merry yuletide celebration. The image of her smiling at him as she lay her head on his lap by the fireplace, and the glowing embers reflected off her hair. It was his definition of a reformed life, a more respectable life.

Graham convinced himself that his days here in Islington would bring him nearer to the kind of life his mother and the local Vicar demanded of him. Georgette hadn't been impressed by any of it. He sighed, before rising to join the others on the field. He wasn't that much of a bowler himself, certainly not William Lilly White who had taken down the most wickets in English cricket that season, but he surmised that on a good day, he knew how to take down a wicket on his own.

Supper was served an hour late that evening. He chose to join a table other than his regular one seeking an edgy conversation to take his mind off Georgette. Supper was one of the things he most enjoyed. It was a time the lads swapped stories and planned naughty escapades into London's unending number of boroughs, unbeknownst to the hall masters. It was a toss between visiting the travellers who camped their wagons at the vacant land at Battersea, where easy women amongst them took you in for a shilling, or a visit to listen to the Italian Street musicians who staged mini operas to the admiration of passers-by on the streets of Whitechapel. One of the lads warned that the Battersea girls were known to give the itch and were better avoided. The others shrieked in mock agony and glared at each other knowingly. Two hours later, five of them found themselves headed into the city hitching a ride on the back of a milk man's cart loaded with vats filled with tomorrow's ration of milk. They rode past the squalor of the city's open sewers. The tightly packed living quarters of the city's poor, with streets littered with heaps of decaying refuse dumped beneath gas lanterns. They wheeled through the Scottish quarters where merry fiddlers played old Celtic tunes accompanied by the odd bagpiper and half-drunk, homesick tradesmen who bellowed their lover's names at the top of their voices.

Along the dingy roads of Peckham was "*The castle and Pheasant*" a popular inn with a modest reputation for keeping calmer patrons. As they approached, Graham noticed that a crowd was gathered outside its doors. Two middle aged board walkers stood on either side of the posts calling out to passers by.

"What's this about then?" One of the lads shouted at the men.

"A meeting of the reformation society." One of the men answered.

"What's that?"

"About how to help the niggers in Africa." The board walker added. "It's free to come in and yer still get a free mug of ale for your sorry lot." He chuckled.

The offer of free drinks caught the curiosity of the lads and they soon hopped off the cart and filed into the inn. There were about seventy people seated on wooden benches when they walked in. Men of varying works of life, from the lower classes, by the look of their disposition, freely chatting among themselves as they waited for the proceedings of the evening to commence. A man walked up towards the podium and addressed the seated audience.

"Gentlemen." He called out to the lads as they began the hunt for where the ales were being served.

"Gentlemen, may I ask that you be seated." He had a practiced tone and studious air about him. "Welcome to the meeting of the London reformation society. Make yourselves comfortable and keep your wits about you."

"What about the ales then?" One of the lads enquired mimicking the man's tone. The other men seated laughed.

"We are all done in now, by the looks of it." One of the men seated quipped as he tapped his pipe on the edge of his seat.

Two eminent looking gentlemen sat by the side of the raised platform, taking the proceedings all in rather stoically.

"Ales will be served shortly." The gentleman announced." But first we must constitute a decent audience and commit ourselves to the wise words of our very distinguished speaker here."

Graham studied the men he referred to. They were far better dressed than everyone else in their double-breasted frock coats neatly quilted at the upper chest to improve their fitting and fashionable long trousers that seemed to have replaced knee breeches these days. Their top hats were impeccably crafted and tilted at just the right angle.

"Gentlemen, how auspicious that we might on a lovely evening such as this be privileged to listen to the thoughts and reflections of our patron and benefactor, the right honourable Sir Thomas Fowell Buxton. He is a member of His Majesty's parliament representing Weymouth and a friend to all Christian men of goodwill across the empire and her colonies."

The gentleman who stepped out was of slender build and in his late thirties or early forties, Graham guessed. He wore small round rimless bi-focal glasses similar to the type that his uncle wore. When he walked to the podium he carried a courteous and country squire air about him. The sort that came with good breeding, private schooling and suggested that he was more accustomed to grander settings than what was provided by the Castle and Pheasant Inn. He had a small book in his hands as he started his speech.

"Gentlemen, I know a thing or two about brewing a decent ale and I am ashamed to say that in my younger days I have out-drunk with the best of the lot in any Irish free house, so trust me good sirs when I assure that the ale is worth the wait."

Graham, as every other man in the room was gripped by the humour Sir Thomas offered and rewarded him with a hearty cheer. Having grabbed the attention of his audience, Sir Thomas proceeded to deliver a compelling speech. Graham listened as he shared his thoughts on the plight of the aboriginal people of South Africa and India and how they were being ill-treated within the colonies. He offered a modern view of how British life itself should be lived.

"We are christian men living in a great christian civilisation." He declared. "It is the duty of every man irrespective of station to be part of the great reformation of society. It is up to the commons as much as the government to build a kinder society that kills its own less and gives a chance to all to reform themselves."

Then he spoke about slavery in West Africa and wondered why it was that Britain had allowed such atrocities as the dealing in the trade of fellow children of god to continue unabated. He spoke of the great vision that he and his fellow evangelicals had and said that it was Britain's duty as a great christian society with all the influence and strength that the good lord had given her, to raise the native people of Africa from the dust and through christian industry teach them how they might use their own resources to end slavery and become a prosperous ally of Britain herself.

These might have been themes that Graham had heard before at the Parochial school, but they had never been delivered with such élan nor authority. He noticed that only two out of all five of them present seemed to pay attention. The others had reverted to asking about the ale promised. A heated argument eventually ensued between them and the inn keeper who then threatened to have them thrown out. It didn't take long before the first punch was thrown by one of them. It was Philip Upcher, the burly south paw from Lancaster with a reading disability. Everyone had always worried about his quick temper. It was enough to have the six of them pounced upon by the inn keeper's men.

Graham found himself promptly grabbed by the collar like the others and dragged along towards the doors.

That was when they all heard his uncle's unmistakeable voice as he approached them from an inner room within the Inn. He had unbeknownst to them, been in the audience.

"You must forgive me gentlemen, I am Reverend Daniel Wilson of the Church of England, and rector at the Saint Mary School and these rascals happen to be my students. If you are kind enough to hand them over, I will sort the scally-wags out if that's all right with you."

Graham stood there with the others in disbelief as the punishment was read out by Mr Damien. It was severe. The six of them were to be rusticated at the close of the school term and return forthwith to their respective parishes and sponsors. Graham was hardest hit by it as his uncle was determined to demonstrate his sternness and make an example of him by singling him out for even further punishment. He was to be reduced to the indignity of sitting with the junior classes till the end of term after which he would be expected to leave the school like the others.

He was pale from shock and he couldn't even dare look his uncle in the eyes as he, along with the others were marched out of the office and handed over to superintendents who were now assigned to watch their every move. As he walked towards his tiny metal bed space within the halls, he dropped his head into his sweaty palms and broke down in tears. The halls were empty at this time as students were in their classes. The tears came in violent fits, he couldn't seem to stop. He couldn't remember when last he had ever cried. Perhaps when his first dog had died when he was seven, or when his aunt Philo passed away a year later. It was exasperating and yet therapeutic all at once. How on earth was he going to explain to his mother that he had gotten kicked out of a school of learning she had fought so hard to get him in to? Whatever would Georgette think of him now? He clenched his fist to absorb the shame that overcame him, hoping that it would pass. With time he rocked himself gently as he now stared at the floor wondering what he was going to do with himself. For the first time in his life Graham felt the urge to pray and ask God for help. So, he did. He knelt down over his bed space and awkwardly began to mutter the Lord's Prayer. He really wasn't sure how he was supposed to ask God for help but he asked aloud as best as he knew how any way. He got up and sat back on the bed still staring at the floor, hoping for a miracle.

CHAPTER 12

LIVERPOOL, GREAT BRITAIN, JANUARY 2ND, 1827.

D espite the cold, the port of Liverpool was bustling
with activity. There were to be found, ships from
every part of the empire. They berthed on a daily
basis while dock workers off loaded produce, artefacts and
people. There were spices from the Indian sub-continent;
tobacco and cotton from the Americas. Jute bags stuffed with
bright red peppers, palm nuts and dusty white elephant tusks
from Africa. Merchant Sailors with three-month-old beards
mixed with clean shaven naval ratings in starched khakis.
The lot of them sent by the sovereign to the farthest
distances within the empire that their schooners would take
them, to protect the shipping routes from the Portuguese,
the Spanish, the French, as well as pirates and other vermin
of the sea. There were returning penal offenders, once
banished to Australia, but now hopeful for a pardon having
served their penance. They huddled along under the watchful

eye of proud soldiers, while worn out colonial administrators staggered on deck, happy to be back home from the colonies and using their eyes to skirt through the many easy women with fresh winter flowers in their hair, who flocked to the piers looking to dispose the starved among them of their farthings.

Graham looked about him in astonishment and felt the excitement well up in him as he walked up the gang way into the waiting boat. At last, a life of adventure beckoned. He had his beloved rucksack and a newly acquired portmanteau in which he had neatly folded new clothes and a few other personal effects. He heard the loud piercing blare of ship bugles eagerly announcing their departure. He remained focussed on the task of carrying his luggage up the ramp and into the boat. She was named 'Princess Regent' and had garnered an infamous reputation some years earlier as a convict ship which transported penal offenders 'down under' to the penal colony in Australia. She was bigger than anything he had ever seen. He reached his third-class quarters and found a suitable bunk in a room he would share for the next few days with eight other farers. He locked up his luggage in the locker provided and sat down on the bed, testing the firmness of the mattress. It seemed suitable. Everything seemed perfect and he felt hopeful. It was a moment of hope which helped to thaw the aching sadness he had felt in the pit of his stomach.

Graham had received his miracle. As the school term drew to a close, he became resigned to the fact of his inevitable return to Abbeydale. He became withdrawn and grew lethargic. Learning became arduous and the urge to drink unbearable. He chatted with no one, choosing instead to stare at the dank ceiling of the student hall and wallow in the self-pity that had subsumed him. He craved the idea of Georgette even more, but he could not bring himself to write to her.

His uncle now never spoke to him. Instructions if any, were passed through his tutors. He suffered the shame of sitting in class with those much younger than him in learning and it was not long before he became the butt of jokes in the refectory. It had gone on for months and just when he felt he had become accustomed to the humiliation, he was summoned by Mr Damien to his office.

Graham found both his uncle and the Reverend Thomas Davey in Mr Damien's office. And just as it had been, when he had first met all three of them, in what now seemed many years ago, the Reverend Davey sat there stroking his beard, while his grand uncle leaned on Mr Damien's desk brooding.

"Sit down Graham." Mr Damien had waved him to a chair by the corner of the room. He did as he was told, watching all three of them guardedly.

Eventually Mr Damien said. "I have a passage of scripture that I would like to read to you, Graham." The other men observed him closely. Mr Damien lifted up a thick leather-bound bible and began to read.

"But the God of all grace, who hath called us unto his eternal glory by Christ Jesus, after that ye have suffered a while, make you perfect, establish, strengthen, and settle you. To him be glory and dominion for ever and ever amen."

Mr Damien looked up and gently placed the bible on his desk then looked over at Graham's Uncle, the Vicar before he then added, "First Peter chapter five, verses ten and eleven."

"Be sober, be vigilant; because your adversary, the devil, as a roaring lion, walketh about, seeking whom he may devour. Verse eight." The Vicar pointedly added from memory.

Reverend Davey stood up from his seat, walked over to Graham and gently placed a hand over his shoulder. "Mr Thomas, how do you feel about a second chance?"

Graham had looked up stunned at what he had just heard.

"A...a second chance, sir?" He had echoed, perplexed. He looked over at his uncle, who stood there watching him without a single expression on his face.

"Yes, Mr Thomas. Mr Damien and I have made a representation on your behalf to the Vicar and he has graciously accepted that you be offered a second chance to redeem yourself. After all, as Christians we understand that we are all living a life of the second chance."

Graham cupped his palms over his mouth and nodded vigorously to keep from uttering any sound. He wasn't sure what type of sound it would have been, given the emotions that were playing out within him.

"But it comes with a condition." Mr Damien said.

"A condition?"

"Yes," it was the Reverend Davey. "How would you like to come work for me in Sierra Leone?"

"Africa?"

"Yes. A new school is being opened for the education of the natives there. I have spoken to the new instructor and we could use a man of your talents and spirit I suppose."

Graham was silent, looking at his uncle. Still, he found no expression.

"Your uncle tells me that you seem quite taken by the excellent works of Mr Fowell Buxton in the eradication of slavery and the industrialisation of Africa, perhaps there should be some providence to the fact that what got you into trouble should be the very instrument of your redemption." Reverend Davey added.

Mr Damien stood up and walked over to Graham. "You are a restless soul my dear friend. A young man eager to make his mark on the world. Perhaps this is what God wills for you, as you yourself have once said, to bring more *darkies* into the church."

"You will be tutored by me personally to such a point as to be able to return to England to complete your missionary training in six months. You will receive room and board and a stipend of twelve shillings. In return you will make yourself useful and open your heart to a more practical form of learning." Reverend Davey said.

All three men looked at him.

Graham searched his uncle's face once again, hoping to get some form of a commitment from him, anything to suggest a sense of personal approval, forgiveness. He still met a blank stare and it troubled him but in his heart he already knew that this was what he wanted. Perhaps it would have been better to start off in India, but this was what fate had dealt him and he was more than grateful for the chance.

"Yes." He had simply said, looking into the faces of the three men and noticing as his uncle looked away.

∼

The eighteen-day journey to the natural deep-water port of Freetown, left him drained and sea sick. He rarely left his bunk as the strange sensation of waves lapping at the side of a boat that rolled endlessly in the middle of a never-ending stretch of ocean jaundiced his sense of balance and calm. It had been agreed, before he left, that he would be allowed to go home for the yuletide to bid his family farewell. The Reverend and Mrs Davey had returned to Freetown in late November, accompanied by their two African proteges. It was expected that Graham would provide the African students with a more intimate account of English life. The Reverend was also keen to have Graham commence work on the cataloguing of plants and other fauna found within the West African bush.

Graham had not told his mother about the trouble he had gotten into. It seemed that his uncle had also been quiet about it, because the parish vicar at Abbeydale had received him with much delight and pride in whatever his modest accomplishments had been to date. He was invited to several of the festivities at the vicarage and offered to the other lads as another example of what was possible if they put their minds to it. Graham found it all bemusing, an anti-climax of sorts to what he had expected. He was also quite conscious about the accolades that he hadn't entirely earned and he had put up a brave face whenever someone praised him. But this did not apply to Georgette. He visited her often at her father's bakery, always buying more sour bread than he or the family needed. He would spy on her during church on the Sundays he was around. He would even follow her when she walked out towards the old paddock overlooking the new water wheel and offer her all the assistance she needed with her baskets as she picked the flowers that were used to decorate the vicarage. She would ask him polite questions about his stay while at Islington and he would answer enthusiastically, painting exaggerated pictures of London and offering adventures that were not entirely true. He never asked her why her letters had been brief and she never offered him anything more than a polite smile. It was the next best thing to paradise if there ever were such a place. Graham couldn't understand why the thought of her made him so happy. It troubled him at times that it seemed that he couldn't breathe when she came close to him, and once when the tip of her frock had touched his fingers as he helped to pass the flower basket to her, he felt that his heart stopped. But the holidays went so quickly and soon it was time for him to make for Liverpool.

On his last night, he summoned up the courage and walked up the lane to her house. His hair freshly cut and neatly combed, his clothes washed. He practiced what he planned to say to her a thousand times in his head, and each time he stumbled on a word or a portion, he would start all over. As he knocked on the door, he could see her father's reflection as he sat in a sturdy rocking chair reading a strip of paper through his monocles. He knocked harder on the second attempt and stepped back a polite distance. No one came to the door until the fourth knock, and it wasn't her father but another young man slightly older than himself. He had healthy bushy hair and a square confident chin with a cleft that was deeply etched into his face. He stood taller than him and offered a pleasant assured air about him. When he spoke, Graham could tell he was well bred and well-schooled. Graham stammered that he wanted to see Georgette. He wanted to say farewell to her because he was leaving for Africa in the morning. He felt embarrassed as the man in the doorway stared at him with what surely must have been a sneer. He was told that she had already retired for the night, but he would be sure to pass on his message to her in the morning. They stared at each other for a moment that seemed to last a lifetime, then the door was shut on him. Graham lingered a moment longer before he turned around and began his lonely walk back home, clutching the ring he had bought and sensing that he was being watched by the fellow who had never left the door way.

T he Reverend Davey was at the harbour to receive him with a retinue of bare feet natives dressed in white cotton shirts over khaki shorts. They all seemed expectant, even excited at his arrival. He was led to a horse pulled buggy ridden by an elderly *mulato* who spoke a very different kind of English with a thick Southern American drawl. The Reverend Daley sat beside him at the back while the natives who carried his luggage walked behind them.

"Richmond is from South Carolina." The Reverend Davey offered as he observed Graham's stare. "He is one of several freed slaves from the plantations in America who chose to return to the continent. He is with the American Southern Baptist Mission which was set up in Bathurst. We work closely with a few of the other missions in the settlement for the education of the freed slaves."

"Howdy mister Graham." Richmond said with a chuckle and a mischievous glint in his eyes. Graham muttered incoherently and looked away.

"Mrs Davey will be home to receive and make you comfortable." Reverend Davey added as he smiled. "You will bathe, put on a fresh set of clothes more appropriate for the heat of the African jungle and rest sufficiently to strengthen your constitution. A few tinctures and plenty of water and you should be well heeled against any encroachment of the fever."

They carried on in silence through the reddish dirt paths of Freetown towards Fourah Bay which lay further out from the beautiful harbour. Graham was taken in by how imposing 'Lion Mountain' was. It rose up before them and towered majestically over the surrounding hills and harbour. The buildings were a mix of old styled American plantation

135

shacks and mud huts with their coverings made from large palm fronds. There was an incessant buzz of darting flies and other obstinate insects next to his face, which caused him to slap himself several times until he was red with pain, and left with very little by way of any self-respect. A crowd of natives trekked right past them, while the Europeans rode in hammocks carried on the head by four able bodied native men with nothing but loin cloth tied around their waists. In the distance he saw open flea markets with bamboo sticks bound together with sturdy vines to make stalls on top of which were stacked the widest assortment of fruits he had ever seen. Jovial old African *mammies* with brightly coloured headscarves watched over their merchandise of mangoes, guavas, pineapples, limes, bananas and other fruits he couldn't possibly fathom which they sold with so much theatrics to the passers-by who approached them.

"Over there." The Reverend Davey pointed to a cluster of brick buildings that made a small arch around a withered cotton tree. "Over there, under that cotton tree is where the town was christened Freetown in 1792, by the early settlers made up of runaway Negro slaves from Nova Scotia in Canada." The Reverend continued.

"They came in fifteen ships brought in by the Sierra Leone company who had acquired the parcel of land from the native chiefs and in the years after, this has become the land where all Negro slaves may return to their continent as free men."

Graham nodded politely. He was too tired to ask questions, and his face hurt.

The Reverend continued his lecture. "Today Freetown is home to freed negro slaves from several of the West African kingdoms. You have the Eku or Yoruba, the Asante and Ga, and even Ibos, Nufis, and a few Hausas and Fulas."

The Davey's lived in the mission compound along with the few other European missionaries who had been sent by the Church Mission Society to work on the continent. The living quarter was a modest wooden and mud brick cabin set up on stilts. It sat in the middle of a field of guava and mango trees, with thickets of tobacco planted at regular intervals to help keep away snakes. Large stone boulders painted white were laid out in such a way as to demarcate the compound in to distinct areas. There were narrow walk paths, a cricket field with wickets made from cut branches, and a vegetable patch where two weather beaten rocking chairs lay side by side overlooking the distant stream. As they approached the building with its large open windows and a hanging hammock by the veranda, Graham noticed a young native man and woman carrying an infant child seated beneath the shade of an orange tree. They were both barely clad and both had one foot each stuck into what seemed to have been a short cut off section of the stem of an uprooted banana tree. It stopped just above their ankle and looked as though they had been shackled into it as a punishment of some sort. It was here that they met Mrs Davey attending to them through a native interpreter. The bizarreness of the spectacle aston-ished Graham.

"Graham!" Mrs Davey called out to him. "How lovely to see you."

He made a polite gesture towards her still staring at the feet of the two natives who glared back at him. Mrs Davey kissed her husband on the cheeks and uttered some instructions to the luggage carriers in their native language. They headed to the house immediately.

"These are a young Mendi couple from the Mendiland in the inner countryside." She began noticing Grahams astonish-ment. "They wear this around their ankles from sundown to sunset as a way of warding off the spirit of an unhappy relative. They seem to believe that some long passed relative wants their daughter dead." She explained and smiled.

Graham looked on dumbfounded, while the Reverend Davey laughed and hugged his wife.

"The intriguing life of the Christian missionary, eh my dear?" He said softly as he squeezed her hands gently.

Mrs Davey smiled and turned to face Graham once more.

"So, tell me how was your passage? Was the boat agreeable?"

"Yes, ma'am." He replied

"Well, come along. We must ensure you have all you need to settle in. You arrive at a most exciting time for the mission and the young Africans of Sierra Leone."

She led him up the dirt path lined with painted boulders into the house.

"The African Institution School starts next week." She announced as she walked into the house. It was dark, but very airy. "Your old acquaintance from Islington, Samuel Crowther will be registered as the first student. Isn't that exciting?"

She showed him to a room with a large window that overlooked a huge Kolanut tree. A little further up was a simple wooden building set against the backdrop of the bay. It was to serve as the new mission school. In front of him lay a full view of the ocean. It provided a cool current of wind, which despite the incessant buzzing of the atrocious fleas, made the tropical heat slightly bearable. Graham threw himself onto the lumpy bed he had been offered. He didn't bother to take his clothes off, nor put the mosquito netting down as he had been earlier advised. He did not notice his old school mate

Samuel Ajayi Crowther walk quietly in to his room. He had come to welcome him. Ajayi smiled down at his limp bulk knowingly, and then proceeded to help him take off his shoes and place them at the feet of the bed. Graham muttered incoherently to himself. Just before he readjusted himself and drifted into an even deeper slumber, he thought about Georgette and what a pity it was that she couldn't be here to see just how beautiful the Atlantic Ocean looked from here.

CHAPTER 13

THE SUSU COUNTRY, SIERRA LEONE, DECEMBER 1840.

~

My dearest Georgette,

I apologise that I have not been able to write you any sooner. The truth is that everything in the last few months has seemed new and strange to me. And even though I make an effort of it, I am yet to truly settle down in to my new circumstance. Africa is savage yet so beautiful. It is very different from the life we live in England and yet it holds the promise of a great adventure and reward. Freetown, where I live with the Reverend and Mrs Davey and the other missionaries is a small town. I dread to say, but too many English men have died here. The most recent, is the colony's lieutenant general, Charles Turner. He himself like many others, has succumbed to the black or yellow fever that sucks all life out of a man in a matter of days, should one be unfortunate to contract it.

It does not help that the weather is extremely hot and humid and the rains which have just begun to fall are a frightful experience with thunderous lightning claps. But I must not frighten you unduly. There is much good news here too. The mission school has started in earnest and I am what the Reverend Davey refers to as a Gentleman in Residence. I am an instructor within the fold, while also helping the Reverend and others to build the school and tend to the other matters of the mission.

There are Europeans here who assist with lessons in Latin, theology and craftsmanship. I sit alongside the natives, (Mrs Davey insists I stop calling them darkies, but rather Africans, natives or negroes) and undertake the learning of several subjects together with them as well as helping them with their English. My old acquaintance, Samuel Crowther, the freed slave who visited Islington is without question the leading light amongst the students here. He was the first to be registered as a student at the mission school and with that accolade, of being the shining example that the Reverend and Mrs Davey see as Africa's beacon of hope to educate her sons and daughters who will rid Africa of its' heathen ways. He has mastered several of the texts and has proven himself in such a short time to be a master of languages and the bible. I have come to realise that his own native language is Yoruba, from a place further afield from Krooland, but his tribes' men seem to be aplenty here in Freetown. We see several of them freed from the captivity of the slaving ships and milling around the harbour in search of gainful work. Sometimes at quieter moments Samuel confesses to be home sick and lonesome from his mother and sister who were separated from him at the time of his capture by the slavers.

There are good past times here worthy of mention too. Our favourite is weekly visits to the Kissi Street flea markets or 'white man's harbour' where we find pleasure in the haggle with the fishermen who bring in the daily catch of sea food. To be found on any day is the biggest marlin or barracuda as one has ever seen. One of Mrs Davey's house

girls, a lovely African girl called Assana in her tribal language is quite
gifted with the stove as to prepare for us the most delicious fish sauces
on the Sabbath days after the divine service has ended. Next week the
Reverend Davey and a few of the lads are planning an expedition to
station hill, to spot and shoot game which we have been reliably
informed are aplenty for the sport.

My dearest Georgette, the days pass quickly indeed, but I confess that
they are made bearable by the thought of you. I hope that you were
told of my visit to your home on the night before my departure. I was
met at the door by a certain fellow I was not familiar with, a relative
of yours perhaps? He had mentioned to me on the occasion that you
had already retired for the evening…

G raham stopped reading and folded the letter back into its envelope. He lowered his head. It had been dated 23 April 1827. Written in the best immaculate cursive script he could muster. Yet he had never sent it. It had stayed instead, in a small leather-bound wallet amongst his few treasured possessions such as the bible his mother had given him. It was hard to believe that thirteen years had passed, and with it the dramatic changes of Africa's seasons. The sort that seduced you to stay longer, even if it hadn't killed you yet. He placed the envelope on the table and poured himself a cup of water into which a pinch of crusty sea salt or drop of peat whisky was always added to take care of water borne vermin. He sipped as he looked about the room in the mission station he now occupied in the new settlement further north from Freetown in the Susu country. He had been asked to move here a little over a year ago to serve as the mission superintendent. Now he along with four others from the Fourah Bay mission, were charged with the work of spreading Christianity to the hardened Susu people of the coastal areas of the Guinea and Sierra Leone. In addition, he administered over the development of the new settlement in line with the aspirations of The African Institution and Colonial government to promote the trade of produce with the tribes of the hinterland.

Georgette had become the one love that never manifested. The ache that had eventually thawed. Banished into the inner recess of a fragile spot in his heart where a dull empty thud still reminded him of how alive he had once been to have suffered the pain and heart wrenching anguish that came with love, rejection and self pity. He had filled the emptiness with a life now dedicated to the improbable. He fed his mind with whatever could be found in the escape into the colony's brutal difficulties, and in a dour manner, he tended his spirit with the love for many, over the love for one. It might have been selfish in the manner in which it had developed after the realisation had come, that she had never been available for him and had been betrothed all along to the man he had met at her doorway that evening. Realisation had come in the manner of a letter written to him by his mother. She had addressed it to the Church mission station at Freetown. The Reverend Davey had handed it over to him barely two days after he had written his own letter which he was waiting to send to England with the missions' next fortnight dispatch.

The man was a distant cousin of her father's benefactor, his mother had informed him regrettably. His name was Edward Bryne from North Devonshire and she was going to marry him. In some sense he had been saved a major embarrassment, he sometimes liked to rationalise.

In the ten years, he had returned to Britain on furlough only twice, and the first trip had been to complete his training back at Islington, while the second had been because his mother had eventually passed away. She had always been the one other person apart from Georgette who had kept him emotionally connected to the old country. Her passing had been particularly heart breaking for him, and it created an emotional void he feared would finally destroy him. He had not been there when she passed and so Graham suffered the anguish of not having been able to say good bye, to the one woman he knew had loved him unconditionally. When he did return to Freetown after his furlough to tend her grave, Graham had thrown himself at Africa. Botany finally became the new love, and adventure, the new mistress. He had catalogued over five hundred plants and species, and extracted the essence of over a third. He had taken part or led in eight major expeditions in to the hinterlands, journeying as far as the Sula Mountains and skirted the banks of the mighty Niger River at Tingi. He had survived bouts of the dreaded fevers, and had once been left for dead at a rapid near Matotoka where the Rokele River dropped three hundred feet into crocodile infested waters. Time had now left him lean and spartan. His face chiselled and resolute and devoid of the flimsiness of mirth. His once pale torso now bore the scars of several bruises, inflicted over the course of countless skirmishes his parties had suffered with savage native tribes in the African hinterlands.

With age had come a certain mellowness and a calmness of thought. It was such calmness that helped him find greater purpose in the search for the salvation of his own soul. But it was not in the way of the other missionaries he now communed with. He had never thought of himself as the ideal missionary in the evangelical sense of the term. He was more a 'frontiers' man, a christian soldier, a practical catechist who bore his own sin and as the Reverend Davey was fond of describing him, he was more of an English bushman and herbalist to the missions.

A young Susu boy came into the room carrying an empty wooden box. As he placed it on the floor next to the improvised mantle place, he told Graham that he had visitors waiting for him outside.

Graham asked him if it was an entourage of the local chiefs he had invited to discuss a matter.

"No masta." The boy replied. "White mans." He pointed at Graham to suggest the visitors looked more like him.

Graham stepped outside to find three Europeans dismounting their hammocks. They were dressed in tan bush khakis and carried rifles. He could tell they were from the colonial government outpost at Port Loko.

"Mr Graham Thomas?" One of them called out.

Graham nodded. "Can I help you?"

They walked over to him and exchanged pleasantries.

"Two days travel through the bloody thicket." One of them grumbled.

"A good time of the year to make the journey." He replied, leading them to the seats that were available underneath a mango tree.

"So, how can I help you gentlemen?"

A few native house helps had come out carrying water and canteens, which they quietly served to the three visitors.

"How is the work of the mission here at Kookodi?"

"Abbeyville," Graham corrected. "We christened the town a few months ago." He added with a smile. "Named after a lovely place in the Yorkshire Country." He explained as the men nodded.

"I see." One of them observed as they sipped from their canteens and exchanged curt smiles. Graham sensed then that something was wrong.

"Seems quite a hurried trip?" He prodded.

"I dare say." The most senior of the lot retorted. "We have a rather difficult task we were called to look into. The Governor himself, you see."

Graham stared at them intently.

"It seems a reclaimed African slave has caused a bit of a cock up."

"Oh dear."

"Yes," the man sighed. "Really dreadful story; A ship berthed at the port a week ago with a cargo of Negro slaves reclaimed from a Spanish slaver. They were all taken in as is the proto-col, to the court of mixed commission for the adjudication of their release warrants but it seems one of the Negroes thinking he was being placed under another toll of bondage killed one of the naval ratings and fled into the Susu country."

"Good God!"

"Snapped the poor fellow's neck with his bare hands!" One of the others added with a gasp.

"It was gathered that the unfortunate fellow was aided by a court messenger to find passage to Port Loko where it seems a community of his Nufi countrymen have settled with the locals. Signals came in conscripting us to find him. The town folk have informed us that a stranger was harboured in the town recently but is making his way by foot intent on reaching the coastal village of Mambolo."

"How dreadful! That's just half a day's trek from here."

"He wouldn't be within your settlement by any chance, would he?"

Graham looked at the man oddly. "Absolutely not! The mission here is closely knit. I practically know every face about the natives."

The man casually searched Graham's face. "We have had instances in the past with the Baptists at Hastings where they harboured a wanted American slaver." He chuckled.

"That's absurd!"

"We will need to look around if you don't mind and perhaps get some of your men to join the hunt party."

"Certainly."

Graham called out to one of his white missionaries and explained the situation. He gave instructions that the soldiers were to be given whatever assistance they required.

"I suggest you set out tomorrow before first light." He advised. "Brother Henkel will arrange a room for you to rest." He shook hands with them then went back into the mission house.

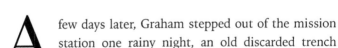

A few days later, Graham stepped out of the mission station one rainy night, an old discarded trench coat flung over his head as cover from the torrential rain that came pouring down with such vengeance. He steadied himself with his free hand and tried to feel his way through the dark void of the court yard. He had come to see a local chief of the Susu people with a retinue of courtiers, but no one seemed willing to help him. The flicker of naked flames from the wick made from thick jute rope thrust into the mould of bee wax did little to shine any light about the area. The wind and the rain didn't help and the woman tasked with trying to keep it alight kept hissing with frustration.

Graham finally found his way to the raffia mat that had been laid on top the mound of damp earth. Three men sat quietly on raffia mats. Their necks were adorned with thick ornamental beads and they had cloth tied around their waists. They were no strangers to Graham and welcomed him as one would a reliable trading partner. Familiar yet reserved. Graham's interpreter was the same boy who had brought in the wooden box and informed him about the colonial visitors days earlier. He stood behind him watching the local chiefs nervously.

The ceremonies were dispensed with quickly, and a thick broth was brought before him, which he politely declined.

"What brings you this time of night?" The senior chief asked through the young interpreter.

"There is an urgent matter." Graham replied. "One that must be addressed quickly so as to maintain the peace of the village."

"What does your master talk about?" The chief asked the boy directly? The boy shrugged nervously and shook his head.

"I don't know, father."

"Ask him to explain quickly. It is late."

The boy turned to Graham and gestured. "My father says you talk now."

Graham said. "Tell him that the soldiers who passed here have found the body of the man who killed the white man."

The boy hesitated for a while. "The man bodi?"

"Yes, he had been killed and his body dumped in the bush!" Graham snapped at him impatiently.

The boy flinched then explained the incident to the chiefs. They seemed unperturbed by the news.

"Why does your master worry about the death of a stranger?" The senior chief asked. "Ask him if the stranger was on an errand to him?"

Graham shook his head. "The death of the stranger brings undue attention to the people of Kookodi." He explained.

"My father says that the town has solved the white man's problem for him."

"That's not how it works." Graham explained irritably. "He was to have been taken to Freetown to be judged by the courts there."

The chiefs laughed loudly. "Tell your master that we have our own ways."

They fell into silence. The colonial officers had already threatened a punitive measure if the natives were that murderously inclined. Such actions made the colonial outpost look inept and could portend trouble for everyone's career. Graham had promised to look into the matter and make things right going forward. He watched as the chiefs spoke amongst themselves and Bala, his interpreter and house boy. The senior chief was the boy's grandfather. He had gathered that Bala's father had been killed in an unexplained incident a few years earlier. The boy had been offered to the early set of Lutheran missionaries when they came requesting a parcel of land to build their initial mission station. The mission soon closed on account of incessant raids by the hostile community and Bala had been returned to his grandfather. By then he had learnt to converse in passable English and could spell basic words. He had been offered to Graham as a helper when he had arrived a year ago to establish the new mission.

"Tell the chief that I am hopeful that we will be able to get the land and people he promised to grow the cotton crop."

The chief grunted, unimpressed.

"My father says when the time is good."

Graham nodded. He rose to his feet and gestured towards the chiefs who still sat watching him." It is late and I must prepare for my journey to Freetown tomorrow."

"My father says you did not take the fire soup."

Graham remembered the last bout of the diarrhoea he had suffered when he had been overtly adventurous with the hospitality. "Tell the chief that he will excuse me this time around."

He grabbed his old trench coat and walked into the rain leaving the chiefs laughing at him.

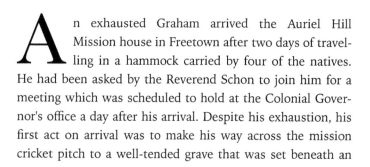

An exhausted Graham arrived the Auriel Hill Mission house in Freetown after two days of travelling in a hammock carried by four of the natives. He had been asked by the Reverend Schon to join him for a meeting which was scheduled to hold at the Colonial Governor's office a day after his arrival. Despite his exhaustion, his first act on arrival was to make his way across the mission cricket pitch to a well-tended grave that was set beneath an old cotton tree, so as to pay his respect to his dear departed mentor.

The Reverend Davey had died from the yellow fever in February 1833, only four months before the British parliament passed the celebrated Slavery Abolition act which had been the labour of love of the Society for the Abolition of Slavery and its' revered promoter, the Rt. Honourable William Wilberforce. In a sad twist of fate, Wilberforce himself had passed away barely three days after its third and final reading.

On the morning the Reverend Davey was buried, a notorious slave schooner initially headed for the West Indies with a cargo of three hundred slaves had docked at Freetown harbour. The West African squadron had captured and escorted the vessel back to the colony, sounding the ship's bugle as was the tradition as it arrived port, to announce its latest victory against the obstinate slave runners. The news of his death had spread quickly all over the colony. The thriving community of freed slaves who now made a life for themselves in Freetown as apprentices, traders, servants, shop assistants and craftsmen sang church hymns alongside the European settlers in his honour. Even the heathen amongst them all agreed that it was a good omen and a tribute to his departed soul that more men, women and children found freedom on the day that he was to be laid to rest. The native hunters shot their dane guns into the surrounding hills in his honour, and the Governor instructed that the Union Jack be flown at half-mast at the colonial office.

Mrs Davey had been devastated. They had had no children. She had been watched over by the few missionary wives who were out done by the bevy of protective African women who along with their husbands and infants were the ardent congregants she and her husband had raised over the years.

The Reverend had asked to be buried under an old cotton tree he had spent several years reading his bible and teaching the early converts bible verses and hymns. It was Samuel Crowther who had overseen the task of lowering him into the ground. He had wept as he barked instructions to the pall bearers. Graham had watched him from afar. Both had exchanged heavy glances that spoke volumes in the sorrowful silence that had enveloped them all within the mission.

That had been seven years ago, and a lot had changed since then. The mission had grown into what was a much larger compound now, with newly constructed buildings that served as chapels and class rooms for the mission's various educational endeavours. The several trees he and others had planted under the watchful eyes of the Reverend Davey were now well grown and offered generous shade to the several children who played around the compound. The mission still pursued its ambitions of bringing civilisation to the people through the word of God and the plough but it seemed to Graham that the fervour with which the earlier missionaries had committed to the cause of evangelism had all but slowed. Particularly after the exit of the Reverend and Mrs Davey.

Mrs Davey had returned to Britain soon after her husband's passing, convinced by the other Europeans despite her reluctance, that a few months of furlough spent in the English countryside would do her a lot of good. She had been escorted to the harbour by a large entourage which included her two favourites; Graham and Samuel Crowther. She had made good conversation along the way, and was even delighted to see that the Lieutenant General had come by the pier to see her off as well. As he stood there besides the Reverend Davy's grave, Graham sadly recalled how she had finally broken down, slipped on to the ground and wept. It had happened just as she was climbing onto the ship's gangway. It had taken the Lieutenant General's steady arms and gentle admonition to calm her down. They had all waved to her as she finally made it on board where she had turned to face them all. She had waved back at them but it was to Samuel Crowther that she had offered her parting words.

"Be of good cheer now, Samuel." She had said. "You have a great commission ahead of you someday." Then she had turned and walked quietly in to the ship's cabin and had never returned.

CHAPTER 14

Graham was ushered into the Colonial Governor's office, by his principal secretary. The Honourable John Jeremie had only recently arrived to take up the posting of Governor of Sierra Leone. It had now become a most unattractive colonial appointment. Sniffed at as a death posting, by those who were offered, given the long list of past Governors who had died from the dreaded fever during service. The Honourable John Jeremie was a man with a remarkable story of his own already. He was a renowned and published jurist, a well-travelled administrator who was hated by the big plantation and slave owners across the colonies, for being a thorn in their flesh. His various legal battles against them had made him famous and a respected member of the abolitionist movement.

While Graham had not known so much about the man he was now here to see, he had been advised by his colleagues at the mission to try and make a good impression. By that they had meant to encourage him to tidy up his appearance and perhaps wear a collar. One of the mission ladies and Sunday School teacher who had once been curious about Graham's lack of a female companion had suggested he be a bit more amenable to trivial pursuits than he had a reputation for.

No one prepared him for the shock of finding his uncle the now Bishop Daniel Wilson seated in one of the Governor's visitors chairs in conversation with a few other gentlemen and sipping tea. Graham went white with a fear he had not felt in over thirteen years, and had to grab onto one of the door knobs to steady himself on.

"Hello Graham." His uncle said calmly. "How have yer been?"

He stammered a response that didn't say much and walked over to the gentlemen seated not sure if he wasn't seeing things.

The Governor rose from his seat and came over to him with a hand extended.

"What a pleasure to finally meet you, Mr Thomas." He was a slightly portly man with a rotund, almost cherubic face. He wore a pair of round rimless glasses.

Graham shook his hand, still looking at his uncle who hadn't bothered to get up. "I am good, sir." He answered then stepped away to one of the seats offered by the Governor's Principal Secretary.

There were four other men seated apart from his uncle, only one of whom he knew.

"Shall we get straight to it then?" The Governor smiled, peering at his timepiece.

The introductions were offered by one of the men he didn't know.

"Mr Thomas, may I introduce the governor who you have already met, your colleague Reverend Schon who you certainly know, Mr Francis Glover of the newly formed

African Botanical Society, your uncle, the Right Reverend Daniel Wilson and Bishop of Asmar Cathedral, Ceylon and a revered colleague. My name, sir, is Dr Joseph Stockport and I am with the British and Foreign anti-slavery society."

"How do you do, sirs?" Graham said with a curt nod.

"You may be aware that in June of this year, the anti-slavery movement held what is perhaps the most seminal gathering of abolitionists under the chairmanship of Prince Albert to discuss and agree a plan that puts a final eradication to the dreadful trade of slaves, particularly by Africans themselves."

Graham nodded, looking towards his uncle.

"Both the governor and your uncle attended the Africa conference and if I may say, came away with very important commissions. One of the agreed actions is the honourable Mr Fowell Buxton's rather audacious plan of sending an expedition of experts up the Niger River to establish treaties for the abolition of the trade in slaves and the introduction of Christianity and commerce with the kingdoms in the interior of central West Africa."

Graham nodded. The entire colony had held its breath in anticipation of the outcome of the now famous Exeter House conference. It had been the largest gathering of abolitionists from all over the world and it had been generously reported by the British papers, late copies of which reached Freetown through the British merchant ships that now visited the colony regularly. It was remarkable that even the attempted assassination of her majesty the Queen, a few months earlier had not been sufficient to warrant it's being postponed.

Mr Stockport continued. "A key aspect of this expedition must be a detailed cataloguing of the botanical specimen to be found along the routes. In addition to our plans to establish a model farm at a suitable spot to be found in the hinterland for the purpose of teaching the African how to cultivate industrial crops." Mr Stockport flicked an imaginary spec of dust off his flannel trousers and readjusted in his chair.

"Mr Thomas, we would like you to consider joining the expedition, given what we are told is your experience and vast skills in this area."

Graham was silent for about a minute. "I am not really trained as a botanist. It is a past time for me at best."

The Governor looked at him and smiled. "My understanding Mr Thomas is that you have more than a passing skill in this area. You see, your uncle and I were acquainted during my time in Ceylon and as you will imagine got to discuss quite a bit. Your colleagues here also seem to hold you in high esteem for this remarkable skill of yours and you do also have the reputation of being an explorer of sorts."

The Reverend Schon coughed slightly. A cue Mr Stockport took up directly. "If it is any consolation, the society will be engaging the services of a much-respected German botanist, though I am not a liberty to say who he is just yet, but he will be requiring of someone of your experience of the African bush and tribal manners to assist his team. It offers you a great opportunity to learn under a renown botanist."

"Indeed." The Governor grunted, still peeking at his time piece. "The Church Mission Society has with the blessing of Lord Russell the Secretary of the Colonies, earlier selected two other colleagues of yours to be engaged in this expedition, Reverend Schon here for his expertise in the Hausa, and the African, Mr Crowther who I understand is a diligent catechist and gifted translator of the native southern languages."

Graham glanced at the Reverend Schon who smiled at him warmly. He said nothing. Then he heard his uncle sigh.

"Yer've grown into a remarkable servant of both god and country, Graham," his uncle finally said allowing his full Yorkshire accent to come through. "Not the uncertain lad I met in Islington several years ago. Yer ma would have been proud."

A respectful silence wafted gently above the brows of the men present and enveloped the room where they all sat and watched him with a quite admiration. Graham got out of the chair and quickly walked to the large Bay windows that over looked the beautiful natural harbour. He counted the two naval chasers owned by the Royal Naval Task Force, four captured slave schooners, several smaller trading vessels and flimsy dugout canoes with which the native fishermen ventured out remarkable distances into the sea. They returned most times in the early hours before dawn with prolific catches of assorted marine life. He knew that the others could see them too, but hoped that they hadn't caught the tears that had dropped just before he wiped them off.

≈

D ear Mr Thomas,

We are honoured to write you and to thank you for accepting to join the forthcoming Niger expedition into the heart of West Africa. In accepting to join us, you follow in the great tradition of Britain's greatest explorers. Courageous men like Hugh Clapperton, Mungo Park and Richard Lander who by volunteering their gifts, including the ultimate sacrifice, have helped push not only the frontiers of empire but also civilisation and Christianity.

Your reputation as a resourceful and resolute man familiar with the character, customs and fauna of Africa will be of immense value to this endeavour. Our colleague, Mr Francis Glover who was present with you at the meeting with the Governor spoke highly of you upon his return to London. *As we prepare for this grand commission, it is our sincere hope that you can meet with us very soon so as to be introduced to Dr Vogel who has been appointed by the society as Chief Botanist for the expedition. It will serve both of you well to acquaint yourselves with each other and compare notes on matters of your joint botanical pursuits.*

Yours sincerely

Members

The London Botanical Society

(January 7th, 1841)

~

G raham had wondered about his uncle all these years. Though he had never written him nor received a letter from him, he had always been at the back of his mind. A hovering moral compass, he used to weigh his own actions. Odd pieces of news did filter through occasionally, particularly when Reverend Davey had still been alive. He had not been aware of his transfer to Ceylon nor his consecration as a Bishop of the church. Their time together at Freetown before the Bishop's return to Asia through the Cape of Good Hope had been stiff and uncomfortable for both of them. He had stayed at the Mission guest quarters at Bathurst choosing to visit the mission schools and riding along with the new Governor to inspect colonial government projects. On the few evenings that Graham was invited to dine with them at the Governor's residence, the conversations between them always tapered off rather quickly. It was however compensated by the lively debates the other invited guests engaged in on a wide range of subjects ranging from the dawn of the Victorian era and its more progressive stance on the eradication of slavery, to matters of state craft in the administration of colonies. Sir Jeremie had seemed to favour more autonomy for the colonies, to the extent that they followed the broad framework of the laws as set down by Westminster. It was a position to which the missionaries seemed aligned. In their own scheme of things, it had become evident that the native agency should be the future of the missions, and the time had come to stop merely playing lip service to the training and development of African clergy within the church. It was what made the coming expedition so important for the broad coalition. The Telegraph of London had called it a Holy Crusade by the friends of Africa and the Negro. Her Majesty's government had committed to the building of three brand new steam ships which would be fitted with modern respiration systems to protect the explorers, from the ravages of the foul air that had become the cause of death of so many Europeans in Africa. This was a grand mission and all the best servants of the realm were needed to make a success of it.

It was on the evening before the day of his departure that the Reverend Daniel Wilson had asked Graham to escort him on a leisurely stroll around the streets of Freetown. The two of them set off towards Regents town with its well-appointed streets and stone houses with shinny corrugated tin roofing sheets that were now fast replacing the earlier wooden cabins built on stilts. Though the weather was balmy, the breeze that rolled down from the nearby surrounding hills helped to provide some required coolness. They walked in silence for a few minutes, each man weighing his thoughts and crafting an appropriate opening gambit. There were several people going about their business, but mostly Africans speaking loudly to each other in creole and other African languages. Several of them would approach them and ask, "Good evening masta. Hope no palava?"

"What on earth do they mean by that?" the Reverend asked bewildered. Graham smiled.

"Palava means problem. So, it's really like asking if you've had a good day."

"Ah! Ey up!" The Reverend laughed warmly finding the Yorkshire equivalent and tapping the tip of his top hat with his walking stick.

Graham grunted politely, kicked away a little boulder and then fell back into step with his uncle.

"Empire!" the Reverend sighed reverting to his more formal tone before shooting his nephew a critical glance, "It remains one, if not the greatest of our accomplishments."

Graham looked back at him but said nothing. The Reverend carried on unperturbed by his apparent discomfort. "A chain of near self-governing colonies where three estates of the realm act in unison to pacify savagery and yet spread British civilisation, salvation and industry to the farthest reaches of the world."

The Reverend stopped abruptly and turned to face Graham.

"It's a long way from the rolling hills of Yorkshire wouldn't yer say Graham?" he asked.

Graham swallowed and looked straight at his uncle. "Yes sir." He replied. He wondered if he was being mucked about with.

"And yet we remain under British dominion. It is a remarkable concept when one has had the privilege of actually experiencing the vastness of that which we lay claim to."

Graham felt obliged to nod in agreement. He had not been beyond the bordering hinterland of Freetown but Freetown had become a melting pot made up of not just the re-captive slaves, but also empire men and seafarers who told stories of the distant lands they had also been too.

"I have served the church in helping to save men's souls both in Britain and now also in Asia, where the good news of Jesus Christ competes against beliefs that have been entrenched for thousands of years. Yet we win them over to our way of life and the blessed sacrament of Christ. Do yer know why Graham?"

He understood that the question was intended to be a rhetorical one so he shook his head respectfully. His uncle had presented a totally new side to himself that he had not previously been allowed to experience and he was tempted to wonder if the credit perhaps was to be given to the generous glass of Sherry that he had been earlier offered during dinner.

"Well, Graham, I have come to realise that we have grown empire not because of ideology nor philosophy nor faith but because of the talent of Great Britannia, found in her sons and daughters. People like yer who are brave enough to leave the dales of Yorkshire behind and do yer duty wherever it might take yer." The Reverend Wilson stopped once again. This time he took off his top hat and dabbed at the thin patina of sweat that had formed on his forehead and brows before looking at Graham.

"I know son that when yer ma died, yer were not able to be at her funeral." His uncle said. Graham stiffened.

"I know what it would have meant for yer to have been there."

Graham tried to say something, but what came out was an inconsequential grunt that got stuck half way up his throat. The Reverend tapped him gently with his walking stick.

"Yer see, Graham my boy, the expedition up that river will be one of the most important ever to be undertaken in furtherance of the empire and perhaps will make every man on board those steamers famous. But yer must never lose sight of an important point."

"What do you mean, sir?" Graham asked intrigued.

The Reverend smiled. "I meant every word of what I said at the meeting with Sir Jeremie. Yer a proper champion, lad. Likes yer pa never could have been."

"Thank you sir."

"But I have to say, yer do behave like him a times. Stubborn Viking blood ever since yer were a wee barn. Distant like me too, and too quick to give up on love." There was a hint of a sly twinkle in the Reverend's eyes.

"Before she died, yer ma told me everything. About the young lass who stole your heart and why you seem to have given up on England. She made me promise that I would bring you back when it was time. You were her only child and she died lonely. In the memory of yer ma, you must return to England when this task is done and settle down to raise a family that will oblige her the wee *cletches* she never carried in her arms." The Reverend stuck his hand into his pocket and pulled out a chain to which was attached an ornate silver locket.

"Yer ma, she wanted yer to have this." He said handing it over to Graham who stood transfixed to the spot, staring at the content in the locket, oblivious to the native passers-by.

"Good evening, masta." One of them greeted grinning and waving the palm of both hands. "Hope no palaver?"

CHAPTER 15

THE BIGHT OF BENIN, 1841.

To the Chiefs, and People of Africa.

Listen to what we have to say. The Queen of England is a great Sovereign, and has sent us to offer you her friendship, and to talk with you as friends and brothers about the way to become wise and rich and powerful.

You know that the great God made all nations of the earth of one blood. White people are Christians, and worship this great God. They can do many things which black people cannot do, and they have almost everything that black people want; clothes, ornaments, tools, and useful articles of every kind. Some of these things we have brought with us to the Great Water, or Kawara, to show you what we mean, and anything else you desire can be sent you another time.

But for such things as these you must give us something of yours in exchange. You have been used to sell slaves for some of these things. But it is contrary to the laws of God and of white men to buy them of you, though some white men have been wicked enough to do so. Now you live in a country where everything grows very quickly out of the

164

ground, and these are the things which we want. They will also bring you much more profit than slaves.

You must dig the ground, and raise cotton trees, indigo, coffee, sugar, rice, and many other things of the same kind; and while these are growing, you can collect elephants' teeth, gold dust, gums, wax, and things of that sort, almost without any trouble.

Now, if you will always have plenty of these things ready for our people when they come, you shall have plenty of our goods in exchange. Perhaps you will say we do not know how to make these things grow. But the Queen of our country has sent good men to teach you how, and also how to build houses, and to make clothes, and to read books, and to talk about the great God, who made all things. Only you must be very kind and attentive to them, and not suffer anybody to hurt them.

You may say again, our country is so disturbed by war, that if we dig and sow we are not sure of gathering our crops. But is not this the consequence of catching and selling each other for slaves? If you wish to be rich, you must be peaceful, therefore, you must leave off this wicked practice. And if several of the chiefs would agree together to do so, their people would be much safer and more industrious and happier.

Perhaps some chief may say again, but what shall I gain by giving up the trade of catching and selling men? First, you will gain much by putting an end to war, for by this means your people will live quietly, and become industrious, and thus you will be able to get large tribute, like the kings and queens of Europe. Secondly, you will gain also in this way. Suppose you sell a man for five pounds, this sum you get for him only once, but if you make him free as our people are in England, and pay him good wages, he will work very hard, and will collect for you so much gum, or so many elephants' teeth, or help you to grow so much cotton and other things, that after paying him his just wages, you will get as much every year by his labour as you would have got only once by selling him and sending him away.

Now then, you must judge for yourselves. Our Queen offers you her friendship, and an innocent trade which shall make you rich and powerful and happy; but it is only on one condition, and that is, that

165

you will promise solemnly to give up the practice of catching and
selling slaves, even if wicked white people should ask you to sell them,
and that you will punish, without cruelty, anyone who tries to do so.
We also hope you will give up the sacrifice of your fellow-creatures
because it is displeasing to God.

Consider well the offer we now make you, and remember that if you
accept it you will please the great God, you will have our powerful
Queen for you friend, all good white people will love you, and will
endeavour to help you, and you will soon become wiser, richer, and
happier than you ever were before.

The Commissioners
In the name of her majesty
Queen Victoria
The Queen of England
and her overseas Dominions
1841.

Graham looked on and smiled to himself as the Commissioners' letter to the kings and the peoples of the African heartland was read out aloud. He wondered how on earth any one would be able to explain these grand ideas to the natives? Given what he had seen in the Susu country, the African had very simple requirements of the European and he wasn't sure being told how to grow cotton was one of them. He remembered the case of the fugitive murderer, and how the Susu chiefs had so efficiently dispensed of justice without so much as referring the matter to the colonial officers. Though it still troubled him, he had let the matter lie, and advised the chaps from the Colonial office in Freetown to do the same.

He knew his place here, however. This was not Susu country where he could lord it over the young administrative types. The Commissioners who led this expedition where seasoned empire frontiers men. He was merely one of the chaps here. Conscripted to do what he was told, and he would be damned if he did not ensure he made a success of it. Graham tore his eyes away and looked on over the horizon at the other iron steamers, as they navigated their way through the narrow tributaries, up the nun river and on their way into the brackish waters of the great Niger River. There were three ships: the Soudan which was the smallest of the three, the Wilberforce which was the flagship, and the vessel he travelled in, and the Albert, named in honour of the Queen's consort and honorary President of the society that had fought to promote the cause of the expedition. The bay provided calmer waters than they had experienced in the week that it had taken them to arrive from the British Colony of Accra. One of the rudders on the Albert had been slightly damaged by the silt, which had forced the expedition to spend the last five days anchored to one spot as the engineers worked to remedy the problem. Now well on their way into the heart of the Niger proper, the excitement within the crew was palpable.

They had left Freetown on the morning of 2nd of July, making several stops along the way in an effort to acclimatise to the humid weather and load enough supplies to last the duration of the expedition. The three captains, each in charge of an individual steamer, had also all agreed that it would be better to go up the river during the height of the rainy season, when the river water levels would be higher and better navigation would thus be guaranteed.

Graham listened on as the man read the letter out loud above the steady chug of the wood fired steam engines. He was First Officer Kenneth Dolton, a boisterous seaman from Cornwall. He read it in his grammar schoolboy accent, to the admiration of all on board the Wilberforce. A few of his fellow naval ratings bellowed out an emotional 'God save the

Queen!' A few others just exchanged thoughtful glances. Graham's interest was however directed at the native interpreters who stood a few paces behind the white Europeans, wondering about the emotions their masters displayed. He knew from his several years of communicating with the local natives, that a lot was always lost in the ineffectual translations of those the mission had entrusted with the work of translating. They were the ones who would be entrusted with the responsibility of interpreting such simple yet powerful words into the local native languages of the various tribal clans that dotted both banks of the Niger River. In the end it was the bewildered native translators who would have the success of the mission in their hands.

They were the resettled freed slaves from Freetown who, over the years, had risen to become young native catechists, assistant school tutors and mission helpers. They spoke several of the languages to be encountered on the expedition: *Ibo, Oyo* and *Aku* dialects of the *Nago*, Nufi, *Ibio, Efik* and *Hausa*. They had been taught to read and write in English at the mission schools, but Graham knew their vocabulary was largely limited to words found in scripture and fewer other words of general conversation. The exceptional one amongst them was his old friend from Islington; Mr Crowther, a close working associate of Mr Schon, who on account of his remarkable intellect and gift for language and other personal qualities, had risen to become a well-considered authority in both teaching and the translation of the Yoruba dialects.

As evening fell, they found themselves forging steadily up the Nun River, bordered on both sides by strange beautiful mangrove trees propped above the muddy banks by eerie looking stilts. The intrepid calls of river creatures were echoed by the distant howls of larger mammals. There was not a soul in sight nor flames from afar which might have suggested a community was nearby in the thick brushes further on. The moon was barely visible, and the inky dark skies were at once haunting and beautiful. Later when the engines had been turned off, and the steamer was allowed to anchor in the middle of the river, Graham went to sleep in the crew cabins beneath the deck, his hands clutched around the content of his mother's locket. For the first time since she had died five years earlier, Graham dreamt of his mother.

A bolt of lightning rippled through the pouring rain. The echo from the ensuing thunder clap reverberated across the dark skies. It shook the sides of the steamer, causing the tin cans already filled with the dirty rain water to spill onto the charts that lay on the massive wooden table in the corner of the captain's deck. Several men stood there huddled over them. They held grim stares as they steeled themselves over the tropical storm. They were now two weeks into their journey along the Niger River and the joint commissioners had an air of concern about them. Unsure of what actually lay ahead of them, the younger officers and ratings frequently gathered around each other, mostly to second guess their superiors.

Today they stood and listened to that which was being said in front of them. All of them eager to dim out the crackle that came with the tropical storm. Yet nature's vengefulness seemed tame compared to the roar that emanated from the man who stood before them angrily waving a sextant. He was the ship's cartographer and he stood there, in a fit of rage, panting. He spat instructions to the porters to save the maps. A few had been blown to the floor by the turbulence. They were precious artefacts. Maps, secured at great expense from the London geographical society. The porters scurried to retrieve and spread them back on top the wooden table, using whatever weighty object they could find to hold them down. The markings on the parchments were already greying and the dog-eared edges frayed from months of poring and shuffling. The odd tobacco stain showed in a few spots and along others, murky markings of ill brewed chicory. You could see the points where a lead tip had cut in deeper than had been intended, as a straight line had been etched along portions representing the barely known turns and contours of the Niger River and her banks. He, along with a few trusted others, had plotted their intended journey in the months of painstaking preparation that had led to this expedition. So, they watched him in silence borne out of the respect they had for him. It was his responsibility after all to guide them towards the confluence of the *Nufi* savages deep into the continent's hinterland. Here they hoped to establish themselves a fort and set about the construction of an experimental cotton farm for the training of the tribal Africans on the science of agriculture and perhaps someday even manufacturing. The Lander brothers who had attempted an expedition by foot several years earlier had written glowingly of the richness and fertility of the hinterlands. Graham recalled that he had once read about how they described massive Baobab trees with trunks as massive as a hundred grown men clustered together in a scrum.

Graham watched as the cartographer used a massive palm to wipe off a pool of water from a set of highlighted markings. They suggested a settlement of sorts. This point was supposed to be where slaves taken by the Portuguese a few years earlier, had reported that a great African chief and war lord lay sway over the land of the *obi*. He was said to control the trade routes into the hinterlands and traded in palm kernels and slaves in exchange for liquor and cowries. The Portuguese had called him *Jo boy* and he was dreaded for his thirst for human sacrifice and the blood of white men. It had been reported in a pamphlet written by a Portuguese soldier in 1789 that the Obi had a large armada of war Canoes which travelled fast across the water and from within which they threw poison tipped spears at strangers visiting their waters. Travel through the *Obi*, was encumbered with the large sand banks that dotted the river water ways as one approached their domain, and it was this great deposit of muddy silt that made the approach a treacherous one.

It had been agreed that the only way to pass through this portion of the journey was to have a party of five row towards the bank in a dingy adequately armed with rifles and gunpowder for protection and a generous tribute of spirits, fine cloth and a bowler hat for the adequate appeasement of the famed war lord. It had been decided that Graham would lead the party given his expertise in securing treaties with African tribal chiefs from the hinterland. He was to be accompanied by one of the porters who spoke the *Ibo* dialect and had once casually referred to the chief as his father. It was a comment that had generated a lot of curiosity amongst the Europeans until Graham had explained that every African considered a tribal lord his patriarch. There would also be two armed naval officers and another missionary also from the Church Mission Society in London, who had insisted on coming along with a gift of a well bound bible for King Jo Boy.

The burly cartographer had finally been offered a piece of cloth with which he carefully dabbed the maps. He refused the help of those who offered to fold the sheets away, choosing instead to superintend over each one personally. Graham looked on bemused at the scene, wiping his own palms on the seats of his starched khakis and contemplating the task force ahead. It had been agreed that the advance party would set out in a day or two after the dreadful storm had abated and a greater sense of reason he hoped had finally come upon them all.

~

There was a large feather, possibly that of an eagle, perched prominently on the small head of the tribal chief. The tip of the feather had been dipped in a reddish dye, the same colour of anthills he had seen many times in the thick bushes around the *Susu* country back in Serra Leone. The man who they famously knew as Jo boy was remarkably small in stature for all the legendary tales that had gone before him. Five other muscular men with elaborate chalk markings on their faces and torsos stood menacingly surrounding him with daggers and long spears. Another much more elderly character with raffia strips tied around his biceps stood to the side of the chief holding a brass pole shaped in the form of a trident. It made an eerie clatter each time he struck the pole to the ground which he did ever so often. His eyes were bloodshot, while his teeth had rotted off in several places.

Graham walked towards him hands extended and closely followed by the interpreter who seemed disdainful of the tribal party that had come to way lay them by the banks of the river. It was midday by the look of the narrow shadows cast, and the searing humid heat was made even worse by the constant buzz of insects. Jo boy raised both hands as though to suggest that the extended hands were an unwelcome gesture.

"Tell him that we come in peace and bearing the good wishes of the Queen of England."

Graham listened as the translator bellowed out a series of brash words, and watched closely to observe what reactions the tribal party gave in response. There were no nods of acquiescence or grunts of approval as he had been used to with the tribal elders within the *Susu* country. Jo boy and his entourage looked on studying them calmly and not uttering a word amongst themselves. After what seemed an eternity, he said something to the interpreter, while staring at Graham.

"My father say make I ask you who you be and where you come from?"

Graham gave a hearty grunt of approval and nodded back vigorously at Jo boy's party.

"Tell him that we are from the land of the great white queen over the great sea, and that we have been sent by her to deliver an important message of peace and friendship to all the African people."

The interpreter bellowed back at Jo boy and seemed to join the chief's party in a loud snigger they all fell into upon receiving Jo Boy's dead pan response.

"What did he say?" Graham asked, obviously curious.

The interpreter coughed nervously and looked at Graham sheepishly. "My father says I should ask what type man you be to do messenger work for woman?"

The silence was more awkward this time around.

"Tell him, tell him an adventurous man, who comes in peace." Graham finally suggested.

"My father ask if you be warrior."

Graham shook his head "Tell him no."

He held his fellow CMS missionary's hand and gently waved the bound bible they had brought along above his head. "Tell him I am a servant of God."

The interpreter looked at Graham strangely and smiled, "Masta Grayam." He began rather demurely, as he turned to give him his full attention. "I no fit tell my father like that..."

"And why not?" Graham shot back,

"Masta e no good to tell my father you be like that." The man whispered. He was now evidently uncomfortable and shifting on his feet.

"Explain yourself man?"

"I go tell my father you be great medicine man of a powerful God."

As it sank in, Graham smiled to himself and looked at his interpreter with a new-found respect. Graham had known him as one of the several adult helpers who had been enrolled into the literacy classes back at Fourah Bay. Several like him were returned slaves, freed by the British naval anti-slavery expedition. They were offered a new life in Freetown. Grateful for what the Europeans had done for them, they happily converted to the Christian faith and a few like him did so with an uncommon degree of fervour. They became dutiful helpers and men who carried out the clearing, building and whatever odd jobs that needed to be done within the mission. In return for their loyalty and diligence, the mission fed them, occasionally clothed them and provided quarters which had grown to become a bastion of sorts for the growing creole community within Freetown. Graham had observed over the course of a few years, how different from the aboriginal Africans, they had become. They were the more fanciful; with their new-found religion, basic literacy, and new European mannerisms. They were now seen as the higher classes amongst their African kinsmen. They took wives amongst themselves only and a few now served as clerks to European merchants or house boys to colonial officers. Almost all of them diligently taking the ways of their masters even if they didn't quite understand it.

He had taken Francis Hamilton Bey as his name at his baptism. A suitable name that had been suggested after the commander of the naval task force schooner who himself had Ottoman roots, and had filled and authorised his release papers to the anti-slavery tribunal at Freetown. It had been an easy choice given that it was the only form of documentation that he had ever had about him.

"Yes, Mr Bey." Graham laughed, looking into the astonished eyes of his missionary colleague who now reluctantly handed the bound bible to him with a painful grimace.

"Give him this beautiful bible," Graham said handing the bound bible over to the interpreter, "and let him know that the Reverend here and I are great medicine men of a powerful God indeed."

Graham sought to share what he thought to be a joke with his obviously bewildered fellow missionary, the Reverend Penrose Streatham. As he turned to wink at him, he found the man bent over clutching at his stomach in agony. He was sweating and his face had turned purple as he retched uncontrollably. Graham watched in horror as the missionary lurched forward in pain and vomited all over Jo Boy's warriors.

CHAPTER 16

THE NIGER RIVER, 1841.

"I am crucified with Christ: nevertheless, I live; yet not I, but Christ liveth in me: and the life which I now live in the flesh I live by the faith of the son of God, who loved me and gave himself for me."

The chaplain solemnly recited the verse from the scripture to the hearing of the men present. After the *amens* were uttered in response to another sorrowful prayer of exultation, the African porters amongst them began pouring sand over the make shift casket of Reverend Penrose Streatham. It was late evening and the sun no longer had the fierce bite. They had become accustomed to fleeing it and conducting their business in the cool of the evening. Even the discordant notes of irritation of the sand flies and other fleas had abated. It was as if they too sensed the enormity of the tragedy that had befallen the expedition. The Reverend had lasted only four days before he eventually gave up his painful fight for life. They had been four days filled with delirious muttering and even louder screams of agony. The headaches and shivers that mercilessly racked through his weak body took their toll, and he lost fluid through every possible orifice. When he lost consciousness, his body went cold and limp. His skin turned a strange blue hue. Everyone except the crew physician was convinced that he had passed. There was still a pale and minute stream of mist from his nostrils when the mirror was placed close to them, however. The religious amongst them prayed fervently that his life might be spared, while the agnostic and more experienced adventurers looked on with a sad yet knowing gaze. It was the dreaded curse. The tropical fever, which every European who ventured this far from home knew all too well about. It was the horrible death that hung like a gleaming sabre over their necks and despite the array of tinctures and exotic brews that they swapped in an effort to give themselves the confidence they knew they needed to push ahead, each man lived in grave dread of the thought of being the one who it came down upon.

They buried the good Reverend with the solemnity that was deserving of such an exit and they once again kept their upper lips stiff and gave each other the curt nod of solidarity that they knew bound them together; One of a common heritage and shared threat of painful death that only men of their race who had the courage to venture this far could ever understand.

It was heartening that Jo Boy had offered them a place to bury the Reverend, even if it was by the look of it, an area where wild animals lurked. He also provided a retinue of warriors who followed them at a distance. The warriors trekked in silence through the thicket by the banks of the river, at once wary, intrigued and disdainful of their strange language and even stranger ways. When they stopped to choose the site where the grave was to be dug, they profusely refused to proceed or to help with the dig. The old witch doctor who had also come along slowing the trek considerably on account of his frailness spat directives to them regularly and chanted incessantly. Hamilton had told Graham that the man who they called a Dibia had questioned the power of their God. Later he had wondered aloud if the dead man perhaps had been afflicted by Ahmadiora, their own god in a pre-emptive strike of sorts.

"It is white worms that destroy the healthy corn cob after all." Graham had learnt the old peeping tom had suggested to Jo Boy.

It had taken the generous gifts they had brought along to warm their way into Jo Boy's acceptance to sign a *'Treaty of friendship and industry.'* But when it came, it was cautiously given and the gifts accepted with limited reciprocity on his part. He refused to renounce the sale of slaves and also refused to accept the gift of the 'cursed book' which his medicine man had warned could have caused the white man to vomit so violently. The liquor he accepted. He had sent twelve tubers of yams and six kola nuts to them at the river bank as a mark of modest welcome, and to indicate that he was not in their debt. Even the parcel of land that they had been granted to bury the good Reverend was revealed by Hamilton to be 'bad land'. The warriors who came along stopped by its fringes and would go no further. As the burial cortege found their way to an appropriate spot overlooking the river, they passed the rotten carcasses of dogs and other wild animals, a rash of broken gourds and other objects of sacrifice and absolution, littered all over the grounds.

It was Graham who supervised the making of the simple cross that would mark the Reverend's grave on the instruction of the expedition's Captain Trotter. It was made from the branches of a sturdy fruit tree found nearby. With its sap still dripping, they bound it together into a cross with the aid of twine they had come along with and reinforced it with two nails deftly hammered into the splinter. There were no rocks to be found which might have served as a tomb stone, so they piled a little of the earthy red laterite soil into a heap and stuck the cross into the soil as far as it could. It was all that they could do. One of the senior officers made a point of attempting to mark the spot on the map they had come along with and were continuously updating. The spot was to be entered into the expedition's log and perhaps to offer the late Reverend's widow a bit of closure upon their return to England. But Graham knew better. All it would take was one tropical rainstorm to wash away everything that they had done.

～

On the evening of the Sixteenth, September, 1841, the expedition arrived the confluence of the great Niger River. It had been twenty-five days since they navigated up the Nun River, and two weeks since they had buried the good Reverend along the sandy banks at Onitsha. Scattered ahead of them could be seen several Lokoja hamlets and villages nestled beneath the crest of the surrounding mountains. They overlooked the muddy brown waters of the Niger River where it met the calmer and cleaner River *Chadda*. There was a certain whiff of grudging admiration amongst the commissioners as they pored over the old maps devised by Mr Mungo Park, the one later updated by Mr Hugh Clapperton and the Lander brothers. They found the mountains and adjoining flat lands exactly where they had suggested the confluence would be. Yet, there was also a sense of ensuing despair as the dreaded river sickness had finally begun to ravage the crew within the three traveling steamers.

Graham looked over board to study the thin blades of brown reeds bunched together in bushy thickets by the muddy bank to the northern side of their steamer. He spotted a few kingfishers and egrets. They were similar to those he had seen in the Susu country. They looked like statues, perched on top of several of the reeds as they looked on at the coming dusk without a sound nor a care in the world. Graham had begun to care and the thought that he could die on this God forsaken river had begun to cross his mind. It was a journey that had now begun to manifest itself as a grave cost and a bush adventure more terrible than he and several of the commissioners could have ever envisaged. Death had come calling, and it had begun to take the men in droves and with such brutal ferocity that even the hardest and most gallant amongst them had been reduced to a pitiful state of utter anguish and fear. What had started off as a glorious expedition and royal commission to advance the glory of empire, was now reduced to an undertaking as they buried one mate after another. The once rambunctious laughter of haughty crusaders was reduced to the soft whimper of a heart wrenching dirge and grown men could be heard weeping softly in the evening as the cold dry harmattan wind whipped their exposed torsos. Twenty men now lay on the deck writhing in agony as the sickness ravaged their bodies. The medical team were barely well themselves, and despite their attempt at diligence, it was obvious that they had been reduced to a forlorn state. Almost all of the Europeans now suffered from incessant bouts of dysentery. Of the one hundred and twenty who had commenced the arduous journey up through the Nun River, only half now seemed capable of continuing the expedition further up the Niger River. They seemed to have come to terms with their frail constitution, having found out that the African Kroomen, and even the coloureds, remained unaffected by the foul air. Dr Vogel, the botanist, had suggested it might have to do with their diet of sturdy gruel or perhaps the dark nature of their skin which made them unattractive to the bite of the vermin about. It was difficult for some of the men who had come on the expedition straight out of Europe to comprehend that the African constitution had become well suited to the harshness of the African interior. But Graham had always known this from his travels throughout the bushy hinterlands of the Susu or Shebroo people. For all their lack of civilisation and science, the tribal chiefs and elders he had spent time with in the inner hamlets and villages had their superstitions, juju magic and native folklores. Graham had come to understand that the African had a rich body of plant knowledge by which they lived their lives fastidiously. In many ways it was not unlike how he had grown up in Yorkshire with roots and toadies that had served he and his family well through the seasons.

An incident on the deck brought his attention back to the steamer. He noticed a few of the commissioners had gathered and called out requesting that captain Allen join them for a brief word. Captain Allen was the only member of this party who had transversed the river some years earlier, in what was a disastrous expedition that had taken the lives of nearly every man who had been on the cursed venture earlier in 1838. It was therefore understood that the commissioners would view his opinion as valuable. After about an hour of debate, it was announced to the men on the three steamers, that the commissioners upon Captain Allen's' assurances of better fortunes had resolved to push ahead with the plans of establishing the industrial demonstration farm at a large parcel of land to be purchased from the native chieftains. Graham was informed that he would be joining the advance party that would visit the *Seriki* or king of the *Nufis* to commence the important task of negotiating the treaty of co-

181

operation and deed of purchase for the parcel of land on behalf of her majesty's government.

≈

Day had barely broken when a loud scream of sheer agony rang out throughout the steamer. It came from 'Krootown'. The part of the steamer where the Black African labourers were quartered, near the charcoal fed steam engines at the far side of the steamer. Paraffin lanterns were hurriedly lit, and Graham, who had barely woken from a bout of fitful sleep joined others and the two sentries attached to guard the section of the steamer as they hurried towards the crowd that had now gathered.

"Snake…snake…Big snake!" Some of the Africans cried out.

"Snake bite person master!"

They were all wailing in anguish by now. Several had their arms wrapped over their heads, their entire torsos shook in bewilderment.

When Graham and the sentries pushed through the crowd, they found Hamilton Bey thrashing on the deck floor where he lay in only a tunic. Foam was coming out from his mouth and his left leg was curled under his torso in a most grotesque and unnatural angle.

"What happened to him?" Graham asked.

"Snake bite him for leg masta." One of the Africans said. He was holding a thick wooden spatula limply in his hand and his mouth was curled in horror as he explained that he had met Hamilton writhing on the floor just a few minutes after he had heard the scream himself.

"Can you hear me boy?" One of the naval sentries asked.

"I doubt that he can under such a situation." Graham muttered tightly. "Perhaps he needs to be moved to a clear part of the deck and attended to by the ship medical officer."

Some of the men gathered around him were asked to pick him up and carry him towards a clearing next to where a few bushels of corn were stacked in jute bags.

"And the snake?" Graham asked the Krooman holding the spatula.

"E haf enter the wata again masta...di snake long like dis...and black!" he squealed gesticulating with his arms and the spatula. Several of the Kroomen gasped excitedly and spat.

"E go die masta. Na bad tin."

"We must see if we can get the venom out quickly." Graham uttered to the men around as he walked after those carrying Hamilton. He was limp by now and his eyes had rolled back into their sockets. Graham noticed Ajayi Crowder move closer as he silently studied the situation.

"We must cut quickly." He whispered.

Graham nodded. "I have a pen knife but we might need some spirit and a good flame."

"I know one of the men here who can help." Ajayi said. "He is from my old country and he is familiar with these kinds of things."

Graham had grabbed on to one of the paraffin lanterns and was now heating his pen knife with its flames. "Go get him quickly Mr Crowther."

Ajayi nodded and pressed through the crowd towards the quarters.

A few minutes later the African had been summoned. He was tall with a lean frame and bald from shaving. His name was Olu. He was also a freed slave who had been taken as a young man and sold off to a sugar plantation owner as far away as in the West Indies. His fortune changed the day he served a guest at his master's table. The man was an English merchant and abolitionist whose ailing wife had taken an interest in his gentle manners. At her insistence, her husband had bought him from the plantation owner and over the next two years he carried her around the house as she gradually lost the use of her legs from the debilitating disease she suffered from. In those years, she had taught him to read and write and recite words of scripture. When she finally died, he had been granted his freedom as she had wished. The English merchant had bought him passage to Freetown and a letter of introduction to a friend of his who had recently opened up a general merchandise trading house at Bathurst.

He had insisted on keeping his African name despite having been baptised by the church. Olu knelt over Hamilton where he lay on top of a wet rag on the deck. He put his mouth to the two incisions that had been made at the point of the snake bite and pulled hard through his pursed lips drawing blood which he promptly spat out into an enamel bowl by his side. He worked silently and methodically, pausing at intervals to study Hamilton's breathing. The men around watched him curiously. Day light had broken and the other steamers were in sight. Labourers could be seen offloading agricultural equipment from one of them.

"He will need herbs." Olu announced finally, turning to Graham and Ajayi who were kneeling beside him, also attending to the stricken man. "We must place it on the wound to draw out more of the poison. There is a special kind but I do not know if we can find it here."

"How will you know it?" Graham asked. He was spotting an unkempt beard and wrinkles had formed around his eyes, blood shot red from lack of sleep.

"We must ask the native people." Olu responded.

Graham nodded and looked overboard to gauge the distance to the river banks. The steamer was closer to the Western bank which showed more vegetation, yet it was to the northern river bank that the expedition sought to land. It was here in the flatter plains that it had been explained to the European contingent that the kingdoms of the Nufis, the Hausas and the dreaded Fulas lay. Barely four miles inland nearer the hills that they could see was a thriving trading town. There would be found an old ally of Captain William Allen from the previous expedition known to him as the king of Koton Karifi. It was the chief that the advance treaty party were to seek out and hopefully purchase the farm land from.

An elderly woman sat alone in the dugout canoe and cautiously paddled herself towards the side of the steamer. Graham stretched to see if she were perhaps hawking something for sale, and found that she was not. They had encountered several parties during the course of their journey along the river. The parties that ventured close had been made up mostly of young men, wearing nothing more than loin clothes and paddling furiously while they their ripped torsos gleamed in the strange afternoon sun and they grinned incessantly at the men aboard the steamer. They always shouted out loudly towards the crew in whatever it was their native languages were. Several wielded menacing looking cutlasses and spears, which they occasionally brandished to the crew as they looked on with astonishment at white men they had never seen before. Rarely had they encountered women during the journey. So, it came as a surprise as the woman all on her own, her flat breast bared for all to see, came even closer calling out to them in a raspy voice.

Hamilton had been left to fight off the effect of the venom in an unconscious sleep, wrapped in an old raffia matting the Africans had woven themselves from the reeds plucked along the banks of the river over the course of the journey. Olu sat on the floor of the deck keeping a watch over him and wiping the sickly sweet smelling sweat that formed so quickly on his forehead. Olu had announced frankly that he had only been able to draw out so much of the snake venom. The man would be dead before the sun went down if they could not get him the mulch of certain bark of trees that hopefully could be found in the bushes around. Ajayi had suggested that it was best they set out as soon as they could to forage around the neighbouring villages. Perhaps if the stricken man was lucky, the villagers would be able to assist them to source what was needed.

Graham, having obtained the permission of the commissioners now sought to leave the steamer with Olu and Ajayi, so they might explore the nearby villages. They chose to take their search to the western bank of the river.

The woman called out again in her raspy voice. Unable to understand a word of what she was saying Graham waved her away with his hands. He noticed her chuckle with amusement. It did not seem to have the desired effect so Graham called out to the Africans who sat in small huddles about the deck. He asked if any one of them understood the woman's language. They all shook their heads and gaped at her.

"Masta she be fish woman." One of them offered. "No palava."

He grunted and walked towards the inner deck quarters hoping to rest his eyes for a while before they set out.

He had barely slept for an hour when he was woken up. Hamilton's condition had worsened. He was now foaming in the mouth and his limbs had begun to constrict in epileptic fits. He found Olu stoically shaking his head in a futile effort to fight off his sense of helplessness.

"Master Graham we must go now." The man announced calmly.

They lowered one of the small boats aboard the steamer onto the river and rowed towards the bank. Hamilton had been placed in the care of the ship's last healthy medical officer. A young internist who by now was beside himself with strain and the premonition of his own painful demise. It took them slightly under an hour to reach the bank and then find a suitable dis-embarkment point. Here the waters were deeper, faster and seemingly more treacherous. They rowed against a strong current which repeatedly threw them against dead tree trunks and odious floating debris. Once they saw a playful group of hippopotamuses that had converged by the distant bank. On another occasion they had to make a quick detour after they spotted two crocodiles lying lazily on top of a rock formation. The horde of circling vultures and egrets suggested that they had just finished tearing into a carcass of some unfortunate water buck.

They found a suitable spot to disembark by the edge of a flat field of wild millet and quickly waded through the cold water towards land. The three of them had travelled light, sharing only a rifle, a few daggers, a sickle and an empty jute bag amongst them. Olu was the strongest amongst them, and adept at clearing a path through the bush so, the task of navigating a tracked path through the bushy thicket fell naturally upon him. There was not a soul in sight and beyond the immediate sound of snapping twigs and the swish of trampled mud, they were greeted with utter quiet. They travelled quickly for what seemed an hour before finally coming to a stream. Carefully stacked under an Iroko tree was a heap of freshly cut firewood. The wood was still wet and sap seeped out from where the blade had chopped into the bark. Graham could hear muffled sounds in the distance and motioned for the others to investigate. Olu acted promptly, leaving the other two men as he pranced ahead and was soon covered by a motley of shrubs. He returned a moment later with an elderly man and two young boys. All three were barely clothed and holding what looked like hoes

"They are Tapa people." Olu announced with slight irritation. "Nufis, but the old man understands our language small." Olu said something to him in the old Oyo dialect of the Yoruba tribe as they were sometimes referred by the Africans back at Bathurst. Both Olu and Graham watched suspiciously as the old man replied in a guttural version of the language.

"He says that he comes from a village not far from here."

The old man kept an astonished gaze transfixed on Graham as he spoke. His two sons had begun to whimper with fear. They had not yet reached puberty but even at that age, their bodies had already begun to be outlined with the muscular frame that was chiselled out by a life of manual labour.

Olu and the old man exchange more stilted words. Graham observed as the conversation was punctuated by familiar amplified gestures of tribal strangers.

"The man says that we can get *Ogun Aransi* at the village. There is a man there who has strong medicine."

"What is that?" Graham asked.

"Medicine for snake bite." Ajayi explained lightly.

"How long will it take to get to his village? " Graham asked stealing a peek at the sun. The shadows around suggested that it was a few hours after mid-day.

"The man say the village is not far." Olu hesitated and looked knowingly at Ajayi, seeking reassurance before proceeding. "But he says they afraid of you. He says you are white spirit."

Graham laughed uncomfortably. It was a dry exasperated laugh, borne out of fatigue, frustration and a sense of foreboding. In his mind the expedition was over. Death now plagued his thoughts. Men were dying and his own health no longer seemed assured.

"Tell him that we need help to save an African man like himself."

Olu paused as though to contemplate the thought. He looked on at Ajayi yet again to help gather courage.

"Hamilton is a stone eater." He smiled mischievously. "He is not from the man's country."

"Stone eater?" Graham asked incredulously. "How can a man eat stone for God sakes, man?"

Ajayi laughed and poked at Olu.

"No Masta Graham, his people, they eat heavy food like-Like this and do not drink water." Olu held his fist in a thick bunch and gestured as though he was intent on ramming the entire fist down his throat.

Graham looked on slightly puzzled. His gaze wavered intermittently between Olu and Ajayi's thick forehead, as he searched for whatever clues their expressions might betray. He found none so chose to move on quickly.

"This is really no time for joking, my man." He muttered. "Tell the man that he has nothing to worry about. Tell him we have a few cowries to offer if that will help."

As Olu relayed the message, Graham felt he saw the man's eyes light up. The old man finally called out reassuringly to the two boys with him. Their whimpers eventually transformed into audible sniffs and then a forlorn silence fell upon them.

They reached the old man's homestead after a brisk ten-minute trek which saw them meander through a winding bush path through the forest. It was a small hamlet of about fifteen huts. The out perimeter was fortified by a wall made from a mixture of swish mud and thick cut branches. In the distance could be heard the sound from pestles that women pounded rhythmically into mortars filled with grains. It intertwined with the echo from the muffled laughter of drunken men, offering the colourful sparrows that darted in the sky just above them, something playful to dance to.

As they approached the major gateway into the village, they found a dozen horses tethered to a few posts made out of cut sturdy tree branches. Three men attended to the horses, feeding them millet stalk. They were naked except for dirty loin cloth that covered their lower regions. They were shaven bald and marked similarly with a deep diagonal gash that began at the upper tip of the side of the bridge of their nose and ran down their right cheek towards the jaw.

"Hausa!" The old man announced with alarm, "Balogun Ijeru's dogs!"

Graham saw the man attempt to bolt into the bushes with his sons in tow. Olu reached out and tackled him to the ground. It was then that Graham noticed that they had been surrounded by fierce looking men wearing amulets and clothing made from animal skins and brandishing spears and cudgels. The first blow that struck him cut a deep gash and splattered blood onto his feet. The force threw him into a thorny shrub and sent his rifle flying in the other direction. He grimaced with pain as he struggled to lift himself and crawl in the direction of the rifle. He barely saw the second blow land at the back of his head. He merely felt a bolt of excruciating pain that lasted for just a moment before it tipped him into an abyss of merciful nothingness.

PART THREE (1841-1847)

BALOGUN IJERU

CHAPTER 17

IJEPETU, THE OYO EMPIRE, THE RAINY SEASON, 1841.

~

I jepetu was usually subdued at a time like this, with no one keen to make trouble. Only arrogant lizards dared dart across open court yards eager to bask in the shadows cast by their own bellies. On days like this, those who went to the farm, hung their hoes on their shoulders and took refuge under the canopy of trees. Then, those who stayed back home, found other ways to preserve themselves from the merciless heat. The women and children would strip themselves and find the nearest river or stream to swim or bathe in. The elderly would use fans made of strips of raffia leaves to chase the sweat off their bodies and lay down hoping to escape the delirium that heat causes by sleeping. It was not so however this afternoon at Balogun Ijeru's compound.

Seven men entered the civic chamber of his large dwellings and proceeded to find seats for themselves from amongst the several stools that lay scattered about the large open space. There was a court jester who approached each one of them. He welcomed them jovially and glowingly recited each person's Oriki as they settled themselves down. He was an old man now. *'Oku igbe!'* they insulted him behind his back; shit carrier! He had spent so long in the services of the Balogun and his jokes were all so stale that even children in the market could recite them. He was now mostly just tolerated rather than revered and even though it was true that he alone could recite the praise verses of every prominent family in Ijepetu, he owed his standing more to the fear the people had for his master whose shit he carried, than his ability to deliver comic relief.

The men who came in were all ranking members of Ijepetu's Ogboni cult. The Ogboni were a revered earth cult made up of ranking citizens found within most kingdoms and towns within the Oyo Empire. They worshiped the earth deities and offered counsel to the ruling courts on civil, spiritual and criminal matters. They were particularly influential on matters that involved the spilling of blood and had to be consulted before the passage of the death penalty on any one found guilty of a grievous crime such as murder, witchcraft or adultery in the case of women. They represented the popular opinion of the town folk, which they shrouded in the mysticism of Ifa and delivered to the ears of a listening king through the authority of their leader, the Oluwo.

The seven of them sat in silence exchanging kola nuts. Unlike several other towns, Ijepetu had never been a kingdom founded by a regent and as such did not have a traditional royal family nor rulers who could trace their lineage back to any of Oduduwa's sons, the first Ooni of Ife and progenitor of the Oyo Empire. The town had been established instead as a military staging post two hundred years earlier. The town's oral historians sang that it had once been a desolate clearing by a stream in the thick forest where warriors had once camped while on a failed defensive manoeuvre against the dreaded neighbours and rivals of the Yorubas, the *Tapas*. This had been during the calamitous reign of Onigbogi who succeeded his father Oluaso to become the eighth Alaafin of Oyo. It was recited in the allegories that a few years into his reign, the Tapa's attacked. As they approached Oyo Ile, Onigbogi fled his palace and took up exile in a location with the Borgus further north. Ijepetu then became home to several demoralised warriors who having lost in the battle with the Tapa were demobilised and sent on their way. The town's fortune then changed dramatical when Oba Ofinran became Alaafin in Onigbogi's absence and raised a new army with which he fought the Tapas to reclaim large portions of Oyo land. Several of the soldiers were recalled from Ijepetu, and the town which by now had grown to become a few encircled encampments served as a military garrison where the Alaafin's cavalry camped.

In the years that ensued, and over the reign of several Alaafins, the inhabitants of Ijepetu continued to serve the empire as warriors and lived on the largesse of the Alaafin and his military General, the Aare Ona Kankafo. The distance of such outposts from the capital was a clever arrangement that kept the capital and Oyo metropolis free of the excesses of idle warriors in between wars, and this provided the Alaafin the peace of mind required to rule.

In return, the warriors, several of whom were of questionable character, and dreaded for their war mongering and penchant for bloodletting, were free to hunt, and farm in between wars. Several bred horses and livestock. A significant few lived as cattle rustlers and slave raiders who pillaged the surrounding villages and hamlets for whatever they could lay their hands on, including slaves. Like many other garrison towns scattered along the fringes of the Alaafin's empire, Ijepetu thrived on the fortune of successful wars. Her warrior clans who served Oyo's expansion from kingdom to empire also prospered through the conquests of hamlets, villages, towns and kingdoms during the several years of civil wars that the empire witnessed. At one time, over ten thousand people lived in Ijepetu town. This was the time when the glory of Oyo stretched from the Savannah lands of Oyo metropolis at Oyo Ile in the North to the Southern kingdoms of the Popo, the Anagos, the Dahomenians and further on to the fringes of the kingdoms of the Ijebu and Bini as well as the Awori by the tip of the great Atlantic Ocean. 'The mighty fingers of Oyo,' Alaafin Atobatele once boasted to his Prime Minister the Bashorun, 'touched the waters of the great sea and further on through the slaves they provided the white man.'

Then a few years ago the disease of treachery and discord that had been eating Oyo from within for several years, came full circle, and anarchy was let loose on the empire. It came in the form of the marauding Fula and their ground swell of Ja'maa or Muslims from Ilorin. Instigated by the late Aare Afonja and edged on by the prominent Muslim cleric of the time named Sheik Shehu Alimi, they rode under the protection of the Sultan Othman Dan Fodio of Sokoto and sacked Oyo-Ile. It was reported that they raped women, murdered children and burnt whole villages and farm settlements to the ground. Oyo reeled and fell to its knees. Unable to find the strength from within itself, the empire lost its' glory and Oba Atiba and his council, the Oyo Mesi, were forced to retreat in shame and establish a new capital at a new settlement of farm lands called Ago. It was the third time in its history that Oyo would relocate its capital on account of a military defeat and by this time, even children knew that the house of Oranmiyan was deeply troubled.

The relocation of the empire's capital to Ago after such a decline in fortunes inadvertently granted Ijepetu a renewed and greater importance to the empire. Keen to shore up the fortunes of his declining empire, Alaafin Atiba had directed that Ijepetu now be transformed from being an offensive southern post that had for over one hundred years helped drive the expansion of the empire's territory, to one now charged with defending her north-eastern borders from their hated enemies, the Tapas. To underscore how serious the new situation was, the Alaafin had now also bestowed greater responsibilities and honour to the position of the Balogun of Ijepetu. For as long as anyone could remember, the position had been seen as purely a military one, appointed from amongst accomplished field commanders reporting to the Alaafin's Field Marshal through the commander of the eastern flank, The *Ekun Osi* and therefore not warranting the Alaafin's direct attention. Now Ijepetu had been invited by the Alaafin in council to Oyo Ile where Balogun Ijeru was to be awarded a stool and royal staff of office before proceeding to the Ooni at the spiritual source of the Yoruba's in Ile-Ife for the spiritual blessing which would recognise him as equivalent in status and rank to provincial kings and a mere step behind the natural born royals and descendants of the lineage of Oduduwa. It would in effect, create a new royal family in Ijepetu which through the Alaafin's imperial proclamation would henceforth be recognised and much respected by the Yoruba aristocracy.

Balogun Ijeru found himself thrust into the glory of a royal station on account of the loss of the empire. Despite its imperial decree, it was an ironic and unbefitting back story which was difficult for the proud Ijepetu warrior clan to swallow. Theirs after all, had always been a proud clan of generals and warriors who would rather die, alongside the *Aare Ona Kankafo*, field marshal of the Oyo army in battle, than return to tell the tale of defeat. It was said that an Ijepetu warrior never return home with a pristine spear. It was unthinkable to the elders of the various families that such a dented spear would now be accepted. It was a fact which was not lost on the Balogun, his rival generals who made up the leadership of Ijepetu, or the citizens of the town. It was an open secret that many despised him and even women were now asking embarrassing questions at the market stalls across the town as to his suitability for the position in the first place.

As Ijepetu's Ogboni in council sat waiting to be received by him, Balogun Ijeru walked over to his secret gourd within his inner chambers and pulled out its' content. It was a small tightly bound leather parcel, the size of a large pebble. He was sweating as he carefully unwrapped it to reveal a lump of mixed bitter kola, dry pepper and chalk which had been dripped with the blood of a sacrificed parrot. It was a powerful charm that had been made for him by his Ifa diviner. An elixir to make the words he uttered resounding like the parrot's, powerful and unquestionable to anyone who listened to him. He wiped the sweat of his thick brow, a droplet ran down the burrow of his thick tribal marks. They were prominent and like several men his age, identified him as an Ijepetu man with standing. The Balogun bit into the lump, breaking off a small portion of the chalk then waited as it dissolved all over his tongue. Satisfied that he had followed the instructions appropriately, he adjusted his robes then sauntered out of the room into the steely glances of his waiting guests.

"Balogun we greet you." One of the men called out to him as he found his seat. Due to the limitations of his position, he was not availed with a horsetail or other regal Yoruba appurtenances of power with which he might signal his royal dominion over other men. The position he occupied was in many ways to be viewed by the elders as that of a first among equals, or that of a senior ranking colleague. But over the years, Balogun Ijeru had instilled fear into the hearts of those around him, and that fear was now his horsetail. The Balogun had carefully cultivated the impression about himself, that he was always the warrior in the thick of the fiercest battle, the man with the most potent charms, a purveyor of the deadliest poison laced on the tip of the sharpest spear, and even the possessor of the most dangerous women. It was rumoured that in his harem were to be found witches, hunchbacks, Ifa priestesses, and even the one Omitirin, the woman, who had been gifted to him several years ago by none other than Oba Osinlokun of Eko, after she had killed a white man.

Balogun Ijeru sat in silence. The Oluwo, leader of the Ogboni was a softly spoken elderly man, who had over the years acquired a reputation of being wise and thoughtful. His name was Babatunde. As a younger man, he had fought alongside Afonja in his several campaigns to the southern kingdoms on behalf of the Alaafin. The two of them had fallen out when Afonja had decided to attack Ile-Ife, an act which was seen as sacrilegious given the reverence the people of Oyo had for Ife as their spiritual home. Babatunde had decided to end his war then, and retired back to Ijepetu to tend his large millet farm.

The Oluwo coughed and chose to readjust his indigo cloth before he spoke. "Balogun Ijeru," He began. "This town, indeed the whole of Oyo owes you a debt of gratitude for the sacrifices that you have made and continue to make for our people both on and off the fields of war." There were audible grunts of approval. "Balogun, eh- no one admonishes the cockerel that chooses to perch on top of a door post, indeed we admire its ambition and vitality, but what is to be said when the same cockerel is found attempting to perch on the top of an Iroko tree?"

The men offered grunts to suggest their disapproval.

"Balogun, must we not advice the cockerel not to be fool hardy in the name of ambition?"

Balogun Ijeru stared at the Oluwo. His eyes were red and his gaze unflinching.

"Ijepetu has been at the vanguard of advancing Oyo for the last hundred years, we cannot be accused of not having done our duty. You and I both served Aare Afonja and stood with him in the midst of death. No one can say we do not know our worth, but where is our revered Aare Afonja today. Killed by the very ones who promised him immunity. Sent to the great beyond by the very ambition that I see lurking here today."

"And what does Ifa say?" Balogun Ijeru finally asked, as he deliberately rolled the beads that adorned his left wrist."Oluwo, what does Ifa say, I ask you?"

The Oluwo paused for a moment and then smiled. "On this matter Balogun, Ifa yet offers all of us a riddle and even your own diviner advises caution and that perhaps to consult your Ori."

"Caution?" The Balogun spat with disdain.

The Oluwo smiled and looked hard at the Balogun. He was much older, and despite all the theatrics that the Balogun was known to put up, the Oluwo was far more advanced than he was in the mysteries of Ifa. The Ogboni were revered and even dreaded by every Yoruba man in Oyo for the influence they had as much as the mysticism that followed membership of the cult.

The Oluwo cleared his throat and began to chant softly from the *Ogunda Meji, an* opus as had been once cast.

> *"Ifa asked who has the skill*
> *To go on a voyage.*
> *Did Sango not say*
> *He could make the trip?*
> *And what happened when Sango*
> *Had travelled far, when he had walked*
> *A great distance and come to Koso,*
> *His hometown?*
> *When he was given kola nuts*
> *And rooster meat to eat?*
> *Sango tarried when he had eaten his full,*
> *He said he would turn back and Sango was*
> *Not able to complete the journey"*

The Oluwo continued the chant with the appropriate poetic eloquence of those knowledgeable in the chants. As he did so, the verses of this particular allegory from the hundreds that could be found within the oral traditions of the Ifa corpus explained to the listener how the other deities attempted and yet failed to complete the voyage of one's destiny until the task finally fell on the *Ori*, the Yoruba deity in charge of one's destiny who amongst the Yoruba was represented by ones' own head.

> *"Ori was the only one*
> *Who could make the trip.*
> *Ori is the only one.*
> *Orunmila says,*
> *Ori covers a dirty person*
> *With dyed cloth.*
> *Ori, the one*
> *Who makes the elephant blow its horn?*

Ori is the only one
Who can complete the journey?
If you have cowries,
It is the work of Ori.
If you want a wife,
It is Ori.
If you want children,
It is Ori.
If you are searching for any blessing,
It is to Ori
That you must bring
Your supplications.

As the Oluwo concluded his recitation, he brought the palms of his two hands to rest on the crown of his head and then used them to gently wipe his face in a symbol of ablution.

As he watched him, Balogun Ijeru fell into an uncomfortable silence. Inside him though, he seethed with rage. How dare this old man who had not had the courage to join Afonja sack a weak Ooni, or stand up to a despotic Alaafin, sit there and preach caution to him? He wondered if it wasn't that they were all planning to block his rise so they might gain the position for themselves. It was unheard of for such an opportunity to have ever been presented to anyone in Oyo within recent times at least, and it did not occur to this old fool that the very fact that it did while he Ijeru served as Balogun was good enough sign that his Ori was good.

"I sense that rather than rejoice with me, your council seeks to go against me on this matter, Oluwo. And on what grounds? That perhaps my Ori is not good or has not been appropriately propitiated?"

The Oluwo sought to dispel the suggestion, but Balogun raised his hands angrily to cut him off. "Do not be the one to place judgement on my Ori, Oluwo. I warn you. It has not spilt innocent blood to warrant the judgement of your council."

Balogun stood up from his wooden seat that over looked the stools his visitors sat on. He had bought the arm chair from a young Anago trader on one of his journeys to Eko. It raised him above the level of those who sat in his visitor's stools, so much so that he could cast his gaze upon the crown of their heads. It had once been mentioned to him by a crafty crown Prince at Apamo, that it was good that a man studied the crowns of the heads of men that sat in his court, for one never knew what strange charms might be lurking there. "I know that even the hyena will eat her young should it try to run off with the carcass that the pack must share. I know that the world tears you down when it seems that too good a fortune befalls you. That is what Ifa says, but should such behaviour not suggest that one is in the midst of enemies?"

"And who, Balogun, are you insinuating are enemies here?"

Balogun laughed, "I do not know, Oluwo, perhaps you might be kind enough to advise me?"

The Oluwo shook his head sadly and stared at the Balogun. "I have known you since you were a child, Adeniran." He called out angrily, addressing the Balogun by his childhood name. "Perhaps that enemy you are so fearful of is your very shadow."

"Perhaps," Balogun retorted. "For even the shadow flees one when darkness falls."

"In the long run you will decide how Ijepetu will be honoured." The Oluwo said. There was a sadness about him as he continued. "But, remember that there is no king without a sacrifice, nor a hero without a curse. Ijepetu is bigger than all of us. We met it, and despite our legends, we shall hand it over. The name you give your children is that which will follow them."

Balogun wasted no time replying the Oluwo. "I will be at Ago'd Oyo at the next Bere festival to accept the stool from the Alaafin, my old friend, whether you people like it or not. Atiba offered it to me of his own free volition and it honours Ijepetu as much as it honours me and my seed. My only advice to all of us, is that we must remember that it is the fear of my anger that keeps me calm." With that Balogun Adeniran Ijeru stormed out towards his court yard leaving his guests shocked and insulted.

The Balogun's courtyard was an expansive open piazza which the Oyo called *agbo-ile*. It was encircled by buildings all around which protected it from the peering eyes of on lookers from other compounds. It served as a communal gathering space for members of the same extended family unit. In the Balogun's case it served for more extensive use given his position. At the far end of the compound was the meeting chamber where he had just stormed out from. There he met with the town's leaders and sometimes visiting dignitaries to administer over the affairs of the town or plot the strategy for battles assigned to the Ijepetu army by the *Ekun Osi* (General of the eastern flank) on behalf of the Alaafin. On each side of the chamber were living quarters designed to have their own mini compounds. Here were housed his wives and concubines who all lived together along with their children, indentured servants and slaves. His own living quarters were to the back of the chamber. It had an armoury of highly treasured muskets, spears, arrows in bulky quivers and an assortment of knives, daggers and a few cases of gunpowder. Next to it was the grain house. There was also a strong room where important sacrifices and supplications for the Orishas were kept. The room served as a shrine to Sango the third Alaafin of Oyo and deified God of thunder who the Balogun, as did several of Oyo's warriors, propitiate as staunch leaders of the Sango cult of worshippers. It was next to this strong room, where a dungeon had been carved out, that he kept the white man captured by his riders two months ago at one of the Tapa villages by the river of the goddess Oya, as the Niger River was known to the people of Oyo.

The soldiers had returned with three captives after a raiding expedition to the fringes of Igbomina land. It was a two day ride out from Ijepetu. Warriors scoured the area regularly to extract tributes from the villagers who fished along the great river. There was also a thriving horse market in the area which was amply supplied by the Hausa people bringing quality steeds and ponies which they sold to wealthy patrons from kingdoms as far south as Bini and Ijebu who sent special buying expeditions for good deals.

The night the captured white man had been brought to him, Balogun had felt the situation was ominous and immediately ordered a consultation from his Ifa Priest. His fear was based on what he knew about two white men he had witnessed in his dealings with the *Iga Idungaran* royal court in Eko. The white man never travelled anywhere alone. They hunted like packs of lions. One never strayed too far from the others. Balogun was concerned that a similar situation existed with this man and that reprisal might therefore be imminent. He had also seen how potent their weapons were and he knew how much they relied on its ability to inflict death. The white man he had come to learn through observation possessed very powerful medicine and was to be feared for his ability to take life. Despite the concern, it had been his close adviser who served as his administrative head, Mogaji of Ijepetu, who had advised him instead to fatten the white man up and offer him to the Alaafin of Oyo at the Bere festival, where he was to be elevated. A white man as a gift of novelty and a token of his own power as new regent of Ijepetu. The idea suited Balogun and the situation was made even better when he discovered that the black men travelling with the white man were men who spoke Oyo even though one of them spoke with a strange accent.

He found his captive lying on the floor. He was covered in a pool of vomit and shivering. He had hardly touched the meal of pap and fried bean cakes that he had been offered for the day. Balogun studied him as he lay there groaning and muttering in his strange language. He looked ghastlier in that state than anything he had seen and his gaunt tired face was like that of a Baboon that had been caught in trap for days. He was clothed in tribal robes; a flowing agbada, with an inner buba and sokoto trousers. They fitted him, but were now all dirty and soiled with urine. Unsure of what the white man's fate was, Balogun called out to one of his sentries, who hurried to his side.

He pointed at the man as he lay like a heap of shapeless soggy millet littered all over the damp floor.

"What is wrong with him this time?" he asked,

"My lord I am not sure that I understand this." The man confessed.

"How long has he been like this?"

"We found him like this in the morning."

"What about the other one?"

"He is well my lord, he rises early and stares."

"Hmmm, a man who stares yet does not talk. Bring him to translate what the white man wants."

As the sentry scurried off to bring the other captive, Balogun Ijeru observed the white man further. He was now worried that the man would be dead before the Bere festival. As he weighed the situation in his mind, one of his children ran towards him sucking on a piece of Agbalumo fruit. The little girl pointed at the figure of the white man and asked her father what was wrong with him. Balogun stared at her amused. This one was an inquisitive one, who certainly took after him.

"White Man!" He explained to her, pointing at him.

"Where did he come from father?"

The Balogun looked beyond her as he noticed one of his wives, the child's mother running towards them terrified. She grabbed the child's hand and made to drag her back to their quarters.

"Forgive me my lord. I did not know when she ran off." Then she turned to rebuke the child who was now crying that her adventure had been cut short.

"He comes from very far across a great river, my child." He shouted back to the crying child. A thought suddenly crossed his mind as he spoke the words. Perhaps there was a chance that a dangerous white man could be nurtured back to good health, he wondered.

"Call me Omitirin, the white man killer at once." The Balogun ordered the child's mother. Just maybe the murderess could nurse this one back to his health, he wondered.

CHAPTER 18

I n the months that passed, The Balogun's white prisoner regained his health. As colour came back to his skin, his sallow face was replaced with a rosy pink glow and his battered lips healed. The fever ceased and the diarrhoea he suffered abated. He had been allowed a few more liberties, such as daily walks around the compound and at other times under the watch of armed guards he could venture to the Balogun's private farm land, where he spent a significant amount of time studying the bark of trees and tending to a vegetable patch. The Balogun would often visit him while there, observing him from afar as one would a strange specie of water buck that usually gathered around *Isale Afon*, the marshlands, around Ijepetu. He would ask him questions through Olu the one that interpreted.

The Balogun's curiosity was always stoked. 'What was it that he sought among the trees and the shrubs?' He would ask. 'What was it he buried in the ground? Where is it that he had become familiar with the native spinach, that he could grind it into salves with which he performed strange things on his own body?'

It had soon dawned on Balogun that his captive was familiar with the land, understood the way of their seasons and could sometimes even mimic the call of birds. He learnt through Olu, that he had lived amongst native people like his, in a distant kingdom with kings of great standing among their own people.

One night as a thunderstorm threatened the peace of the evening, the cult of Sango worshippers to which the Balogun belonged, gathered as they always did every month within his compound to propitiate the deity. Olu who he had instructed be brought before him, revealed to him that the white man had mentioned that he came from a clan of herbalists himself. The thunder crackled furiously through the sky illuminating the thatched roofs of nearby huts and casting eerie shadows of Baobab trees on to the swish mud walls. The subdued followers all dressed in white cloth with dyed red bands tied around their foreheads, smacked their lips together to produce strange smacking sounds they believed would ward off the wrath of their deity on such a terrible night.

"An herbalist?" Balogun had asked incredulously, his eyes widening.

"Yes, my Lord?"

"How can that be? Does the white man practice our ways?"

"No, my lord, he has his own God. But he told me that his ancestors were familiar with the power of roots."

"*Alagbho!*" The Balogun laughed. He called out the title given to those within the community who prepared the potions and elixirs from roots and herbs for patients across every hamlet, village and town within Oyo. It confirmed the suspicions he had held about the white man all along. He had seemed too comfortable and familiar with the land. His palms hard and calloused, his finger nails chipped away like those of a man who could cut thickets and chop firewood.

The story the captives had told when they were brought before him was also suspicious. They claimed to have been travelling on the river of the goddess Oya on a great canoe made from iron, searching for farmland and hoping to meet the kings of the lands bordering the banks of the river to stop them selling slaves. It was an impossible tale for any sane man to believe. A white man far away from the coast, claiming to be working for a woman regent could never be thought of as a normal occurrence. It would take a significant amount of supernatural powers, or stupidity to attain such a feat.

There had been three of them, captured along the outskirts of Igbomina and matched to Ijepetu. He had ordered that the second black man be returned to the place they claimed to have crossed the Oya River. It was a careful ruse that the soldiers of Oyo had practiced against their several adversaries for many years. A decoy was always released to return from whence he came, to ward off any repercussions, and for scouts to secretly follow at a distance so as to locate where exactly the enemy lay encamped.

The ploy had fallen on the one who called himself Ajayi. They had kept him away from the others and lied to him in the morning that only he had been spared as the other two had been killed and thrown to the wild animals. The Balogun's most senior wife had supervised a few of the wives from his household who had been ordered to prepare the man a parcel of cold pap and a gourd of water. Then the party set off on their way back towards Igbomina.

The scouts had returned a week later to report that they had left the man by the river bank overlooking the land of the *Tapas* across the river. They had indeed seen one of the ships he talked about. Moored along the river like a great iron canoe in the distance.

That had been several months ago, and through all those months which then turned into years, the Balogun had worried that danger lurked in the bushes ready to pounce. But it never came.

"We must see if he is as powerful as he claims to be then." The Balogun announced before turning his attention to the fresh oil pressed from red palm kernel which lay unperturbed in the open gourd overlooking the effigy of Sango, the dreaded god of thunder and deified third Alaafin of the Oyo empire. He led the other worshippers as they dripped the deep red palm oil on top of the effigy of the patron deity of the court of the Alaafin of Oyo himself.

Dreaded and fiercely revered, particularly by those from the warrior class who understood the complexity and the tragedy of rage and war. The legend had it that Sango's mother had come from a lowly village in the *Tapa* country. The irony was never lost to those who worshipped him. That one so revered could have the ancestry of their arch enemies. Sango who had lost his powers of destruction to the genitals of a woman and who in rage had brought death upon his own seed and then fled to the land of his mother in shame. He remained the most violent of all the gods in the Yoruba pantheon of Orishas. A deified ancient god king and mighty handler of the double axe with which he still shattered the world of its calm with ominous thunder.

∼

It was Omitirin the white man killer, who the Balogun had tasked to tend the white man back to good health. His hunch had been right after all. It had occurred to the Balogun that the time of her usefulness had finally arrived, and perhaps a way to shake off the dark cloud of misery that had set over her all these years. So, he sent for her once again. When she arrived, she knelt before him silently and cupped her palms outwards together in a sign of reverence. Her head was bowed and her gaze was upon the floor. The Balogun reached with his right hand and lifted her chin up towards him. The person knelt before him was no longer the child slave who had been gifted to him years ago. She was now a full-grown woman endowed with strong ample features chiselled into her rich attractive face, her luscious hair packed in thick cornrows and adorned with simple cowries. Her bosom ample but never suckled by a child, her thighs generous, and her legs long and lean from years of trekking long distances. He studied the outlines of her full lips that flinched slightly upon his touch and her forehead, determined and yet vulnerable at the same time. She would have been very beautiful if not for the eyes. He looked into her eyes and saw what he had found in them all those years ago when she had been chased and dragged back by his soldiers on the night she had attempted to flee at Agodi, his transit camp. They were defeated. Distant and forlorn, and lost to the world around her. In the years that she had now become a member of his household, it seemed that all sparks of life had left her, and now she merely went through the motions of living through those large distant empty eyes. They were dark and ominous like deep wells that fell into unending depths of misery and loathing, and despite all his hardness it saddened him to look into her eyes.

He had ordered that she be shackled on the journey back to Ijepetu, to keep her from escaping and taking her own life. Then she had been handed over to his senior wife upon their arrival with the hope that she would be tamed and groomed by one more elderly, and settled into his household. He remembered how her condition had worsened as she became gravely ill. He had thought she would give up and die. But she had not. It was a remarkable thing and he silently admired her for it. He admired her for not dying. This one he thought to himself should have been a man. Had she been one, she would have made a formidable warrior. With life, however came a new sickness. It was a similar sickness he found in the eyes of several slaves he had held captive or men who had lost their loved ones to death that came with war. A sickness that ultimately overcame them when the final flicker of hope was extinguished and left them at the very moment their anguished minds realised that they would never be reunited with their families, nor be able to hold their loved ones again. It was a sense of hopelessness that he himself had once known all too well in the past when he had also had to bury his children after murderers had come visiting at night.

"*Yindi-Yindi*, you will take this white man and cure him of his *Iba*." He had said to her at the time. " You will infuse his pap with the herbs that my herbalist will make for him, and ensure that he takes enough of it to help the fever break in the coming days."

The Balogun had laughed drily. "A white man is not supposed to be in these parts, their skin is too pale and more than enough to lure the bad spirits."

"It is only Olodumare that cures." She had replied. But following that she had been very effective. Every morning, for the next three months she would arrive at his dark room where he had been imprisoned, carrying a bowl of steaming hot Ogi, the sour pap made from fermented millet which she had infused with the herbs she had been given by Balogun's personal herbalist. In the early days the Balogun would watch her from afar as she knelt on the damp floor, propped the man up by her laps and fed him the bitter mixture. One could tell that it was tough going at first, as the man just lay half dead, muttering manically in his strange language and shivering as the deep fever racked through his body. Yet, despite her own frailties, she held him up and patiently fed him like the child she had never been able to conceive nor bear him. It infuriated him at times and saddened him at others.

The white man's shivering had stopped by the third week and by the sixth he could sit up by himself. Seeing the progress, the Balogun no longer bothered to watch over proceedings, content to leave the matters to Omitirin and his retinue of guards. She continued to care for him. She changed his food to include more solid meals like yams and bowl food like *Oka*, made from the ground flour of the bark of yams and served with dark green Ewedu soup and she would watch as he attempted to cut tiny morsels with the tip of his fingers rather than wholesome portions before dipping it into the gourd of Ewedu soup laced with peppery stew and garnished with chunks of game. She showed him how to eat Oka with Okro and with Ewedu and Efo tete, all of which required a different hand motion in order that one might enjoy the combination with the soups appropriately. By the seventh week he had begun to direct conversation to her through Olu the lanky interpreter who had been captured alongside him.

Balogun's men had reported back that the white man had asked her several questions, about Ijepetu and the Balogun and the people. He would place the palm of his right hand on his massive hairy chest when he was offered any assistance or food or an item for his comfort, which he finished off with *'tank you.'* She was told by Olu, the lanky one, that it was the white man's own greeting of thanks. So, she had taught him to say, *'Mo dupe'* which was the way the Oyo would say it, 'I am grateful.' The day he uttered it correctly of his own volition, she had glanced at Olu and the attending guards then looked back at him and smiled. Yet the Balogun would never realise that there had been times over the weeks she had been assigned to look after him, when she had despised him, as she despised all men and particularly those of his kind from the scarred memories she still had of the past. Then it had turned to dread as he stirred and got healthier, and now, she simply pitied him. He was like a fish taken out of water and left to flutter and thrash about on the riverbank. Alone and afraid and far from his own kind, and now he could say, "*Mo dupe*".

Underneath her robe was a dagger which she had always kept for her protection in the event that he might attack her. She felt its blade touch her outer thighs and looked away from him. That evening she had thought again about her mother and her brothers as she had always done over the years since she had become the Balogun's property.

As the months passed, the white man requested that they give him a small parcel of land where he could build a shrine to his own God. The Balogun was intrigued by the request and granted him his wish. Not before long, a small hut had been erected. Inside the building, he had placed a symbol of his god in the form of two pieces of wood bound together with a piece of twine in the form of a tree with two branches. He had nailed it to one of the walls and beneath it he placed a table where he kept a book he claimed contained the words of god. There was an old tree to the back of the new hut, and there the white man and Olu spent time grinding and mashing leaves and roots into salves which he offered to anyone who came to him complaining about an ailment. Sometimes the Balogun himself would send for a salve out of curiosity and marvel at its efficacy.

One day the Balogun had come to inspect the shrine the white man built, and asked him about his god. He asked him what it was that the god could do. The white man had replied that his god was the one true god. He was all powerful and could indeed do all things. The Balogun had nodded his head in understanding.

"This is true of Olodumare." He had simply replied. "He can do all things but he sends the Orishas to do his bidding among men."

The Balogun had asked the white man who his god sent to do his bidding.

"It was his only son he sent." The white man had replied, "Jesus. It was he who when he came down from the heavens had been born as a child and then grown up to be killed by his enemies and hung on the wooden cross to die for all men."

The Balogun had listened patiently to the white man tell him the story of his god. Then when he had finished, the Balogun had shaken his head in disagreement.

"Our Olodumare is too fertile to have had only one son." The Balogun had countered him.

"He had several sons and daughters, and no one would have ever dared nail any one of them to a tree."

Balogun Ijeru looked on at his fellow devotees as the rites of worship to Sango were completed and walked out of the Shrine into his personal living quarters. The rain had subsided by now and the crackling of lighting had receded into the distance, leaving the welcome smell of damp fresh-ness. All over Ijepetu on a night like this, men would huddle with their wives and concubines and children would be encouraged to play outside and catch the flying termites that would come out in droves. The termites would be attracted into waiting gourds and calabashes of water that reflected the light off the various flicker of palm-oil lanterns. Later, the children would gather them into large piles and offer them to their mothers who having performed their conjugal duties to their men would then spice them with salt and fry them in open vats till they became crunchy delicacies. It was above the din of happy children chasing after flying termites, and giggling women with wrappers tied loosely about them, that his courtier announced the arrival of an unexpected yet very important visitor.

Alaafin Atiba's son had walked into the Balogun's quarters with a retinue of fierce looking warriors and sat himself down next to the Balogun's elevated stool of office without much ceremony. He was drenched, but had made no effort to either dry himself or take off his outer garment. As Balogun hurried out to meet the first son of his benefactor and over lord of Oyo, he sensed that things were not quite right.

"Aremo." He greeted him using his traditional title of crown Prince, with a show of concern." *E kabo o.*"

Aremo Adelu gestured back absent minded and folded his hands in indifference.

Balogun drew back cautiously and then chose to sit himself down on his elevated chair. As he did so, he remembered an old verse once sung by a famous Ijepetu griot.

> *'It is only a bastard that hears his Oriki being recited and still fold's his arms about him in indifference.'*

Both men let a little bit of silence linger as they sized each other up. The tradition dictated that it was the Balogun who had the responsibility of showing the required deference and appropriate sense of hospitality in the situation. He beckoned to his chief messenger to approach him quickly, and whispered a few instructions into the young man's ear, then watched him dash off to fetch the Mogaji of Ijepetu, his chief councillor, political adviser and enforcer.

The Balogun turned to face the Aremo once again and greeted him more profusely this time around. "I trust that you did not see the rain." He asked the drenched man politely.

"Ah! We thank God for the coming harvest." The Aremo replied sarcastically. He was much younger than the Balogun and even more cunning than his illustrious father Atiba Atobatele, and current Alaafin of Oyo.

"How is the *Ekeji Orisa*?" The Balogun asked respectfully, using the revered cognomen of the Alaafin which addressed him as being an equal of a deity.

"My father thrives." Aremo Adelu answered, before he let out a massive sneeze.

Balogun nodded as though approving of both the sneeze and the response, and allowed another moment of polite silence before he went on. "We rarely see a great masquerade in the evening market." He chided gently, prodding for a reason for the visit.

Aremo Adelu looked up at him. "My father is king of the palace, while to me belongs the joy of roaming freely amongst his subjects." He responded flatly. It forced hearty laughter out of the Balogun, as the import of the response was not lost on him.

"It is well my lord," Balogun Ijeru retorted jovially. "Long may both of you reign."

The Balogun watched as the Aremo's face betrayed a moment of deep hurt. He watched him lower his gaze to the floor and mumble a brief reply to the prayer.

The timeless traditions of the royal court of the Oyo Empire was based on an intricate system of great powers across various organs of government, wielded by the Alaafin, his family and chiefs and yet effectively tempered through a range of shrewd checks and balances which the traditions had the various organs cast upon each other. The Alaafin was revered as a god, but was never allowed to leave the palace and mingle, nor speak directly with the people. It effectively left him a prisoner within his palace. The eldest son and crown prince therefore played the important role of serving as the Sovereign's trusted envoy on matters of personal importance. Several Alaafin's had used this as a key manner in which they circumvented the rival authority and influence of their Prime minister, the Bashorun, who across most of the empire's history had wielded great political and military power over the Alaafin. Over time, it had brought equally immense power and prestige to the position of the Aremo or crown prince, such that, there had been several instances of Aremos plotting the murder of their own fathers in the past. All in a bid to assume the throne for themselves. The Oyo Mesi led by the Bashorun, which served as the supreme governing council of the empire had then found an ingenious solution after the problem had come to a head when Aremo Awole had murdered his father, Alaafin Abiodun of blessed memory, in cold blood in 1796. The Mesi then decreed that henceforth, the Aremo would have to take his own life at the time of the passing of his father, alongside the other retinue of close relatives who tradition had long demanded followed the Alaafin to the afterlife. This happened either at times when an unpopular Alaafin was deposed and asked to end his own life or at the end of his reign on account of death by natural causes.

Aremo Adelu would be expected to end his own life along with his father in the event that he did not succeed him.

Adelu finally stood and removed his outer gown which he handed to one of his men. The Mogaji of Ijepetu walked into the chamber at about the same moment and came closer to pay him the traditional obeisance. The Mogaji was a stocky man with a thick tribal mark carved across both his cheeks. Aremo Adelu watched him through hooded eyes and then turned his gaze back towards Balogun.

"I do not see your *Ilari* here with him or have you compromised him?" It was intended more as a snide remark, or perhaps a reproach. The Ilari were a peculiar class of royal eunuchs, named after their strange half bald hairstyle, who served as the Alaafin's ambassadors to all the major courts within the kingdoms. They acted as spies within the royal courts of Oyo's vassal kingdoms and enforced the collection of all the taxes and tributes levied by the empire on the vassals. They carried a mystique of being in possession of potent esoteric powers which made them as much feared as they were equally loathed by their vassal hosts.

Mogaji looked at the Balogun uncomfortably.

"With what Aremo?" Balogun shot back at him. "After all we have nothing to hide. Kabiyesi's tributes are secure." The Aremo nodded, saying nothing.

"You can assure your father our supreme lord that he has no reason to be concerned about Ijepetu's loyalty."

"The Olu of Igbon and the Ese of Iresa do not seem to agree with you Balogun." The Aremo retorted.

"*Lobatan!*" The Balogun spat softly. "Finally the heart reveals itself."

"Surely, you of all people know that the concerns of Oyo's eastern flank cannot be taken lightly, Balogun?"

"And what are the concerns this time?"

Aremo smiled knowingly. It was his turn to prod at Balogun's underbelly. The petty rivalry between Balogun Ijeru and the Oba's of the two most prominent satellite kingdoms within the *Ekun Osi*, as the kingdoms, towns and settlement to Oyo's eastern guard was referred to, was legendary. Despite his famously oversize ego, Balogun Ijeru *was* a non beaded leader of a provincial Oyo town and was outranked by both other traditional rulers.

"They have sent word to Kabiyesi that you have persisted in your ways of blocking their routes to the Tapa country, unilaterally extracting trade taxes from their own indigenes along the very routes and not as much as paying the required obeisance."

Balogun Ijeru cursed softly. "Aremo, they must be reminded that good words tease out kola nuts for friends from the bag, while bad ones draw out the arrow from its quiver."

"That may be so Balogun, but let us not also forget that it is injustice to the orishas that causes the loud roar of thunder." Aremo replied swiftly.

Balogun stared back at his uninvited guest through dark brooding eyes. "So what is it you want Aremo?"

"It is not what I want, as much as what Oyo needs my lord. That there should be peace amongst the kingdoms and sufficient strength among the Ekun osi in these times of great peril. The Tapas and the Fulas lie just outside our borders and wait to annihilate us. Is it not shameful enough that they have sacked us twice from our ancestral land? I tell you that my father worries, and for a man who he has promised great honour it would be wise that you desist from antagonising those he leans on for the defence of the new capital."

"Your father is a great man Aremo, and I, and indeed every Balogun of Ijepetu before me serves at his mercy."

"This is true, Balogun, but you seem quick to forget that the tradition right from the time of Adegbesin the son of Jegbe, stipulates that the road to Oyo for all kings and town heads of the eastern flank must go through the Onikoyi as Ifa allowed. Remember the oriki;

'of the three kingdoms of Olugbon, of Aresa and of Onikoyi, there was no other authority on earth and Olugbon is the eldest, Aresa follows, and Onikoyi the youngest of them all'

Balogun heard as the Mogaji, his chief adviser, heaved a deep sigh borne out of the acceptance of a superior argument, and his eyes immediately darted across to lock with his in a flash of animosity. The Mogaji tore his eyes away quickly and re-fixed them conveniently beneath the gaze of the Aremo.

"You are a very knowledgeable and wise crown prince." Balogun offered coyly.

"I have my father and perhaps lessons from Bashorun Oluyole to thank for it."

"That Ibadan man who refuses to reside in the same town as his sovereign?" Balogun said with disdain. "Honestly your father allows too much."

Aremo sighed." These are no longer normal times for our people my lord General, and my father's stool is no longer as strong as it might have been at the time of his ancestors."

Balogun Ijeru contemplated his words briefly and then spoke.

"Perhaps the same may be said of Ikoyi and Igbon. Only a fool or one not experienced in warfare will fail to realise that Igbon is living on borrowed time. It lies right on the route of the raiding Fulas who continue to grow stronger by the day. Their town walls are porous and their people caught up in enjoying the spoils rather than the act of war. Their soldiers are more interested in slaving for their harems rather than to trade for arms or cowries. I tell you to mark my words that a day of reckoning will come for Igbon as much as it will for Ikoyi."

Aremo Adelu shook his head. "I never thought I would hear an Oyo man pray for the down fall of a sister community my lord."

Balogun scratched his armpit and gave a condescending sneer. "Aremo, I have instructed my senior wife to arrange a hot meal for you and your party. I fear that the rain has weakened you and you may not readily recognise the cold truth of reality and confuse it instead as evil. Perhaps you should ask *Aare* Kurunmi in Ijaye and Bashorun Oluyole in Ago'd who you speak so highly of what they honestly believe on this matter."

Aremo Adelu laughed as he rose to his feet. "I was warned that you are a difficult man to reason with."

The Balogun also rose, "I beg to differ Aremo. I will be just a moment." He said. He left the room, returning shortly with a small calabash covered with a white cloth on top of which were placed four large kola nuts. They were round, well-formed and resplendent in their dark red and purple colours. Balogun breathed on each of the Kola nuts and offered a prayer to his long-departed father, that his father might continue to protect his guest and him from evil, and

224

strengthen him in this world. He offered one of the Kola nuts to Aremo who bit a chunk off. He chewed for a few seconds before handing the nut back. Balogun received it politely and offered a portion to his Mogaji. He then wrapped the remaining three nuts in the white cloth and handed the parcel to the Aremo.

"This you will offer to the three Obas on my behalf as a token of my respect. Plead with them on my behalf to lead me to Oyo-Igboho on my forth coming pilgrimage to receive the honour your father in council has promised me."

The Aremo received the parcel carefully, pleased that his admonition seemed to have at last found acceptance. Balogun watched him curiously and then finally added. "And tell them that I said a day will come when they will need my help too."

Aremo Adelu nodded his approval as he tucked the parcel into the pockets of an already wet inner pouch then he and his entourage awaited the late evening meal promised by his host.

Later, after dispensing with the formalities and thoroughly washing their hands to rid them of the heavy sludge of the delicious bean soup, they settled onto large raffia mats that had been spread out on the floor by the entrance into the Balogun's private chamber in the piazza.

As they picked their teeth and spat out strands of the goat meat caught in between, Aremo Adelu glanced at the Balogun and heaved an exaggerated sigh of concern. It was the cue that his host had been waiting for all evening. A crown prince of Oyo did not come visiting the provinces after all for the sole purpose of admonishing a Balogun to be more hospitable with his superiors. There was trouble brewing somewhere within Alaafin Atiba's Kobi and he had sent his trusted son to Ijepetu to extract an important favour. Balogun

Ijeru let his own gaze fall on his visitor and ever so subtly signalled that he was waiting to hear what the matter was.

Aremo wasted little time. "Balogun Ijeru, Ekeji Orisha sent me to you on a delicate matter as well." The Balogun raised an eyebrow and cleared his throat to urge him on. "Aare Kurunmi is proving rather difficult on certain matters that if not handled quickly might threaten the coming Bere festival. You might have heard of this."

The Balogun scratched his buttocks and proceeded to slap a wayward mosquito to its death on his laps. He said cautiously. "All lizards lie flat on their stomachs, so it is difficult to determine which one has a stomach ache."

Aremo smiled and retorted jovially. "This is true my lord, yet Soup should not move around noisily in an elder's belly, not so?"

The Balogun caught on to the request the Aremo just made for secrecy.

"You may speak with confidence Omo Oba." Balogun whispered gently, choosing to address Adelu with a more intimate title that acknowledged his personal privileges as a son of the Alaafin.

"Kurunmi's quiver seems filled with bad arrows these days Balogun. He is causing my father problems and Kabiyesi now fears that Kurunmi and Bashorun Oluyole seem intent on opposing his wishes on the matter of how the tributes and taxes from the Egbados should be marshalled."

The Balogun grunted. What Adelu was insinuating was that Alaafin Atiba was facing the threat of being deposed by his two most senior courtiers and might not make it to the reassurance of the next Bere festival. If Atiba did not survive it to the next festival then he could very well forget about ever being elevated to the status of a beaded king, or the offer of his own royal horse tail and stool.

"And what about the other members of the mesi?"

"Oluyole has them in his pouch." Arelu confessed.

"People cannot live together without quarrelling, but reconciliation must always be given a chance." Balogun Ijeru advised.

"I would not expect a warrior of your stature to solve a quarrel by talking my lord."

"All wars ultimately end in talk Aremo." The Balogun suggested.

"Then how do you suggest that this matter is handled, my lord general?" Adelu asked.

Balogun Ijeru studied his countenance curiously. "But that is not why you are here Aremo. Tell me, what is it that Kabiyesi wants of me?"

"A major distraction," Adelu announced promptly. "A major battle against key Fulani villages and towns within the fringes of Ilorin that will occupy Kurunmi enough to let him leave the comfort of Ijaye."

"And you need Ijepetu to act as the fodder?"

"Aare Kurunmi will not commit to another northern war, unless he is dragged or lured into one. Should you start one and escalate it, he will have no choice once he is pointed to it."

"I fought with your father and Kurunmi at Kanla, where I saw the folly of holding out against the Ilorin people. The Eso has become too quick to abandon battles in recent times. Besides a hunter with only a few arrows left must not shoot with careless abandon."

"This is true, my lord, but, are we not all wiser?"

"We might be, but what do I gain for all this Aremo?"

"The Alaafin's favour and all spoils for you and your men to keep."

The Balogun laughed. "Have I not had my fair share of spoils already?"

"This is true, my lord but the demand for slaves grows and still fetches plenty cowries at the coast."

"The white men and their thirst for slaves." Balogun wondered aloud. "It is only Olodumare that can understand what it is that they do with all of them in that strange land of theirs."

"It has been suggested that they eat them." Adelu whispered in confidence." Or use them for sacrifice."

Balogun shook his head in disbelief. "Then their god must be very thirsty for blood indeed."

"And possess very powerful magic." Adelu muttered. Then he asked, catching the Balogun unawares;

"When are you going to show me the white man you have been hiding here all this time, or did you think that the Palace would not get wind of this?"

CHAPTER 19

The women's quarters within the Balogun's compound were a series of mud cottages located to the left of his private chambers. They were covered from the view of his public piazza by a grove of Agbalumo fruit trees which the women of the compound had planted themselves and tended over the years. The trees held a powerful symbolic significance for the women of the compound. They treated it as a shrine to their fertility and an ode to their harmonious existence within the Balogun household. When the sun came out, the children played beneath the shade of their expansive branches so their mothers could keep an eye on them, as they went about their daily chores.

There were fifteen women who shared the quarters with their children, servants and slaves. They came from different towns and villages from all over Oyo and were now joined in a collective cause. They shared the same man as their husband, lord and master. They carried on their lives under his dominion as wives with a strict ranking in order of seniority. Some had been taken in traditional marriage ceremonies which bestowed greater status on them, while others had been added to the harem as concubines. A few were daughters of men who indebted to the Balogun, had offered them as servants with conjugal benefits. Despite the ranking, all their lives revolved around communal duties which ranged from taking care of the children, cooking meals for the family and household members, tendering the Balogun's several farms and petty trading during the evening market. They gossiped about one another, sang folk songs as they groomed each other's hair and sometimes wept on each other's shoulders when overcome with humiliation, fear or homesickness. The younger wives unsure of what to expect often whispered to one another in embarrassed hush tones about how bland and painful it was to sleep with the Balogun. The more mischievous hid their conjugal displeasures in a labyrinth of songs with hidden jibes and derogatory epitaphs to their husband's manhood.

The only other person they dreaded besides the Balogun himself, was the first wife and matriarch of the household who they simply referred to as *Iya agba*. She was stern but kind and had been with Balogun Ijeru from the very beginning, betrothed to him when he was but a young man. It had been two of her children who were murdered in their sleep, by enemies who snuck into their homestead one night, several years ago when she had still been his only wife, to extract their revenge on the father. It was a story that none of the younger wives ever had the courage to tell out in the open. No one dared mention the two harmattans it was said that she had roamed the outskirts of Ijepetu like an unkempt mad woman looking for her children, even after they had been buried by her husband. One evening she had torn the garments off her body in grief, clutching at her naked breasts, wailing like a stricken dog and cursing her destiny and her enemies.

Iya agba had seen death, but she had also seen life. She acted as the mid wife at the birth of all her husband's children from all the other wives and concubines who had come later, after she had stopped giving herself to him. It was she who oversaw the careful burying of the placentas and the healing of the women after child birth. When the Balogun was away on expeditions, at the time of the birth of a child of his, it was she who over saw the *Ese te aye* ceremonies where the Ifa priest prophesied the child's future and the child was named. Iya agba saw to the circumcision of all the children, their scarification with the appropriate facial tribal markings and she recited the Oriki for every child within Ijeru's household.

One night several harmattans ago, the Balogun had returned from his yearly journey to the coast and handed over a young Omitirin to her to look after as a slave in his harem. She was dishevelled, gaunt and sickly, and her eyes no longer looked like those belonging to a human being. The only other time that she had ever seen so much agony and pain contorted into the face of one person had been when she had caught her own reflection in a stream one morning after she had tried to stab her husband to death for being the cause of the murder of their children.

She had tended to Omitirin's bruises including those her husband had inflicted on her virginity. The poor child would not sleep. Her eyes had grown wide and wild like a caged animal's. She did not eat either. It was only so much that the body of a child could take. She eventually slipped into long bouts of unconsciousness and raging fevers and it did seem that she would eventually succumb to death. Then one morning as she sat outside on a stool supervising the other 'junior wives' as they fried *akara* bean cakes for the morning meal, she saw the emaciated figure of the child crawl off the sleeping mat and stagger out towards her, breathing heavily and asking if she could be led to a stream or river to have her

231

bath. Iya agba had stared at her incredulously at first. Then she had broken down where she sat that morning and wept.

Things had improved for Omitirin from then on. Although she still withdrew into herself and stared at the world around her through hostile and distant eyes. Sometimes the other wives would gather their infant children at her feet and encourage her to pick them up and nurse them. It would take many days before she paid them any notice. The time went by as it always did in Ijepetu, punctuated with the joys of new births and naming ceremonies, marriages and the celebration of funerals of brave old warriors who had caught the arrow in the endless inter-communal wars that now raged all over Oyo towns regularly. Several settlements were now being displaced by all the violence, and greatly fortified garrison towns like Ijepetu had become attractive to refugees. There was a saying amongst the griots that it was only an army in search of death that would dare venture towards Ijepetu, and that the only sound of war the people of Ijepetu ever heard was that of their victorious cavalry returning home triumphant. Yet Ilorin lay but a day's ride away, and with that knowledge lingered the dread of the terrifyingly deadly Fulas and the havoc that they were capable of unleashing.

Iya agba had taken Omitirin under her wings and protected her from the scornful glares and maltreatment of the other junior wives. In time a chorus of complaints arose that Omitirin did no work, but no one ever dared report her to Iya Agba.

The Balogun rarely visited the female quarters. The last time he came calling had been two harvest seasons ago, when he had complained about the nature of the ground millet and stormed the cottages in a fit of rage, bellowing at the top of his voice. The women had scattered in every available direction, fearful for their wellbeing and nonplussed as to the calamity that would befall whoever's error it had been that the millet had not be well ground. The culprit at the time had been a young indentured servant who had been given to the Balogun by her father as a recompense for an old debt. He had dragged her out of her living quarters towards the middle of the public piazza and inflicted a severe beating on her.

This morning however was different. The Balogun walked in quietly. He came unaccompanied and unannounced. His head was bent downwards and his shoulders drooped.

"Where is your senior mate?" he asked the few who he found outside their cottages basking in the mid-morning sunlight. As they looked up shocked to find him standing in front of them, they became immediately contrite that they were to be found lazing about. They promptly dropped to their knees in obeisance and pointed in the direction of the cooking stead.

The Balogun found Iya Agba seated on an old stool by the fire pits, across which five large earthenware cooking vats were placed.

Iya agba did not get up when she saw her husband approach her, but she knew immediately that there was trouble, so she re-tied her wrapper more tightly around her torso and waited for him to speak. The Balogun hesitated for a brief minute and kicked a small empty basket that lay in his path. His eyes darted around the cooking stead, but he did not acknowledge the greetings of his other wives.

Eventually Iya agba beckoned to him and addressed him as *Baba Deola*, which honoured him as the father of her long murdered first son. It was her way of reminding him of just how far they had come, and it always drew the same expression of guilt and hurt from the man that an entire town dreaded. It had become her own power over him.

The Balogun always chose to address her by her unofficial moniker within the clan. He did so now. "Iya agba, did I not send for you?" He began, which they both knew was a lie.

"What troubles you my lord?" She responded choosing to ignore it.

"We cannot talk here." He complained aloud to the hearing of the others. It was his own way of differentiating her status from that of the other women. They might all be his wives, but they were not all his trusted companions. Iya agba nodded calmly and rose to her feet laboriously. Arthritis had started to set in one knee, as had glaucoma in the eyes. She followed behind him as he walked towards the Agbalumo trees, dismissing the children in all directions with the wave of a hand.

They sat together on a bench that had been placed there by one of his court guards.

"There is trouble." He muttered ignoring any required preambles. "There is trouble."

"What troubles you my lord?" Iya agba asked gently. "Has the Aremo left?"

He nodded and looked into her eyes.

"He has. The dog!" he muttered and drifted into a moment of brooding.

"What did he want?"

"He knows about the white man, and has asked that he be delivered to the Alaafin's palace within seven days."

"But did you not tell him he was being prepared as a gift to be presented at the Bere festival?"

"He would not hear of it."

Iya agba sighed and re-tied the wrapper about her bosom yet again. "Your adversaries around are working against you again my lord."

"It is obvious." He agreed.

"Someone has taken the matter to the Alaafin's *Kobi* ahead of you."

He nodded.

"And you choose not to get counsel from your Mogaji?"

"Not on this matter. Can one truly know who is speaking the truth, or to be trusted at a time like this?"

"Could it be Ilari Majeobinu?" Iya agba enquired of the Alaafin's vassal to Ijepetu and court spy.

Balogun Ijeru scoffed. "That one would not report even his own shit to a fly with all I do for him secretly. I have him in my pouch!"

"Then Oluwo Babatunde, perhaps?"

"It could well be. The obstinate maggot!"

"Or it might be no more than the loose talk of town folk, after all a few people have seen the white man about. Surely news like that is bound to spread."

"This is true." The Balogun admitted. "But it is the things that he did not say that bothers me. This morning before he left, Adelu asked to admire my muskets. An unusual request which I still chose to honour, but when I asked that a sample be brought to him to inspect, he insisted on visiting the armoury himself."

"That he comes unannounced and then demands to inspect your armoury can only mean they believe you are building up arms towards an unsanctioned battle?"

"That is what it seems. He offered me a lame excuse of the Onikoyi of Ikoyi and Ese of Arese being offended with my manners."

"When did the two Oba's become your enemies my lord, do you not pay them tributes?"

"Beyond their arrogance and love for the easy life, I do not have grudges with them."

"My lord, are you not being naive or swallowed by the idea of your importance?" Iya agba finally reproached him. "The Alaafin sends no other than his crown prince in the dead of night to visit you and inspect your armoury and then directs that you hand over a white man you are harbouring. Can that not only mean that they do not trust you?"

"So, it would seem." Balogun muttered.

"They worry that you may be planning to be in alliance with the people of Ilorin against Atiba, and buying muskets directly from the white man." She explained.

The Balogun cursed out loudly in disgust as the truth began to dawn on him.

"You do not lie! So that is why they prod me to go and instigate trouble with Ilorin? To weigh my loyalty to the Alaafin, and yet find a ruse to send Aare Kurunmi to keep an eye on me."

"But to weigh your loyalty to Atiba against what my lord?" His wife asked curiously. "What would you stand to gain if you went against Alaafin Atiba. He is your friend after all?"

"Beyond slaves to trade and cowries to be made, I do not see what else there is. What is to be gained in siding with the Muslims if not their eventual betrayal and one's untimely death as Afonja himself soon found out? Atiba knows that he keeps my loyalty for life with the kingship he is offering me."

"Then are you sure that this is actually Alaafin Atiba's doing? Surely he himself will know this?"

"Then who?" Balogun snapped.

Iya Agba studied her husband's terse face. It had always been part of his gravitas for as long as she had known him. A strong man's face, dark and unsubdued, deeply etched with the Ijepetu tribal marks with the prominent diagonal slash that began at the bottom of each cheek and ran right up to the bridge of the nose. Now even those were crossed with deeply etched worry lines. She offered him a popular proverb on rivalry.

"One does not compete with another for a chieftaincy title and yet show him the way to the king's house my lord."

A long smirk grew across his face as he rose to his feet at that very instant. "You show him the way to his demise instead." Balogun completed the proverb slowly as he stood arms akimbo and finally turned to face his wife, and for a fleeting instant revealed the deep respect and admiration he had always had for her.

"Oluwo Babatunde!" He exclaimed, as the truth finally dawned on him. "That cursed son of *Esu* has played his crafty hand indeed!"

"I advise caution my lord." Iya agba added quickly.

"The Oluwo has the ear and admiration of the people, particularly the women and the elderly. It will not serve your interest to be seen as antagonising him."

"I would rather slit his throat and throw him to wild hyenas." He retorted.

"But what good will that serve a man who seeks to establish his lineage as the natural rulers over an entire town of equals? More than force you shall need tact and wisdom. More than dominance you shall need love."

The Balogun shifted on his feet, uncomfortable with the turn his wife's counsel was taking. Tact and love after all were the domain of women. What he understood was force and domination.

"You need the people to see that you have the authority of Ifa on this matter of your ascension. It must be made clear that whoever goes against you no matter how loved by the people or highly placed, aggrieves not just you but both Obatala the lord Orisha and Ori, the owner of all Ori's himself."

"And by that you mean a public divination?" The Balogun mused.

"Yes, my Lord. One for the entire town to see and honour and not just a few."

"And what do I do with the white man?"

Iya agba paused and looked away into the distance in contemplation. "Did Ifa itself not warn of the return of the white nago? Did Ifa not foretell the coming of troubles, *Oko mi*, an ill wind bringing nothing but trouble and revenge between brothers?" Iya agba spoke gravely referencing a rarely recited odu from the Ifa corpus. "The sooner you wash your hands of him and hand him over to Atiba, the sooner he will be Atiba's problem and not yours."

Balogun Ijeru heaved a long sigh and looked on at his first wife.

"You have spoken well, Iya agba." He said, and then he re-traced his steps back across the open piazza towards his own private chambers. He left her there, still sitting under the

238

shade of the Agbalumo trees staring at him as he walked away.

~

All the Bales within Ijepetu, and their Mogajis, were ordered to gather at the Balogun's compound on the day after Ijepetu's market day. For six days the *Aarokin*, who served as Ijepetu's town crier, chief bard and historian visited all the town's major quarters belting out the Balogun's message with his gong and husky voice, to the amusement of children caught up in the theatrics of his performance, and the disdain of several traders he had taken undue favours from, by virtue of his position within the court.

Over two hundred people gathered at the Balogun's communal piazza curious as to the reason for the summons. The more important members of the town were granted their prominent spots at the front. They were composed of members of the Ijele ruling council, members of the Ogboni cult and the twelve prominent Baloguns, heads of Ijepetu's other twelve warrior families who were recognised as the descendants of the earliest settlers. There were only two women amongst the gathering, Iya agba and the Iya Oloja, Ijepetu's most prominent woman and leader of the town's market women. No woman could ascend to any of Ijepetu's other positions of authority, except that of headship of the trading class of market women. It was through this position of authority that they were given recognition and representation in the affairs of the town. While Iya agba being Balogun Ijeru's first wife was accorded respect and reverence and allowed to attend such civic gatherings, she was not recognised as a queen in much the same way that Ijepetu had never recognised a natural born king.

Balogun Ijeru sat in his elevated chair surrounded by members of the Ijele. His Mogaji was in charge of proceedings and had his stool to the right of the Balogun's in line with tradition. This was why his position was always referred to as the Otun, or right hand, as was the case across nearly all royal courts in Oyo. The Bales who served as leaders of each clan clustered within shared villages, compounds or homesteads, were the land owners and Barons of Ijepetu through whom the administration of the town's affairs were executed. They had full authority to manage the affairs of their clans and communities, as long as their decisions did not go against the edicts from the Balogun in council.

The Mogaji worked with the Balogun's guards and other courtiers to clear a path way through the mass of Bales seated on dyed raffia mats for the town's most prominent Ifa priest to walk through. The priest had a small retinue of staff who walked dutifully behind him carrying baskets filled with various fruits, palm nuts and its oils and other items of worship. He was a slightly bent elderly man and he made his way slowly through the crowd. He wore no upper clothing apart for a series of brass chains that adorned his neck and strips of leather on to which several leather pouches and small gourds of charms and elixirs had been sewn. Slung across his shoulder was a medium sized bag made of dried animal skin. In it were the sacred appurtenances of his calling. A brass Okpele divination chain carefully encrusted with sixteen half palm kernel nuts, passed on to him over five generations of Ifa priests, a wide divination palette carved out of Iroko wood and an ivory tusk. Every one present knew him and nearly every family present would have had course to consult him for advice on all sorts of matters. He, after all was the Babalawo; The cultural philosopher and spiritualist of the people. An inheritor of the precious mysteries of Ifa passed down through the generations from the time of the

Orunmila the second son of Olodumare. With each frail and cautious step he took, he announced himself as several things all woven into one. Part priest, confessor, diviner and intercessor, part herbalist and natural doctor. One who could help you find your Ori when it seemed beyond you and one who could damn it to a lifetime of ruin.

Balogun Ijeru watched as the man made his way towards him, milking every moment of attention. He sniffled a smirk as he recalled the old bastard's several past indiscretions. How many times had he been caught trying to sleep with the wives of men who had gone to fight in wars. The Balogun looked away and stole another glance at Oluwo Babatunde, his arch rival. He sat there silently swatting flies with his gnawed hands and looking up into the sky as though expecting Olodumare himself to save him from the humiliation that they both knew was coming. The members of the Ogboni council sat about him looking dutiful and dignified but he could see that the worldly amongst them exhibited nervous ticks every now and then. They all knew what was coming, and not one of them he knew would summon the courage to go against a divination given in front of the entire town folk, even when they suspected that it had been arranged.

When the Babalawo finally reached the central clearing, they paid each other the perfunctory obeisance, and the Balogun listened as his Mogaji cleared his throat and began welcoming all. The Aaorkin was in a good mood. The Balogun after all was always generous when he wanted something, and he had been duly compensated. He came with the support of recently recruited praise singers and seasoned drummers who belted out the early verses of each prominent family's Oriki. It honoured them as much as it softened the ground in his patron's favour.

"There is a reason why Ijepetu will forever flourish." The Mogaji was bellowing about him. He was regally dressed in the full complement of a flowing agbada and sokoto robe and his cap was newly sewn.

"And that reason is because we fear God." He concluded grandly. "We seek the wise counsel of Obatala in all our matters and we give the Orishas their due." He looked towards the crowd and added solemnly."May Olodumare lead us on to the right path."

The crowd replied with a thunderous "Ase!"

"Ijepetu needs Olodumare's words now more than ever. It is the foolish antelope that darts about the forest without an eye out for the passing hunter. Is it not right that on the day the market opens, we send out for word of who might be coming, less our produce goes to waste? It is the way of wise men to seek counsel on matters of great providence and Ijepetu is not lacking in wise men."

The Mogaji turned towards the old medicine man and spoke quietly.

"Baba Agboluaje, we have requested you to help us approach Ifa on this sensitive matter so that we might go towards the ordained path with confidence."

"The Alaafin, our great lord and protector has offered this town an honour the likes of which has not been heard of in this land since the time of our own forebears. A great honour which will transform the standing of every man from this town and raise the profile of our warriors and our General." The Mogaji then turned to give the Balogun a respectful glance of approval.

"One would have thought that such great honour would be quickly accepted, but we have a wise leader, a God-fearing leader and a man who looks to his ancestors for guidance."

Balogun Ijeru stared coldly into the Mogaji's eye, betraying no emotions. He watched as the man stared back equally as cold then dropped his gaze carefully as he carried on with his speech.

"Baba, we need to know what Ifa says on this matter of our leader's ascent to the stool, as offered by his good friend and benefactor Kabiyesi Atiba."

The Mogaji signalled to the servants who stood in a huddle by the side of the piazza, and they immediately approached the centre clearing, carrying baskets full of farm produce and cowries. One of them dragged a hefty goat.

The crowd watched as the Babalawo's helpers took possession of the items and carefully carted them away. The Old Babalawo beckoned to the Mogaji to come closer and then whispered into his ears. The Mogaji glanced over at the Balogun abruptly then turned back to snap at the Babalawo. It seemed like both men were on the verge of arguing when the Balogun immediately motioned that the Mogaji approach him. He did as commanded.

"What is it?" The Balogun hissed with veiled annoyance.

"My lord, Baba says that he cannot do the divination here."

"The old dog had better not embarrass me here today." The Balogun continued. "What does he want?"

"He says he prefers to cast his Okpele inside the house."

"His house?" Balogun Ijeru asked incredulously.

"No Balogun, inside your quarters."

Balogun Ijeru raised his head to see Oluwo Babatunde and his retinue of loyalists had approached them.

"Is there anything the matter?" The old man asked with false concern.

The Mogaji spun round nervously, while the Balogun cursed under his breath. "There is no problem." He assured. "The matter is being resolved."

The Balogun waited as Oluwo Babatunde returned to his place and was now whispering with his loyalists. The crowd had broken out in a hum of several small conversations that now enveloped the entire piazza in one din and the Babalawo stood slightly bent, peering at him through rheumy eyes. Balogun Ijeru beckoned at him to approach.

"Baba, what is it that you are doing?" He asked angrily." Do you want to disgrace me here?"

The old man shifted uncomfortably and adjusted himself carefully.

"On the contrary my lord," he began. "It is so that you are not disgraced."

"What do you mean by that? You had better be careful with me old man."

"My lord, it is not right, nor wise that I cast the Okpele for you in public like this."

"And why not?"

The old man shifted some more and briefly glanced at the crowd. He sighed as his glance finally rested on Olowo Babatunde and his entourage. "You have placed me before men who cast long glances, my lord."

"Long glances?"

"Yes, men who can see far even though they pretend not to be watching and therefore men who can see how the Okpele drops."

Both Balogun Ijeru and his Mogaji fell silent and stared at him as they realised the point he was trying to pass across.

"I cannot read what is not cast before these men around us on a day like this Balogun. It will not be good for Ifa, nor will it be good for you nor I."

"So, you want some privacy then?"

"It is wiser, is it not, that Ifa be more generous to you in the shade?" The old man asked solemnly.

"Let him do it inside then." The Balogun instructed.

"As you wish Balogun." His Mogaji replied.

"And you will have to be there with me my lord." The Babalawo added. "You know that we cannot cast the cowries on matters of your Ori without you being present."

"It is true. I will join you." Said the Balogun before shoving his nervous Mogaji back to update the crowd.

Despite the assurances that the Mogaji had given, members of the Ogboni council had insisted that they be present when Baba Agboluaje did the consultations. The *Bales* of the town were occupied with the portions of food that Iya agba's army of cooks had spent the past two days preparing for. There was silence in the Balogun's chambers, in stark contrast to the mood outside. Baba Agboluaje was sweating by now as he settled down on to the animal skin mat that adorned the cold clay floor and arranged his paraphernalia in front of him. The Mogaji's worried eyes darted about the room, flicking from Oluwo Babatunde's bemused look to that of his over lord the Balogun, who looked like he was on the verge of killing someone.

It seemed that Baba Agboluaje's every move had become laborious and painfully slow. He never looked up, choosing rather to concentrate his attention on a large wooden dais placed on top of the mat before him. His assistants gathered around him, shielding him from the late afternoon sun that cast a long shadow about the chamber. From within the leather pouch he carried around his arms he pulled out the divination chain and placed it to the side of the dais. He watched as one of his assistants emptied fine sand carefully on to the surface of the dais from a small calabash he carried. The members of the Ogboni council sat a short distance away facing him, and with full view of his paraphernalia spread out on the floor before them. They watched closely and in silence, exhibiting no emotions.

"Shall we begin Baba?" The Balogun uttered loudly. "The day is far spent as it is already."

"As my lord pleases." The Babalawo muttered as he proceeded to lift the Okpele divination chain and cast it upon the dais. He accompanied his one deft motion with chants and oral exultations and punctuated them after a while with moments of thoughtful silence as he studied the binary patterns left by the throw of the chain. He threw several more times, using his index finger to etch the corresponding marks into the patina of sand, nodding thoughtful and chanting appropriate verses from the relevant Odu of the corpus, then he would sigh. This went on for what seemed a lifetime to the men within the room, and when it seemed like his arm might have begun to ache, he would cast the chain again.

Finally, it was Oluwo Babatunde's voice that rent through the anguish of uncertainty that everyone in the room shared.

"It seems that Ifa is reluctant to speak." He mocked in a grave voice that left no one in doubt of the disdain which he held the proceedings. He did not bother to look at his adversary, nor did he give the old diviner the traditional obeisance befitting an occasion of such importance. "It seems that Ifa is reluctant to speak today." He repeated.

The old diviner sat up and stared back at Oluwo Babatunde. His eyes were glazed, his eye brows deeply furrowed, his face troubled, and for once his voice cracked.

"There is trouble coming." The old Babalawo said in a weak voice that no one seemed to have heard. "There is trouble coming my lords." He spoke louder this time, so that everyone heard him.

It stopped the Oluwo in his tracks. "What trouble baba?" He asked as his glance darted towards the Balogun in apprehension. Both men locked eyes even as the old Babalawo gestured for one of his assistants to help him up from the floor. He gently dusted the seat of his worn sokoto and held on to his staff with a sudden firmness that belied his age.

"What trouble?" It was Balogun Ijeru who now asked in a cold voice.

"My lord, it would seem that you have deeper problems embedded within your household." The old man said quietly.

"What does that mean?" The Balogun snapped.

"Unfulfilled destinies, my lord. And defiled Orishas."

The Balogun rose to his feet irritated by the turn of events. This wasn't what he paid for. "Speak plainly old man." He retorted. "What are you talking about?"

"You, my lord, might have unwittingly stopped the kadara of a man whose kadara it was not yours to stop…"

"Not mine to stop?" The Balogun asked irritated.

"Yes, my Lord. Ifa says that there are two rivers that have not been allowed to flow their courses. Ifa says that Oya the tempestuous one and Yemoja the maternal one, both of who suffered from the wrath of Sango. Ifa says that who will tell Sango that he will be destroyed by his lust of Oya, the harbinger of the drought. Ifa says who will placate our mother Yemoja who has been grievously offended and has tied the womb of her servant. There is trouble coming for the propitiators of Sango."

There was a moment of deafening silence as everyone contemplated what it was they had heard. It was the Balogun who broke the silence this time around.

"This is not what I brought you here to tell me, old man." Balogun Ijeru said shaking his head. "This is not what I brought you here to say."

The Babalawo readjusted himself and coughed nervously. "It is the way of Ifa my lord." He said. "It is the way of Ifa to play tricks on men. But within the odu lies your redemption like any other man." The old man looked towards Oluwo Babatunde and then back at the Balogun.

"Men must not allow ambitions and rivalries blind them to the odus of Ifa my lord. It is for you to probe deeply into what Ifa offers you and then perform the appropriate rites my lord. A man desperate to paddle a canoe must look for calm waters and not be in a hurry to paddle down a rapid. To do otherwise is to go the way of Sango, is it not?"

"And what do you mean by that?" The Balogun asked sensing the veiled threat in the old man's admonition.

"You know what he means!" The Oluwo finally snapped at the Balogun. "Are you that far gone in your arrogance that you now question a deity generous enough to forewarn you, Balogun?"

The Balogun turned and stared coldly at the Oluwo. He returned to his stool and then comported himself.

"Is this not all too convenient for you Oluwo my brother?" The Balogun asked quietly as he turned away to watch the Babalawo return to the dais to cast his divination chain once more.

"Hmm, two rivers now allowed to flow towards their destinies," he muttered aloud. "And an Orisha defiled. Ifa now tells me that I am a destroyer of destinies and a defiler of an Orisha. Is it not all too convenient for all of you?" He repeated, waving his hands at the members of the Ogboni council who all sat transfixed watching the proceedings with fear.

"You are indeed a fool Ijeru!" The Oluwu spat disdainfully. "You are like the arrogant hunter who goes digging holes to entrap the rabbit, not realising that Olodumare is digging a befitting hole for his own downfall."

At that moment they all heard the old Babalawo laugh out knowingly, as one would when a realisation had just hit one.

"There is one amongst your wives who has yet to conceive." The Babalawo announced aloud. "One who is yet to bear you a child!" The old man declared.

The Balogun stared at him in confusion, shocked at what he had just heard.

"Who is she?" The Babalawo asked.

The Balogun jumped up from his raised stool as if he had been bitten by a scorpion. His face betrayed his shock from the Oluwo's stinging words.

"Yindi-Yindi." He muttered in a subdued voice. "Omitirin, the white man killer is the only one."

CHAPTER 20

IJEPETU, THE OYO EMPIRE, THE DRY SEASON, 1846.

Balogun Ijeru had begun to prepare his army for the battle against the weaker satellite towns and fringe settlements of Ilorin, as he had been directed to by Alaafin Atiba of Oyo. The signal had gone in code to the seven leaders of the various flanks, who made up the seven regiments that Ijepetu was famous for sending into battle as a single ruthless striking force against its rivals. Seven vultures were released into the inky morning sky, each trained to find its way to the piazza of each Balogun and head of a clan of warriors. A dog would be slaughtered and then offered as a carcass for the unsightly birds to scavenge on. War brought death and vultures followed death.

Warcraft within the kingdoms and city states of the Savannah land east of Oyo, were always preferably fought during the dry season. There were many reasons for this. For one thing, the ground was hard, so, the horses could ride swiftly, covering ground to strike quickly at an unsuspecting adversary and retreat back home. Farmlands were also dryer, and barns stocked with grain and other produce from the last harvest, which made the towns more vulnerable as it offered the unique advantage of inflicting greater punishment on the civilian populations through arson and other acts of attrition. The other truth was that it was easier to raise an army during the dry season as idle farmers or part time mercenaries waiting for the coming of the next rains favoured a spare vocation in marauding and enslaving captives from towns other than their own. Even soldiers preferred their hoes to bows and arrows when the new rains came, heralding the commencement of the new planting season.

This campaign, as agreed, was to be waged as a quick strike and cunning ruse. A way to attract the attention of the one-man Oba Atiba feared the most, Kurunmi of Ijaye, Oyo's Aare Ona Kankanfo. Balogun Ijeru had been assured that once he had the fight underway and ensured it had caught the attention of the surrounding kingdoms and towns within the Ekun Osi, Atiba would find legitimate cause to direct his field marshal to attend to the war. No right-thinking Aare would dare refuse to attend to military matters that threatened the existence of the empire. With a protracted war on the northern front of the new and yet unestablished capital, Atiba hoped to be able to buy himself time and keep both his dreaded general and the Fulas occupied and at bay. It was a further price that Balogun Ijeru was expected to pay for the honour that he craved of being elevated to greater rank and establishing a royal lineage. But Balogun Ijeru also saw it for what it was. He had no choice but to execute the battle as further proof of his loyalty to Alaafin Atiba.

Balogun Ijeru made sure that the vanguard of Ijepetu's army supported the war, as did Ijepetu's council of chiefs. After all, expeditions sponsored by the Alaafin were usually more lucrative than those privately sponsored by the Balogun or other vassal towns within Oyo. Yet, despite what was at stake, this was a war that the Balogun had increasingly become reluctant to fight.

One night, two weeks after Baba Agboluaje had revealed the odu about Omitirin to him; he had done something he had never done before. He quietly slipped out of Ijepetu, when the town had become still. Accompanied by just one trusted slave, he had ridden a fast horse through the night to Ile-Ife. There, he sought private audience with the Ooni of Ife and revered spiritual leader of the people of Oyo and beyond.

Ooni Adegunle who was referred to as *Abeweila*, which loosely translated as 'one who stood under the shade of a large okra leaf ' was a direct descendant of Ooni Lafogido and had barely spent three years on the stool of his ancestors. He was a young man barely in his twenties, and not thought of yet as a great spiritual leader. Such however was the reverence with which the stool as well as the household of Oduduwa was held, that all Alaafins and lesser nobles alike came to be blessed and anointed with the sword of Oranmiyan, the dutiful youngest son of the first Ooni. They came to the source to offer prayers to Oduduwa his father and founder of the Yoruba nation. It was Oduduwa who had carried out the errand that Olodumare the god of all creation had initially tasked his elder brother Obatala with, and thus expanded the creation of land for the first humans to settle upon. Ile-Ife was the home of all 400 deified orishas, worshipped across the land, and the Ooniorisa was revered by the people as the only one who could directly intercede on behalf of humans with the 400.

Balogun Ijeru was ushered into the Ooni's civic chambers for the audience he sought, by one of the king makers and a brother at arms of his from past military campaigns. He met the young Ooni seated in the company of his retinue of priests who attended to the daily ceremonies across the several shrines and temples dedicated to propitiating the 400 Orishas of the Yoruba pantheon. It was said that there was a festival of worship every day in Ife and people who sold live-stock and other articles of worship which sometimes included slaves, made a fortune.

The Balogun paid his hosts the most respectful obeisance possible for a man of his station and waited as he lay flat on the cold dusty floor to be allowed to approach.

"My father," The Balogun began. "I greet you. Long may your head carry the sacred crown of your forefathers, and long may your royal slipper adorn your feet."

The young Ooni watched him unmoved. His eyes were tired. He was draped in a simple flowing white cloth, and his feet rested in a pair of slippers crafted from the skin of water buck. He clasped a trident tipped staff intricately adorned with tiny white beads in between both his hands.

"The Ooniorisa greets you too." One of the courtiers who stood beside him responded on his behalf.

Balogun Ijeru nodded and beckoned at his accompanying slave, who dutiful passed on two bags of cowries and kolanuts to one of the Ooni's attendants.

"The Ooniorisa thanks you for the gifts." The spokesman continued." What brings you this far my lord?"

Pleased with the manner of acceptance of his tribute, Balogun Ijeru adjusted himself to a kneeling position and supported his weight with both his hands.

"I am here to ask the Ooniorisa's advice on a delicate matter that gravely troubles me and my people, my lord."

The Balogun's old friend moved towards him and announced to the hearing of all present, "The Balogun is a well-known friend of the people of Ife my lord. He and I have fought on the same side for many years. He has travelled far and his visit at this hour will suggest that it is a conversation requiring the Ooniorisa's quiet contemplation."

"Your words are sacred Kabiyesi." The Balogun added respectfully. "I was hoping that it would be spoken into your ear."

The Ooni was apparently tiring of the ceremony. He waved his hands to indicate that he was open to being consulted more privately. The room was soon cleared of most of the priests leaving only the Ooni and three others, including his chief priest and custodian of the sacred *Aare* crown. The Balogun thanked the men for their kindness and began to reveal his dilemma. He explained how he had sought to know the mind of Ifa on the matter of his coming coronation only to be presented by his priest with riddles of two rivers and a disrespected orisha. Could there indeed be such an interpretation he wondered, or was he merely being deceived, he asked looking into the eyes of the men who sat before him.

It was the Ooni's chief priest who spoke. He was an elderly man in his eighties who came from a lineage of artisan bronze casters. He also had a great reputation for his mastery of the oral traditions of the house of Oduduwa and in addition to the mysteries of Ifa, kept the Oriki of the royal lineage of Ife.

"My Lord," He began in a hoarse voice that revealed his age. "Orunmila is Olodumare's chief messenger through Ifa and every man of the calabash assumes that sacred trust." It was an obvious rebuke to a man they all believed should know better.

"I am mindful that this will be looked upon as disrespectful of Ifa my father, but does a troubled spring fearful of being lost to an uncertain river not seek boulders that can help change its course?" The Balogun replied defensively.

"You must not forget that Ifa speaks for all Orishas my lord general. When we speak to the palm kernel we are speaking to Olodumare himself and when the kernel is cast, Olodumare himself speaks back to us."

The Balogun said nothing. He chose instead to chew on the words. He found them bitter for his taste.

"It is not wise to doubt the words of the man who casks the kernel on your behalf." The chief priest admonished.

"But, can another not give another reading, or perhaps another interpretation? Surely, we have all seen the Okpele fall differently in different hands."

"Another can, my lord general. It might be true that the palm kernels fall differently as Ifa chooses to reveal its odus to the man it chooses to reveal it to. But destinies are like the different paths that lead towards a town through the forest of ignorance. They may be different paths but like all path ways through the forest, they eventually lead to the same spot, do they not?"

"Yes, my father, but men have been known to get lost in the forest?" The Balogun replied with a hint of sarcasm.

The young Ooni laughed out in amusement, inserting himself into the discussion for the first time. He looked at the Balogun with tired yet beady eyes then rose to his feet, eager to take his leave. He was a young man with responsibilities ahead of his years, and tonight in his stomach were mixed strong herbs that required sleep.

"Balogun Ijeru," Ooni Eleweila addressed him. "It is late and I am mindful that we commence the rites for this year's Olojo festival in the morning. But I will advise a great man of your ilk not to over complicate the ways of Ifa, particularly on a night you have travelled far and swiftly." He reached out to the Balogun and tapped him gently on his shoulder. "My late father was fond of saying that when an archer releases the arrow from his bow, he knows where he intends for it to go, yet, he must pray that the wind helps him carry it there. It is for you to decide how you choose to find your path and in this search, it is usually fool hardy to force a path on any man. After all, it is also recited that Ifa is the path for everyone and yet also for no one. Is it not so?"

With this, the Ooni and his chief priest, retired into the Ooni's private quarters and left the Balogun kneeling and pondering.

The Balogun had returned to Ijepetu just before the first light broke across the sky. He had refused to retire to his chamber to sleep, making his way into his armoury instead where he consumed himself with sharpening the blades of his favourite sword over the dampened slab of slate kept for such purposes. His Mogaji found him like that in the morning, eyes reddened from a mixture of anger, worry and remorse that had crept into his consciousness.

"Balogun, are you unwell?" Asked the alarmed Mogaji.

"I am fine, Mogaji."

"You look like a man who has been burdened with bad news my lord."

"I said I am fine." The Balogun snapped. "What is it?"

The Mogaji nodded cautiously. "You asked that we bring the white man to see you this morning. He is being held at the civic chamber along with Olu."

The Balogun nodded. "What is the condition of his health?"

"He seems fine my lord, but can one really tell with an albino?" He chuckled. The Balogun merely grunted an incoherent response and waved the Mogaji away.

Minutes later, he found the white man standing in the civic chamber with three guards keeping watch over him. He was shackled at the ankles while his hands were tightly bound with twine. His entire chin had become covered with a thick beard which threatened to cover his lips and mouth, while the hair on his head had now grown down towards his neck. His interpreter Olu who spoke a different version of the Oyo dialect also stood shackled next to him. He looked much more at ease than his white co-captive did. He in-fact looked as though he was enjoying himself, given all the attention surrounding him. The Balogun was aware that his soldiers, the town folk and children alike, all flocked to Olu's quarters and the white man's shrine regularly to listen to him narrate the story of how he had been captured and sold into slavery and carried in a giant canoe across the great water to the white man's strange land and forced to work in great sugar cane and tobacco farms as a slave. They asked him about the land to which he had been taken, and about the ways of the mysterious white man. Was it true that they ate people?

He told of his experience crossing the frightening ocean, shackled like an animal to the other captives on the floor of the wooden cabins throughout the journey to a strange land they had never heard of. He spoke of how men, young children and their mothers, who died at sea, were tossed overboard to be fed on by the fishes. He explained that these were the lucky ones. Spared a life of torment and pain by Olokun, the Orisha of the deep ocean through the dignity of dying at sea. He referred to them as '*Awon ti Olokun gba*'.

Olu told them about life on the West Indian farm plantations. Some of his stories made their eyes open wide with amazement while others brought them laughter. Like the music they played and the secret marriages of young slaves who yet miraculously found each other again in the midst of anguish, and the strength of the Yoruba slaves who found secret ways to worship their Orishas, away from the prying eyes of their slave masters. Olu also told them stories about pain and loneliness in the strange lands, about death, and the wickedness of the white men who maltreated them. He showed them the mark his first owners had burnt on to his flesh just above his breast, with a piece of burning metal. He told them how he had screamed with pain on the day that he had been marked, and how a strange white woman had given him the balm that had healed him. Olu said that not all the white men were bad. Some exhibited kindness, like the white woman who he carried on his back for several years and her heartbroken husband who had eventually given him his freedom, and the white man, Master Graham, who he had been captured with. He and others like him were priests and worshiped a god that did not believe that men should be sold as slaves. They lived by the word of their god written in a book that all could be taught to read, and they worked to return him and others like him to their native land and had taught him many things.

The Balogun studied his white captive carefully, looking for anything that could help him better understand his emotions.

"Ask him for me…" He began, as he looked towards Olu."Ask him for me if he is eating well?"

Olu nodded and proceeded to translate the question. "He says he is well."

"That is good. Ask him if there is anything he would want me to do for him."

"He says he would like to return to his people."

The Balogun nodded thoughtfully. "It is understandable that one should miss the familiar comforts of one's own people. It is like that for me as well when I leave this land of my father to fight in distant towns during the times of war." The Balogun reached across for a sizeable wrapped pouch he had set on the floor next to his elevated chair. He carefully unwrapped the parcel, took out a musket and showed it to his captives.

"Ask him if he knows how to use this?"

He watched as his white captive studied the musket from afar. It was obvious that he not only knew what it was, but also how to use it.

"He has fired one before, has he not?" the Balogun chuckled knowingly. "He has killed a man before."

"Which white man has not?" The Mogaji muttered.

"Ask him if he knows how we might be able to obtain more guns like this from his people?"

The Balogun watched intently as Olu spoke to the white man with animated gestures. He studied their eyes and watched the way their lips moved. Getting the sense that there was a good prospect that the white man would be able to source muskets, he moved towards them nodding eagerly, as though egging them both on to offer the response he was looking for.

"The white man says he does not know." Olu announced.

The Balogun stopped in his tracks. "He does not know?" He asked in disbelief. "Does he attempt to lie?"

"No, my lord, he says that to acquire such requires that one is wealthy and live amongst his people far from this place."

"But can he acquire them in large enough quantities to fight a war? Ask him"

"He cannot." Olu reported back.

"*Ra-ra.*" The white man added, choosing to interject with the spattering of Yoruba he had picked up over the years. It meant no.

"Then of what use is he good for?" The Balogun snapped. "Tell him, that I can provide him with slaves and cowries if he can provide me with muskets and powder."

It soon became clear to the Balogun that the white man was either unwilling or unable to provide the weaponry he sought, so he eventually gave up and fell into a fit of brooding silence. He could feel the weight of fatigue from the lack of sleep now taking its toll on him. He now realised that he was indeed left with no choice but to proceed with the alternative line of action that was available to him. If Baba Agboluaje's divination was to be believed, then it would seem that the white man spelt trouble. As the old dog of a priest had told him in no uncertain terms.

This one was a bad spirit that must not be allowed to linger much longer within his court and Ijepetu. He could cost him his stool if his matter was not properly handled. If only he had been able or willing to help him source weapons thereby making himself useful in some way, then perhaps he could have been released to find his way back to his own land and people. Now all he represented was a dangerous loose end that could not be allowed to linger for much longer.

CHAPTER 21

On the morning that Balogun led Ijepetu's warriors out for battle against its northern neighbours, he gave instructions that both Omitirin, the white man and Olu his interpreter, were to be escorted and marched under strict watch towards Egba land. Baba Agboluaje had found out after three days of questioning, that the cursed white man killer indeed had deep seated problems that had to do with her past. The old dog suggested that it was this which had set her on a path of years of personal misery. He had warned that if not promptly attended to, it could cause Balogun Ijeru his coronation and his defeat in battle.

His army stole away just before dawn, riding swiftly with the object of inflicting mayhem on the villages of Asawa, just north of Aresa within an hour's ride of Ijepetu. As he rode, Balogun Ijeru was riled with disappointment on how he had been offered a seemingly innocuous, yet deeply poisonous vine by Oba Osinlokun. How cruel was one's fate that he was seduced into nurturing the very thing that would have destroyed him? How devious that he had been held all these years by this weakness for her. For her pain and vulnerability, her deeply etched sadness and nearness with death, which had wrapped her in this shroud of mystery and mystique. He had looked upon her as a strange enchantress who had enveloped a cold bitter stone of pain he also kept deep within his heart. The murderous woman child that strangely reminded him of death, as much as she reminded him of his own murdered daughter.

∾

B alogun Ijeru looked towards his flanks and for a moment took comfort in the sight of his lieutenants as they sat tall and confident in their saddles. They rode with equal determination and the quiet contemplation of men who had seen several battles behind them. There were three hundred and fifty men on horses, all armed with spears and swords and one hundred and twenty dane guns and muskets between them. They were the middle of the warring pack, following a day after the dozen scouts and spies who would have entered the villages by now and ascertained the state of the enemy. In the rear were another three hundred and fifty infantry men and archers who would arrive Asawa later at night by foot under the cover of darkness. It would be their task to mop up whatever was left of the settlements, round up the prisoners and process the spoils which would be taken back to Ijepetu by a retinue of captured slaves under guard. The cavalry would rest tonight and ride out the next morning to the next target.

Baba Agboluaje had counselled that Omitirin be returned to her homestead at once and allowed to complete the appropriate rites and supplications that would propitiate Yemoja, her patron Orisha so that her *Ori* be returned to a state of calm and by extension the Balogun's household also. It was a task that was to be completed before he entered Oyo, triumphant from his strike against the Fulas, and finally able to claim his stool and royal horse tail from Alaafin Atiba.

He rode fiercely, whipping viciously and digging his stirrup deep into his trusted mare. He had ridden her to battle several times in the past and they knew each other's temperament.

Like war, the Ori was not to be toyed with. There were rites that were to be performed to appease the Orisha and reset the balance, and order of things. There were destinies of all those concerned to be repaired. As they approached the outskirts of Asawa, they found the secret codes their spies had left for them. A piece of red cloth tied to the bushel of maize and left by the road side indicated that the village was safe for the taking.

They rode the horses around in a cyclical formation and surrounded the village. Muskets were pulled and shots released into the morning sky. The people of Asawa caught unawares screamed in fear and ran in every possible direction terrified for their lives. Mothers called out to their errant children, running to scoop those they could spot nearby into their arms even as they escaped the crushing blows of horse's hooves. Their husband's had gone to the farms to clear the foliage. Then as the guns were lowered and swords became unsheathed, the bloodletting that came with Ijepetu's sacking of an unsuspecting town commenced in earnest.

When Balogun Ijeru had finally succumbed to the insistence of his war council that he obey the instructions offered by Ifa, it was to the Oluwo that he sent his Mogaji with the gift of a bale of fine woven cloth and a bag of cowries. It was to signify a request for a truce between both of them and an alliance to be forged for the purpose of persecuting the war at hand. A war that was supposed to bring honour and favour to

Ijepetu from no other than the Alaafin himself. Yet there was also a request put in by the Mogaji to Oluwo on the Balogun's behalf, that the Oluwo help source the best *Bere* grass that the whole of Ijepetu had to offer, as tribute to be presented to Alaafin Atiba by the Balogun and the people of Ijepetu at the forth coming Bere festival.

The *Bere* grass was the reed with which the people of Oyo rethatched the roofs of their homes every year in a ceremony that symbolised the renewal of life and purpose. In bringing the finest of the thatching grass from all over Oyo to the Alaafin so that his palace may be thatched before theirs, they honoured his reign and renewed their allegiance to his sovereignty. In return, the Alaafin was obliged to perform the necessary rites of praying for the continued peace and prosperity of all his peoples and to feed them over the week of communal celebrations, when the town of Oyo played host to visitors from all over the empire.

It was an important gesture of goodwill and honour for anyone to be tasked with the responsibility of sourcing the Bere grass with which Ijepetu was going to honour the Alaafin.

There was shock when the people of Ijepetu then woke up to the news that that the Olowo had been killed few days after the first few batches of Bere reeds were delivered to him, by the field urchins who he had despatched to the surrounding fields to harvest the Bere grass. People said that the Oluwo had been bitten by a snake that lurked within the reeds collected and stashed in his barn. The snake had sunk its fangs into him when he had gone to inspect the grass. The venom had disposed of him in less than a day. It was a bad death, unworthy of a man of his station. The old man's family and the Ogboni in council had hardly recovered when the vultures were then released to signal war.

Women were wailing all over the various compounds of Asawa. They cursed as their barns went up in flames. The men who had tried to resist had been cut down with swords and machetes, and children tugged at the lifeless bodies of their mothers who had caught an arrow as they ran in search of safety. Ugly mongrels darted under whatever shrubs they could find, howling in unison at the mayhem that had been unleashed upon their humans.

The Balogun and two of his lieutenants approached the house of the village head of Asawa. It was a simple farmer's dwelling with a heath located towards its back. Low lying shrubs revealed old ridges and tired plant stalk from the previous year's farming season. The soil was stony and dark reddish in colour and did not seem rewarding for any farming activity.

The Village head himself was huddled with his three wives and several children who all shook with fright and screamed as they realised that they were being surrounded by Ijepetu's warriors. The Balogun surveyed the scene and pushed forward with his sword. Unsheathed, the blade reflected light upon the faces of the children. He saw the angst revealed in the faces of the women as they almost squeezed the life out of the children they had clutched towards their bosom in fear. He listened to them as they muttered the strange prayers of the Muslims. Scriptures from the Koran recited in Arabic. He said nothing, as there was nothing to be said in these matters, but a well-practiced sequence of motions that had become Ijepetu's way of persecuting its viscous wars against its victims.

He signalled that the village head be separated from his family and taken towards the communal grounds where he would be forced to accept defeat and stoop in allegiance to the Balogun's authority. They would plunder Asawa of all its resources. It's barns of yam, millet and other grains would be ransacked, while its smeltery would be looted of whatever iron utensils the bellows might have cast. They would separate the older children from their parents and march them down through the winding bush paths towards their destiny as slaves to be sold several times over until they filled the cargo ships of the white man by the coast and crossed over to the other side. He would make a point of returning within a week through Ikoyi and Arese to ensure that the people there could see what he was capable of. The rulers of Ikoyi and Arese might seek to hide their envy at how much prominence he, Balogun Ijeru and his dogs from Ijepetu had begun to earn from all this. They might hold on to their grudge that he had insulted them by going to battle against their own northern neighbours without having shown them the courtesy of asking for their contribution towards the war effort as was customary amongst the Ekun Osi. But they would dread him and know not to find his trouble. He knew also that in the hypocrisy and the treachery of the lavish praise they would heap on him as he passed through their towns on his successful return, the news would spread and soon get to Aare Kurunmi down in Ijaiye. Eventually he would return to Ijepetu. There, he would make to wash himself and propitiate Sango for his victory and prepare himself to attend this year's Bere.

The Oluwo's removal from the scene had now paved an easier road towards Oyo for him. The old dog had become such a thorn in his flesh and if the rumours that Atiba's own court spy spread about him were to be believed, it was possible that he had begun to plot his removal from the leadership of Ijepetu altogether. It had been easy enough to make necessary arrangements, after all Ijepetu was filled with all sorts of snakes, including those who walked on two legs. The white man would be a simpler matter. The journey that all three had commenced towards Abeokuta would ensure that he was far removed from the consciousness of the Ijepetu people when his own story in this world finally ended as well. It was better this way as having lived amongst the people for this long, they had grown fond of him and Olu his interpreter. His salves and other medicines had been a cure to many and there were several children from prominent families who had been released to him to teach how to speak his language. His smattering of Yoruba, still elicited laughter among the womenfolk, but they rewarded him with morsels of food in freshly wrapped banana leaves and even enquired about his health and his libido at times. They say the older women were convinced that he did not have a manhood as men were supposed to, but there had been enough children who had reported back that they had seen him with one when he pissed in the morning.

The curious town folk would gather in his hut on the day of Ose, a day of rest amongst the people of Oyo, and listen to Olu interpret the story of his god. The Balogun had forbidden any one from his own household to attend those sessions. He had heard how such sessions had torn wives from their husband's households in distant places like Eko and Badagry where the rulers had allowed small communities of the white man to settle among them. If there was anything he knew, it was that the white man was not to be trusted nor allowed to thrive, so he had kept a tight leash around him all these years, ensuring he was given the *adi* portion to drink regularly, which would keep his spirit subdued. It had always been his greatest wish that he might be useful for the trade of slaves, and certainly for the power and ruthlessness of the white man's muskets and gun powder.

The Village head of Asawa had been dragged by the Balogun's soldiers towards the communal gathering space and forced to kneel. His people watched his humiliation in a huddle guarded by soldiers. Several fires still raged about where barns and homes had been set ablaze. Billows of thick dark smoke wafted into the sky. Word had already arrived that a few of the neighbouring hamlets had been emptied out as the inhabitants, fearful for their lives, had escaped into the nearby forests and hills to seek refuge from the mayhem that they knew was coming.

The village head, though elderly, carried himself well and exhibited a sprightly strut common with farmers accustomed to a great deal of labour. He knelt proudly, his head slightly bowed to the side, his eyes squinting as the rays of the late afternoon sun hit him directly. One of the Balogun's deputies spoke out towards the people who looked on in fear. He told them that they were now under the sovereignty of the Alaafin Atiba, and that they would be expected to pay tribute and taxes and henceforth receive instructions on the matters of importance from the emissary of the Alaafin in the person of Balogun Ijeru. He warned them that any act of defiance would be punishable by death, not only to the erring individual but his entire family. Yet submission and loyalty would be rewarded. The village head would be allowed to continue to look after the affairs of the village as long as he remained obligated to Oyo. As a final act of submission, he would be expected to prostrate before Balogun Ijeru, as an act of obeisance and swear his allegiance in the presence of Sango.

The crowd gasped when they heard these things. Not only was the village head a Muslim, he was also an imam. It was one thing to be invaded by one's neighbours, but it seemed a cruel act of humiliation for the devout Muslim, a man who prayed towards Mecca, to swear an allegiance to Ijepetu's pagan god.

The Balogun, observed as the blood drained out of the man's face, his head fell further into a dejected stoop. The Balogun looked on patiently, his face revealing no emotion. It was part of war, and something he had witnessed time and again as powerful men caught in the throes of death and defeat had to be weakened and broken into submission. It was all part of the ritual of the warrior and the simple code by which he had lived his entire life by. The strong would always dominate the weak and the weak would always heel. The Balogun looked to the distance and observed the man's wives and children looking on in horror. There was no amusement in the sight. He signalled to his soldiers who all guarded the man and they all immediately aimed their muskets at him. The Balogun walked towards his hostage and lifted the man's chin with his right hand. He saw that he was weeping and reciting from the Suras. He was breaking, but a glint of self pride and stubbornness still lurked there somewhere in those eyes. The Balogun slapped him with the back of his hand drawing blood from his crushed lip. He heard him groan in pain as he fell to the ground. He was walking away from him, his back towards his crumbled body when he heard the man scream *Allah u Akbar*! Balogun Ijeru felt the blade of the dagger pierce its way through the skin of his torso and into him. For a moment, he was utterly surprised by just how easily it had gone in. For a moment there was nothing. Just the eerie sensation of the deadly blade piercing through his flesh, then he watched as it was retrieved so as to stab at him again. He saw how the blood followed, it almost like an gushing spring, then he felt as the pain ensued. He opened his mouth and gasped softly in disbelief, then fell, clutching his torso and giving in to the pain. He heard the muskets ring out and smelt the familiar burnt taste of gun powder all about him. He could have sworn that he heard his dead children call out his name, just before the cold enveloped him and dragged him into the darkness.

PART FOUR (1847)

OMITIRIN

CHAPTER 22

AKINDELE VILLAGE, 1847.

It was the smells that I remembered. The smell of the forest, of old rotting trees mixed with the pungent earthy smells from the tiny mounds that the bush rabbits made, and that of antelope dung scattered about the musky undergrowth. It was the smells from my childhood, rushing to greet my nostrils that made me know I was nearing Akindele.

I had only been a child when I last trekked through these forests. A tender girl of fourteen, who was all too trusting of the world. I was innocent and naive, given to the things that ma'mi placed before me as good, and unconcerned with that which was not my own to be concerned about. In those days, I would walk through these same forests bare feet, clapping my hands as I sang folk songs along with Ayanke and our other friends. We would giggle as the twigs snapped and made funny sounds beneath the weight of my clumsy feet. I found laughter in the most unexpected places then, and joy and wonder in the turn of every path way, or every butterfly that rested on a leaf. It was not that there was never sadness in my heart. I still remember that people died and babies were sometimes still placed on top of ant hills when they died too frequently and returned as *abiku*, only to die yet again. It was not that there was no pain and sadness then. It was just that I remembered that I had been happy and that I had felt safe, and loved.

As we walked through the forest listening to the taunts of the distant monkeys. The footpaths were all unfamiliar. Even though they were well worn into the forest, they seemed new to me. They had been cut into entirely new and deeper parts of the jungle where farms that did not exist at the time I played here, now lay.

It was with great gratitude to Olodumare that I had made it this far, and despite the incidents of the past few days, and those of the prior weeks at Ijepetu, all of which had brought me to this moment. I remained unsure of how the Orisha could have so blessed me to be able to return to my village after I had given up hope of seeing my family again. I had died so many times over, and attempted to bury so many memories in shallow graves within me. It had been twenty-five years. Each of which had been filled with deep sorrow, and a sense of anguish which eventually rested like a thick unrelenting mist upon my head, and would not leave me, nor let me rest.

It had all begun a few months back when the Balogun's Babalawo had called me into my master's chamber and sat me down before both of them. It was obvious that Balogun was troubled. His behaviour was strange and subdued, very unlike the bashful man that he was, who had sought to dominate my entire life over the twenty-five years that I had been a member of his household. He sat quietly looking at me strangely, pensive and even afraid. Then Baba Agboluaje had started questioning me about my childhood, about Akindele and my life as a child. How was I to tell them at the time that I had started to forget things. I could no longer remember ba'mi's face and Adewale my brother who teased me so much when we were children. I did not know how one confessed that kind of thing in front of the man who had been the reason for the sadness that lay in my chest. Yet Baba Agboluaje had not let me rest. He probed deeper asking me about ma'mi and my place in my father's house. He asked me questions about how I eventually came to be sold into slavery and why I alone had been cast into slavery without any other member of my family. Was there a debt owed by my father at any time, he wondered, or had my mother had me for another man. I told him that she had not! Yet, he would not let me rest. For three days he returned to the Balogun's quarters and summoned me to knell before him as he continued to wonder about me aloud.

It was on the third day when he asked me whether I found joy near water, that I had begun to stare at him and Balogun, wondering what kind of question that was, and why anyone would ask such a thing? He asked me about the streams and the rivers I played in when I was a child. Something stirred within me. Yes, I thought to myself, there was a time when I did. I remembered how happy I had always been as a child playing in Yemoja's River. Did he not see that I was in fact named after water? A name that I had borne with so much sadness and heaviness after my mother had explained why she gave me such a name. I shook my head vigorously and yet began to weep.

I had never told anyone about my consecration in to the sisterhood of Yemoja nor how I had been seized by the evil

Fula that morning I had gone to prepare myself. It was a secret that I had carried and learnt to bury deep within my heart all these years. The shame and the disappointment of an unfulfilled promise from the women in my lineage all the way to me. I had come to believe that such a destiny as that which I had been afforded could only have been meted out to me because I was unclean or unworthy in some way. Had ba'mi not always warned us that a person's Ori would always catch up with the person? I had come to accept that my Ori was not good. I told them everything. I told them about my mother and my father and my brothers and about the kind sisters at the Popo. I told them about how I was going to be a good person who was being prepared to bring 'rere' to the world and how the Fula took it all away from me one morning by a river.

That night I stole away from the women's quarters, alone and visited Baba Agboluaje in his own house. I had prepared myself, washing my body and soft places and adorning a piece of fresh cloth which I scented with a potion I had stolen from one of the Balogun's newer wives. He was surprised to see me, and enquired as to my mission. I placed the basket of fruits that I had specially picked that morning, before him and I threw myself at his feet and wept. I begged him to help me find my way back to my people and to help me influence the Balogun accordingly. He was an old man, but there had always been rumours that he still enjoyed the waist of women, so I let my wrapper drop slightly so he might see the ample curves that I carried. He stared at me for what seemed an eternity. I could see his old crafty mind working, his nostrils flared and his eyebrows became hooded as tempta-tion coursed through him. It did not last. He pulled away from my gaze and returned to the mat where he had sat, and stammered incomprehensible words at me.

"I will help you." He said to me carefully. "Wait here." He left me kneeling there as he retreated into his inner chamber and returned with a tiny vial of ground herbs and powders.

"Take this," He said. "And wash your face with it. Then, approach your master as you have approached me tonight." That was all he said before he waved me away with his hands, the way one waved away trouble that was bigger than one could handle.

I took the vial, fleeing back in the dead of night, careful not to be seen by the guards as I returned to my modest hut within the compound. I waited till the evening of the next day and did as he told me. I bribed one of the younger wives to take her turn to serve the Balogun his meal and prepared myself as I had the night before. My heart throbbed with fear and uncertainty as I served him the roasted yams and thick fried peppery stew he loved so much. Perhaps it was my clumsiness and unease that drew his attention, but I was surprised when he asked me what was wrong?

"There is nothing wrong my lord." I whispered

I had never seen the Balogun look at me like that in all the days that he petted me, nor in the days that he forced himself upon me urging me to call him by his title. His eyes calmed down, he became sober towards me and one would have thought that he was seeing me for the very first time.

He called me into his inner room after that and had his way with me, repeatedly. He was forceful and gentle at the same time, angry and yet sad. For the first time in all the years I had lain with him, he was attentive towards me. I moaned out with a pleasure I had never experienced before and it left me devastated with shame that I could be like this. He ordered that I returned to him the next day and the day after that. It was as though he was trying to tell me something. It was almost as though he was trying to tell me that he was sorry and urging me not to be sad again.

I found solace in spending time with the white man, *Alagbho* as the Balogun fondly called him or *'tank you'* as I chose to call him, and his servant, Olu. I would sneak into the small shrine he had been allowed to build and sit on the mat at the back and watch as he taught the children from other compounds how to pronounce sounds. Olu would translate for him. The white man himself would try to say the word in our Yoruba and after he might have disgraced himself with the way he would say it. He would add *'tank you'* and make funny faces at the children which made them laugh. It was a happy place to go to and it made me forget my pains. It was here I listened to him talk about his god, and marvelled at the stories he told about the magic he performed, a god that could walk on water, one who fed an entire village of people with just a few fishes, but yet could not save himself from the wickedness of people. I wondered about such a god with suspicion, until the day I learnt that he himself had once gone to cleanse in a river, in search of the praise from God.

A few days later it had become known to us that war was coming. Iya agba herself had called me to her quarters and sat me down by her sleeping mat, just as my own mother use to, and she looked at me with deep sorrow in her eye.

"I had always known that there was a secret about you." She said. "But why did you not tell me?" She spoke to me as though she was a mother and not a senior wife, and surely, she could, have been as old as ma'mi if not even older.

"What pain and sadness you must have carried, you this one." She said with a gentleness and sympathy that showed in the way she shook her head as she starred gravely at the floor.

"To have been called away from such a life of honour." She clucked her teeth and she shook her head again. It was then she told me that I had to be allowed to return to perform the rites to free me from the life of emptiness that I had lived all these years. She made me swear to her that I would return to Ijepetu and the Balogun's household.

"You have made a life here and it is not too late for you to have a child." She pleaded. "You have suffered what few women will have the courage to bear but may Olodumare bless you with child."

I stared at her, blinking repeatedly and sweating profusely. A child was the last thing I had ever wanted. How could I have wanted a child to come into a wicked world like this, I wondered? How could I tell her that I dreaded the thought of bringing a daughter to this world? How would I reconcile my shame with the birth of a daughter? How could I be wicked enough to pass down my curse? I looked away and wiped a tear. Then I looked back at her and took her hands in mine.

"You have been like a mother to me, Iya mi." I said softly. "And you have carried your own burden as well. Let us rest in the knowledge that not all women share the same blessings from Olodumare."

"This may be true." Iya agba agreed. "But do not talk like that. If there is anything that I myself now know through the things that I have seen in this world, it is that life will always find a way. As we grow older, do we not realise that life is made up of the stories that we can tell each other?"

I asked her what she meant by that. She looked at me and smiled ruefully.

"Yes, Omitirin, stories celebrate the moments of our lives. We might be blessed to live through each in the present, but how quickly they are spent, to become only memories that we spend the rest of our lives protecting with all our might, from fading with time. So, let us create memories worth fighting for."

I thanked her for her kindness and returned to my quarters.

Balogun sent for me two days later. I prepared myself once again. I was surprised to see that he was not alone. I was ushered into his public chamber where all the prominent leaders of Ijepetu were seated along with other members of the town council. There had been a rumour that the Olowo had met with a terrible accident and lay dying in his home-stead. The town had been thrown into disarray and it seemed that there was a calabash filled with trouble about to be smashed on to the floor in the Balogun's quarters. When I entered It was the Mogaji who met me? He told me to wait till the matter on hand was dispensed with by the men who sat there in council. He was immediately over ridden by the Balogun who waved for me to come. I walked towards the men all seated in low stools whispering as I knew they usually did when the trouble before them was plenty. I knelt and greeted all of them conscious of the disdain with which all of them except for the Balogun looked at me.

"I have arranged for you to leave before dawn tomorrow morning." He said to me. I stared at him unsure of what exactly he meant. Even though I had hoped and prayed to one day be re-united with my family, I could not believe that I would be allowed to leave. I did not even know which road out of Ijepetu would lead to my people's land. I had never ventured out of Ijepetu in the twenty-five years since I had been forcibly dragged into this town. The Balogun had been a man in his early forties then, bashful and full of vile with which he oppressed those around him. Now he was in his sixties and still a man for whom many spat in disgust.

"I have arranged for two men to escort you to your father's land and you will find your village and make peace with yourself." He said.

I still stared at him waiting for the wickedness that he was about to reveal but he continued. "You will travel with the white man and Olu, both of who will carry on towards the coast. May Olodumare show them mercy."

It was then I started to pay attention to what he was saying. I had heard the rumour from the women quarters that they were to be driven away from Ijepetu on the prompting of the town council. The two of them had grown to become one with the people of Ijepetu and this was not news that would be well received by the people who themselves had grown fond of them. I looked away from the Balogun towards the others, hoping to find whatever clue in their gestures that might reveal more. They all made the point of looking away, which left me with no choice but to ask aloud.

"Is there a reason of this my lord?"

He did not answer me. He merely looked at me and then looked away towards Baba Agboluaje. The old man took it as his cue to speak, first he coughed in fits as he usually did, before looking at the guards and then back at me.

"You will take only a few clothes my daughter and the items which I will give you for your prayers. It will be better that you go with that which you need and not that which you might hope for."

I did not understand what riddle Baba Agboluaje was teasing me with, but I could sense that I was being told to ask less questions and do as I was told.

"You must return in time for the festival of the Bere." Baba Agboluaje added. This only succeeded in confusing me further. So, I retreated into the safety of the symbolic. I knelt in a show of submissiveness to the council of these ravenous and conniving potbellied men present, yet determined to find my own way through this. I left them there, still whispering amongst themselves, like people who had grown afraid of their own shadows.

I could not sleep that night. I tossed and turned as I weighed what I had been told and wondered aloud to the geckos that shared my hut if it was true that I would be reunited with my mother. I wondered how she would look. I was caught up in a strange mixture of hope and fear, excitement and trepidation. The type that almost causes one's bowel to move. I wondered if she would be able to recognise me? I was no longer the young innocent Omitirin whose corn rows she used to plait with her deft indigo dye stained fingers. No, I was a woman almost forty years of age who had seen wickedness and pain and loneliness in this world and who also had blood on her hands. I was Omitirin the white man killer.

I rose from whatever sleep I could find to see that two ruthless looking guards had been assembled at the piazza just as the Balogun had said. They were not men that I recognised. The white man was there with Olu and I found it strange that they did not seem to be bound in any way. The parcel that had been prepared for me by Baba Agboluaje was handed to me by one of his assistants with verbal instructions on what I was expected to do with the items contained within them. The Balogun was nowhere to be found. I was later to learn that he had ridden out in battle with his soldiers. It was Iya agba who came to me instead. She had two head-ties wrapped around her bosom and carried a small basket followed by her nephew, Adereti, her late sisters second son who had lived with us in the compound.

"This is dry meat, and this one is fish," she said to me, pointing out the tiny wrapped parcels of food neatly arranged in the basket to me.

"I do not trust the food one can buy on the road these days." She said. "Too many kidnappers and marauders all over Oyo these days. All these Hausa people that are of questionable character." She rambled on. I saw that she was pensive, like a mother sending off her daughter on her first errand to a neighbouring town where the men were known to be notorious.

"Adereti will go with you my husband." She added, using the term of endearment reserved for only those family members a woman is fond of. "He will help you with your heavy load."

Iya agba then suddenly dragged me towards her just as I was about to kneel in respect. She stopped me and hugged me instead and whispered fiercely into my ear." Be careful and watchful Omitirin. Trust no one."

Then as soon as she released me, she was gone.

Every healthy horse that Ijepetu could spare was being ridden towards Asawa that very morning. So, our journey was to be on foot. The leader of the guards told us that it would take us a little over four days to get to Egba land. We would travel fast during the morning and rest for a while just after the mid-day sun then continue our journey towards evening. We would spend the nights in well frequented resting spots at the outskirts of known towns for safety. The various kingdoms and towns of Oyo had fallen upon troubled and quarrelsome times. There were bitter rivalries amongst neighbouring towns and petty jealousies amongst settlements. In-laws who once lent each other's farming utensils, now lent each other spears and daggers instead. Men like Balogun Ijeru had become lustful for strife, and now because of the white man's ships waiting at the coast, men had become hungry for slaves and the cowries they could command.

They covered the white man up with enough clothes so as not to reveal his pale skin. They used the dark slurry of burnt charcoal to darken his face and decked him with a *'Fila abeti Aja'* the popular cap of the farm people and royals alike. It barely covered his strange and unruly hair but at least it made him less conspicuous.

At first, we travelled at a cautious pace. We meandered through the less travelled bush parts towards the farming districts on the outskirts of Ijepetu. We were all silent, I watchful, remembering what Iya agba had cautioned and my instincts on edge with fear and worry that she should suggest such. The men moved well ahead leaving Adereti and I walking together slightly behind them. Once a while the guards would fall back and ask me if I was tired. They treated me as though I were their master's treasured wife. I remained polite but averted my eyes and did not encourage talk.

By the late evening of the first day we had made good progress and found a safe camping point at the farm produce market outpost of a small town. We were not the only ones who sought to pass the night there, but we kept to ourselves and the guards made us a fire with which we roasted coco-yams and heated red palm oil we ate them with. I remembered the last time I had travelled like this. It had been with the Balogun as I returned with him to Ijepetu from Agodi where he had forced himself on me so painfully, and laughed into my eyes like a mad hyena. Then I had been shackled at my feet to stop me from running away again. Now it seemed strange that I walked freely. We slept with little incident and woke up to the welcoming sounds of diligent birds and small kingfishers revealing that a small river or a stream lay nearby. We found it and washed ourselves. We refilled our gourds with fresh water from a pleasant brook and carried on with our journey. We reached the village of Kosobo by midday and hid from the several passers-by under the shade of a giant Iroko tree. The village was not far from new Oyo from where Alaafin Atiba reigned. The guards had evidently been instructed to detour round Oyo, less any one close to the palace or an inquisitive road spy stopped to ask us too many questions. It was here by the well that we heard the news passed on from traveller to traveller that the villages around Ilorin where being attacked by the ruthless dogs of Ijepetu as the dreaded warriors of Ijepetu were called. A few of the traders balancing their wares on their heads as they walked briskly past us to the surrounding hamlets, would relate the same piece of news to those they passed. 'Do not go near Asawa today. Balogun Ijeru and his dogs have ridden there. There is bloodletting going on there.' The men would stop them to hear more. But as usual no more could be said, so they would recite Balogun Ijeru's Oriki instead:

Ijeru of Ijepetu
An incorrigible man with a dubious past
He is difficult to control
He is difficult to fight
He behaves as if there is no God
He kills in different clothes

I flinched when I heard them recite this and quickly walked back to the protection of our guards. Was it the same for him all over Oyo I wondered, that the people feared him as much as they held him in contempt.

We trekked deeper into the forest so as to pass by Oyo and begin our approach towards Agodi in Ibadan. Olu and the white man spoke to each other but did not say much to me, but as we approached the end of the third day we sat in a clearing under the lights of a proud full moon and made a fire that cast away the night's darkness even further. I sat there with the men, watching the embers glow and listening to the rhythm of fire, the crackle and subdued hums of charred twigs which enveloped me in the symphony that came with destruction. I remembered the meat and dry fish that Iya agba had packed for me and offered generous pieces to Olu and his white master. They accepted gratefully and nibbled at first, the way men usually did when they did not trust the woman's food. The meat was sweet and the fish dry and well-seasoned. Soon they were biting off larger pieces and chewing like hungry dogs.

"Your master does not seem happy to have left Ijepetu." I suggested to Olu as I tried to make small talk.

Olu looked at me in between his chewing. "Why do you say that?" He finally asked.

"Because he has not greeted us *tank you.*" I laughed.

He smiled back and looked at his master in sympathy. He translated what I had just said and I saw the white man reveal a part of himself I had rarely seen through the months I nursed him back to his health. It was not that he smiled back through that thick beard of his, it was that for the first time he had hope showing in his eyes. I understood the language of his eyes better than I understood his language and I could see that we came from the same place. I could see that he too wanted to go home.

He was wearing the small neck chain around his neck, with a small object dangling from him. I had seen him with it so many times before back at Ijepetu. He would stare at it then put it away in his pockets.

"What is that thing your master always wears?" I asked Olu pointing at the chain.

'*Tank you*' smiled and looked at me. He pulled it off and gave it to me to examine. I studied it curiously, noting the symbol that was on it. It was the same as he had placed on the wall of his shrine.

"It is a cross." Olu explained. "It is the sign of the white man's God."

This I understood. Our carvings likewise were simply the symbols of our orisha. It was not the wood we worshiped. I remember that Iya had once admonished us at the convent of Iya wa several years ago, it was merely the representation of the spirit of the Orisha, but to place it in the alcove and propitiate it daily helped our hearts to reach out to Olodumare through worship. "It must be very powerful." I added.

The white man laughed as he put the chain back on.

"He says that it belonged to his mother, and she gave it to him to protect him after she died."

I smiled back at him and nodded. Mothers I marvelled. Were they not all the same after all. I told them about my mother and how she also had given an article of faith to protect me. Mine lay lost under a boulder in the river near my childhood village. I told them about my time spent in the convent of Iya wa, and how the Fulas seized me while I had gone to prepare myself.

As Olu relayed my story, I saw the white man look on at me with a quiet astonishment. He would shake his head and look at me again.

"Tell him that I will show him where I played as a child with my brothers and was happy, and when I find my mother I shall ask her to make him a dyed cloth that he can give to his people when he returns to his own home."

Olu nodded and translated what I had said for him. He looked at me and smiled. He then turned back to Olu and spoke more of his own words. When Olu turned back to me he had stopped eating. His face was quiet and thoughtful.

"He says I should tell you that you should not be unhappy for your life any more. He says that in the holy book of his God, there is a story of a woman like your mother, who made cloth. Her name was Lydia and she was good inside like you and one day she joined the servants of his God to help them teach the people about the ways of God and God heard her prayers and blessed her with happiness. He says that he prays for you that one day you learn about her yourself and learn about his god the one true god and be equally blessed."

I looked at the faces of both men, then rested my gaze on 'Tank you'. I saw that his eyes no longer looked back at me. Despite the light from the full moon, his skin seemed to have turned as red as the glowing embers of the fire and he shifted with an embarrassment I had not witnessed in him before.

"Did she have children?" I asked quietly.

I know that they caught the slight murmur in my voice, as I tried to sniffle a thought and an unnecessary teardrop. I did not know where such a thought had come from. Only that I had begun to think about what Iya agba had said to me about memories and about children. I wondered now if a woman's happiness could truly be separated from the joy of her having her own children. Perhaps this was what hope does to people. It seduces them with the thoughts of what is worth fighting for again. My mother's true happiness, after all had been in having a daughter who could help take away her shame and now that I was to be reunited with her, I feared for what she might make of her only daughter returning to her with no grandchild to present her.

Olu said the white man did not know if the woman ever had children, but she had had a family. I nodded my head as I wondered what type of life a woman like that might have lived. A childless servant of other people's one true god, a dyer of cloth, a woman who was happy because she had a family. I wondered what ma'mi would make of such a person.

I woke up, startled by a loud commotion. As I steered and raised both my arms out to stretch, I heard both Olu and the white man shouting at the top of their voices. I immediately jumped to my feet and orientated my eyes in time to see two of the guards wrestling both of the men on the grass. They had daggers drawn and by the look of things were intent on driving it through their hearts. I screamed out impulsively.

"What are you doing? Leave them alone!"

I flung myself at the nearest one of them, screaming and thrashing at his back.

"Leave him alone!" I kept screaming. "Why do you want to kill him?"

The guard had such a massive frame that my arms barely wrapped around his torso. He flung me away like a bushel and I landed a short distance away. That interference had given Olu some time to reposition himself however and he being a man of considerable physical stature himself, was able to take advantage of the moment of respite and lunge for his assailant. He clawed at the guard's eyes, grunting like a wild animal as he did so. I heard the guard shriek with pain as blood spluttered about, staining the inky darkness just before dawn. The other guard it seemed was more successful.

The white man lay beneath him writhing in pain as the guard's thin blade coursed its way into his right thigh. Both Olu and I threw ourselves at the guard. I tore at his hair, while Olu snatched him by the back of the neck and yanked him away from his master. The ensuing fight disturbed the ground beneath us and we tossed about the bush like people possessed by some bad spirit. The guard was unusually strong and he almost subdued both of us until Olu grasped at a fallen branch and promptly finished him off with the decaying log of wood.

I lay panting on the cold ground, clutching at my chest and wondering where I had gained such madness from. I gathered my strength back and crawled towards '*Tank you*' who still laid on the ground. Olu helped his master up. The white man was limping badly and blood flowed from the deep gash where the dagger had stabbed him. We did not wait a moment longer before we beckoned at Adereti, Iya agba's nephew, who had stood there terrified, to help Olu carry the white man. Then we fled into the thick of the forest.

CHAPTER 23

AKINDELE VILLAGE, 1847.

Akindele was no more. So much had changed in the years I had been away. The smells might have been the same, and the call of the distant frogs, but huts I had once played in were no longer there and my entire village had disappeared. My family was nowhere to be found.

As we searched about the communal square where I had once learnt to sing and dance, all I could find were the remains of old things, dilapidated swish mud huts with fallen roofs, broken earthen pots, loosened baskets that had decayed into the ground and now my own shattered dreams.

We had not stopped fleeing until about noon on the day after the attack and the heat and bites from obnoxious insects the size of a small child's fist, would not allow us go any further. We were lost in the middle of a thick forest, unsure of which direction would take us to the nearest village or hamlet and fearful that we were being pursued by the guards who might have regained consciousness. We had hidden behind a small outgrowth, panting like baboons, and desperate for drinking water. We had found no nearby streams so we settled for whatever we could glean off the available leaves with our patched tongues, and when that did not do, we had suffered in silence and pressed on all the same.

It had taken a full day and a night before we finally came to a farm clearing where we saw a billow of smoke and heard the barking of hunting dogs from a distant homestead nestled in between cultivated fruit trees. It was there we had met a group of farmers and hunters who initially convinced they were being visited by a spirit had taken to their heels at the sight of the white man. It had been only after much pleading and explanations that I had been able to persuade them to help us. They found us a guide who came along with us and showed us the paths through the forest towards Akindele.

Now, as we walked through what had once been my village, I clutched at Olu in shock, asking aloud for what had happened over and over again. It took us the better part of the afternoon to find a human we could talk to. He was not someone who I knew and he was not a mentally balanced person. He ran in circles chasing his own shadows and when he did attempt to answer our questions he muttered inco- herent nonsense even though it was in our Egba dialect, which I had not heard spoken by anyone in so many years.

My family compound was also no different. The adjoining huts had crumbled into piles of rubble and everywhere surrounding it, including my mother's beloved dye pits, over taken with thick bush. That night before darkness descended, I searched about everywhere for an item that I could recog- nise, which could perhaps offer me a clue. I found nothing. It was as if my family's very existence had been plucked right from this place without any trace.

The white man watched me intently, nodding frequently as Olu narrated my ordeal. He would mutter a gentle 'pele' or sorry which was one of the few Oyo words he had managed to learn, and strangely I would nod back grateful for whatever solace I was offered. But we did not sleep that night. I questioned my Ori and questioned Yemoja and I questioned my sanity. But I did not allow myself to shed a single tear, because I knew there was a perfectly sensible explanation for all this, and I was determined to get to the bottom of all this in the morning.

When morning came, I rose before the men and immediately began to trace my way through the over grown bushes and abandoned paths towards the Popo of Yemoja towards the river, at the outskirts of Akindele. I was sure that I would find answers there. But it was worse there. The compound had all but been burnt to the ground and not a single soul was to be found. I sat there for a very long time shaking my head and talking to myself like the mad man that we had encountered. As evening came, Olu and his master found me sitting on the ground under an old scared tree by the Popo. They had another person with them. This time a woman who carried a bundle of firewood on her head. They had found her near where I had left them and she had offered to take them towards Ake where she claimed another white man had arrived with a group of *Saro* people from Freetown and Badagary to establish a shrine to the white man's god.

I had not eaten, nor did I feel hungry. I was at this point in a mental state I was unsure I had ever experienced. A constant nagging in the very pit of my womb and a queasiness that did not leave me, until I ran towards the bushes and started to vomit.

"Are you all right my sister?" she asked me in our dialect.

I answered her that I was fine. Then I turned to face her and asked her whether she knew what had happened to the people of Akindele.

"It was *Suponaa*." She whispered with dread. "It was the Orisha of the small pox that visited the village suddenly several years ago and wiped out almost everyone." She added.

"Not many survived, and the few that did were forced to abandon Akindele and flee to distant towns, as those in the neighbouring towns would not take them in for fear of displeasing him."

I asked her if she had known my mother or father. I tried to describe them as I had last remembered them now almost twenty-five years ago.

"I am not from here my sister, I only come this far occasionally because My legs travel fast through the forest I am simply in search of food and firewood to prepare food for my children, but we all know what happened to the people here. May Olodumare forgive them for whatever atrocities they committed to warrant such punishment."

They all looked at me in silence. I could see *'Tank you'* observing my every countenance. As though he himself now expected that I would immediately go raving mad. But I knew I would not. I knew that my family would have survived this and would have found a new life in another town not far from here. I would go and find them in the morning. Now I simply re-adjusted my wrapper about my bosom and despite the urge to vomit again, I chose to walk with a sense of purpose towards the alcove by the river where over twenty years ago I had gone to wash my sins away.

～

All I had on as I slipped into the river, was a tightly tied wrapper which covered my nakedness. The water was not as cold as I had remembered it to be. Perhaps it was because of the difference in the time of day, or perhaps it was that all that had happened within such a short space of time, now came up to meet me and urge me to release them in torrents of anguish into the river. Yet I refused to submit to such emotions and willed myself to carry on. I had been through so much after all, and one extra day of waiting was not going to take away the joy of finding my mother. So, I held my breath instead and dipped under the surface towards the boulders that still remained where they had been all these years.

It struck me as I noticed myself wade through the waters with such conviction that I had never doubted that the boulders would still be here. This place where the waters recede, which had offered me calmness at one moment and yet so much pain at another. The memory had always been with me over the years. And even when I had feared that I had begun to forget my mother's face, the boulders upon which I had steadied myself had always been vivid and clear in my mind's eye. As I lurked under the waters, I stretched my hands out to survey the river bed and then discern whatever murky item I might have caught in my hands. I did not have to look for long before my fingers touched what I knew I was looking for. I found the figurine my mother had given me within the area I remembered that it had fallen. I lifted my head out of the water, spluttering and coughing as I sucked in air in to my lungs. My hands followed with the figurine tightly caught within my grasp and I began to use the river water to wash away the mud that had formed around it. It was as I remembered it. The water had decayed it slightly in some parts, but it was still relatively in a good condition. I felt no emotions. I simply felt compelled to do my duty of retrieving her and cleaning her properly, and so I did just that.

I did not perform the rights that Baba Agboluaje had directed of me because I realised now that I had become empty. I could find nothing within me with which I would have wished to complete the rites. Not until I had found my mother. So yet conscious of the nagging fear of what I knew I might learn tomorrow, and oblivious to the strange queasiness that did not want to leave my throat, I carried on cleaning her dutifully and carefully like ma'mi would have wished. When the tears finally came, they were not my own. They were a silent type. Cold and bitter torrents of unreconciled loss from a strange place, that rolled down my cheeks. And as I sang one of the hymns I had been taught not far from here at the convent of Iya wa, I refused to own them.

When I was sure that she was presentable, I wiped the tears away from my eyes. I waded back carefully and resolutely through the water towards the bank of the river. It was at this moment that I saw the white man watching me from behind a tree by the river bank. He had removed the necklace he wore around his neck. The one his mother had given him. His face was beaten by fatigue and pain, but his eyes shone like bright stars on a calm evening as he kept staring at me. He stretched out the necklace in his hand and offered it to me. He was crying. I took it and wore it around my neck. Then, I lifted my eyes to see him smiling at me, the way as a little girl, I had always dreamed that Sango would look at me; Like his goddess.

AFTERWORD

The Reverend Samuel Ajayi Crowther was ordained as a Church of England minister for service with the Church Missionary Society (CMS) in 1843. He established a mission in Ake, Abeokuta, in present day Nigeria in 1847, from whence he aggressively evangelised christianity amongst the Yorubas of the Old Oyo empire. He rose to become the first African Bishop of the Anglican Church in 1864. Ajayi became famous for leading new converts to bury or destroy their traditional figurines.

The themes that I have explored in this novel are ones that have fascinated me and I hope that in some way, the telling of this story helps them find a valuable place within your thoughts and conversations. It is important that Africans come to terms with the need to reconcile their culture with their history. It is even more important that these powerful human stories from our past, locked within the ethos of Africa's various artefacts that were mostly lost or stolen during the colonial era, and now lay imprisoned in the various museums, galleries and private collections in the West, be allowed to find their way back home. Because it is only then that Africans can truly finish telling the stories of their past.

Rotimi Olaniyan

ACKNOWLEDGMENTS

Many thanks to friends and associates who have helped this story find its strength along the way. To my parents who unbeknownst to them, seeded a powerful thought. To my wife and kids, who gleefully stood back and watched me write. Many thanks indeed to Sue Shepherd who read the very first draft and always urged me on with the wonderful words of Mariam Williamson. Thanks to Tolu Daniels and Yinka Akran who made me read better. Gareth Gelder and Doris Edwards who saved the narrative from my ego, and a certain Derek who I have never met but who does not realise he is an Orisha.

ABOUT THE AUTHOR

Rotimi Olaniyan has lived, schooled, or worked and built a business in Nigeria, South Africa and the UK. He received his Doctorate in Business Administration from the Nottingham Business School in the UK in 2015, and currently lectures there as a member of the marketing faculty.

His literary penchant is for African, diasporic and historical narratives that he argues have not yet been sufficiently told. Those that highlight important stories through the lenses, themes, characters and plots that explore the shared history of Africans and the rest of the world.

He spends his time between Lagos, where he wanders along the beach, bare feet, South Africa's Western Cape, where he crawls vineyards and Nottingham, UK, where he tends a modest garden.

'Where the Waters Recede' is his first novel.

www.rotimiolaniyan.com